Outlook to 2060 for World Forests and Forest Industries

A Technical Document Supporting the Forest Service 2010 RPA Assessment

Joseph Buongiorno, Shushuai Zhu,
Ronald Raunikar, and Jeffrey P. Prestemon

The Authors:

Joseph Buongiorno, Professor Emeritus, Department of Forest and Wildlife Ecology, University of Wisconsin, Madison, WI; **Shushuai Zhu**, Assistant Scientist, Department of Forest and Wildlife Ecology, University of Wisconsin, Madison, WI; **Ronald Raunikar**, Economist, U.S. Geological Survey, Menlo Park, CA; **Jeffrey P. Prestemon**, Research Forester, Forestry Sciences Laboratory, U.S. Department of Agriculture, Forest Service, Southern Research Station, Research Triangle Park, NC.

April 2012

Outlook to 2060 for World Forests and Forest Industries: A Technical Document Supporting the Forest Service 2010 RPA Assessment

Joseph Buongiorno, Shushuai Zhu, Ronald Raunikar, and Jeffrey P. Prestemon

Contents

List of Figures

Outlook to 2060 for World Forests and Forest Industries: A Technical Document Supporting the Forest Service 2010 RPA Assessment

Joseph Buongiorno, Shushuai Zhu, Ronald Raunikar, and Jeffrey P. Prestemon

Abstract

Four RPA scenarios corresponding with scenarios from the Third and Fourth Assessments of the Intergovernmental Panel on Climate Change were simulated with the Global Forest Products Model to project forest area, volume, products demand and supply, international trade, prices, and value added up to 2060 for Africa, Asia, Europe, North America, Oceania, South America, and selected countries. Scenario A1B presents a 5.5-fold increase in world fuelwood use that leads to high prices of fuelwood and industrial roundwood, driven by especially strong demand in Asia for large imports from South America and Europe. World roundwood consumption reaches 11.2 billion m³ in 2060, exceeding the increment of forests, particularly in Asia. Even under scenarios A2 and B2, the harvest in Asia is unsustainable. However, scenario A1B and a low fuelwood demand lead to a global harvest of 3.6 billion m³ only and to a sustainable forest volume. The world consumption of manufactured wood products grows modestly under most scenarios, with slight changes in prices. Consumption and value added in industries increases more rapidly in Asia, due to the fast economic growth of China and India in all scenarios. As a result, Asia is a large importer of industrial roundwood from South America and Europe and of paper and paperboard from Europe and North America.

Keywords: Energy, forecasting, Global Forest Products Model, industries, Intergovernmental Panel on Climate Change, markets, policy.

Introduction

During the last three decades, international trade of forest products has expanded rapidly. As a case in point, China's rapid economic growth has had profound effects on the forest economies of the Asian Pacific and the United States through demand for raw materials and exports of processed wood products (Katsigris and others 2005). Therefore, the forest portion of the 2010 Resources Planning Act (RPA) report anchors the national assessment in an international context, with specific focuses on U.S. imports and exports and how domestic production and prices relate to developments in the global forest sector.[1] Using the Global Forest Products Model (GFPM) (Buongiorno and others 2003, updated in Buongiorno and Zhu 2011a), the authors of this document developed projections for world regions and selected countries that were consistent with the more detailed national projections of the United States Forest Products Module (Ince and others 2011).

In addition to trade, climate change is an issue that may impact world forests. To address this potential impact, the 2010 RPA Forest Assessment is linked directly to Intergovernmental Panel on Climate Change (IPCC) scenarios (Nakicenovic and others 2001) on projections (including global and regional economic activity, population, land uses, and greenhouse gases and biofuel consumption [see also Alcamo and others 2005]) that could have major implications for forests and forest industries.

The objective of this study was to assess consequences of the IPCC projections for the world's forest economy. We looked at four scenarios. Three scenarios (A1B, A2, and B2) adopt the IPCC assumptions, with varying but large future biofuel production. A fourth scenario assumes the same economic and demographics as A1B but a lower demand for energy wood.

In this paper, we first describe the GFPM structure and calibration, then discuss the three IPCC scenarios as they were implemented in the GFPM, and next present results, consisting of projections to 2060 for forest area and forest stock, and for the prices, consumption, and trade of wood, wood products, and other papermaking fibers. We also offer global projections for the main regions and for selected individual countries in each region.

The Global Forest Products Model

Theory and Structure

The Global Forest Products Model (GFPM) is a spatial dynamic economic model of the forest products sector of the world economy. The model simulates the evolution of competitive world markets for forest products and recognizes 180 countries (table 1) and their interaction through world economic trade. For each country, the model simulates changes in forest area and forest stock, and calculates consumption, production, and trade of up to 14 commodity groups (fig. 1). In each projected year, the model computes prices that clear world markets for all products.

---

[1]The assessment is mandated by the Forest and Rangeland Renewable Resources Planning Act of 1974.

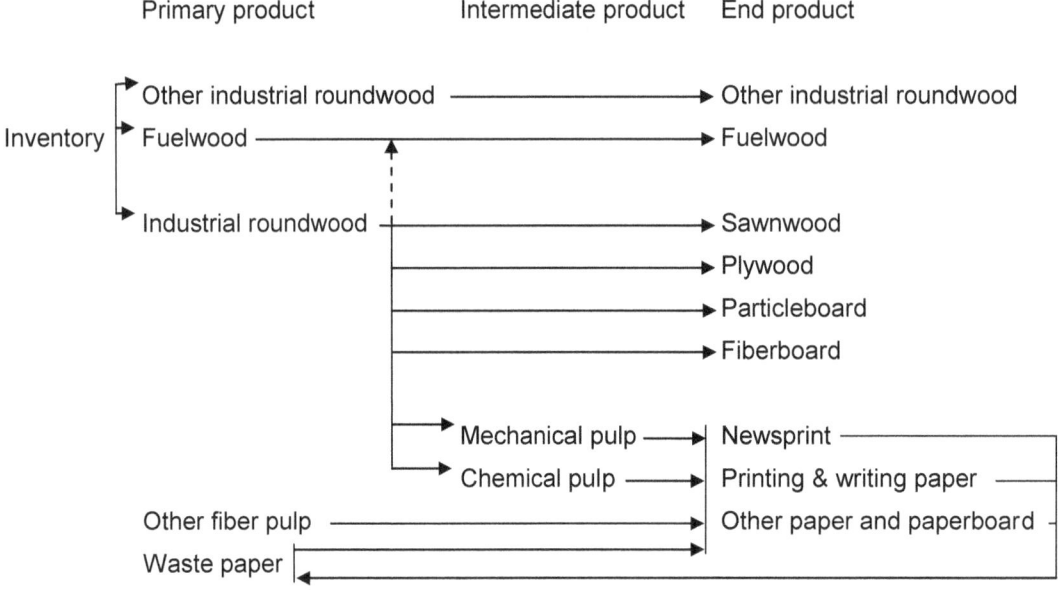

Figure 1—Within each country, the Global Forest Products Model describes the flow and transformation of wood products, from the forest inventory to the end products and paper recycling.

The GFPM is a dynamic system due to its difference equations: the equilibrium in a particular year is a function of the equilibrium in the previous year, but the two equilibriums are computed sequentially, not simultaneously, thus avoiding the strong assumption of perfect foresight. An earlier version of the GFPM and several applications are described in detail by Buongiorno and others (2003). The most recent version, including the software, documentation, and one data set, is available at http://fwe.wisc.edu/facstaff/buongiorno/.

Figure 1 shows the flow and transformation of wood products in each country. At one end of the flow is the supply of raw materials, including fuelwood and industrial roundwood, which depend directly on the forest inventory. At the other end is the demand for end products, sawnwood, wood-based panels, and paper and paperboard. In between is the transformation of industrial roundwood into intermediate (pulp) or end products.

Additional sources of raw materials are nonwood fiber pulp and the waste paper recovered after consumption of paper and paperboard. In this particular application, part of what used to be industrial roundwood may be diverted to fuelwood if and when, due to high biofuel demand, the price of fuelwood approaches that of industrial roundwood (dashed arrow in fig. 1). The GFPM has a static element that describes the world spatial market equilibrium in a particular year, and a dynamic element that simulates the changes from year to year.

Global equilibrium

Computation of the spatial equilibrium in any given year relies on Samuelson's (1952) demonstration that this equilibrium results from maximization of "social surplus," which in the GFPM is the sum of the producer and consumer surplus. Equivalently, this is the value to consumers of all end products in all countries minus the costs of supplying the raw materials, transforming the raw materials into end products, and transportation (equation 1 in appendix A).

The essential constraints that describe the equilibrium are the material balance constraints that ensure that, for each country and product, the total supply is equal to the total demand. The left-hand side of the equation refers to the total imports and domestic production of a country. The right-hand side expresses how much of the particular product is consumed as an end product, used as input in the production of another product, or exported.

In the GFPM, the final demand and the raw materials supply are represented by econometric equations. The intermediate demand and supply are represented by input-output coefficients, and by the corresponding output-dependent manufacturing cost, which covers labor, energy, and capital. The marginal manufacturing cost depends on the level of production, and the transport cost depends on the export price of the product and the import tax duty. With local linearization of the demand, supply, and manufacturing cost equations, the problem describing the global equilibrium has a quadratic objective function and linear constraints.

The dual solution of this quadratic program gives a shadow price for each material-balance constraint, which is the market-clearing equilibrium price for each product and country in the particular year considered. In the absence of trade limits, the export price is the same for all exporting countries, while the price in importing countries is equal to the export price plus the transport cost. Price distortions may occur in individual countries due to trade inertia constraints used in the GFPM to express the incomplete adjustment of trade to changes in economic conditions.

Market dynamics

The dynamic element of the GFPM describes endogenous and exogenous temporal changes in the conditions of the global sector. For example, one type of exogenous change refers to the yearly shift of the demand for the end products due to economic growth. For a given price, the demand for a particular product in a country in the current year depends on last year's demand and on the rate of Gross Domestic Product (GDP) growth (Simangunsong and Buongiorno 2001).

The wood supply for industrial roundwood and fuelwood shifts endogenously over time according to how forest stock changes (also endogenously) (Turner and others 2006). Forest stock changes as a result of forest area change, harvest, and growth of stock on the remaining forest. The change in forest area in the GFPM depends on the level of GDP per capita according to an "environmental Kuznets curve" (Turner and others 2006), which implies that as GDP per capita increases, forest area decreases at a decreasing rate, then forest area increases at an increasing rate up to maximum, beyond which forest area increases at a decreasing rate up to a point where forest area stabilizes. The endogenous rate of growth of forest stock, without harvest, is described by an inverse relation between growth and forest density as the ratio of forest volume to forest area.

Technical change in the GFPM is represented by exogenous changes of the input-output coefficients and of the manufacturing cost. Given these changes from one period to the next, the GFPM calculates the global market equilibrium in the next period, and the process is repeated until the end of the projection.

Model Calibration

The demand elasticity parameters were based on Simangunsong and Buongiorno (2001), updated with more recent data, and the timber supply parameters were based on Turner and others (2006). The main database for production, import, and export data was the Food and Agriculture Organization (United Nations) Statistical Database (FAOSTAT) (FAO 2009). The GDP and population data came from the World Development Indicators (WDI) data bank

(World Bank 2008). The data on forest area and forest stock were from the Global Forest Resources Assessment 2005 (FAO 2006). The demand elasticities are presented in table 2. In all countries except the United States, the price elasticity of supply of fuelwood and industrial roundwood, i.e., the percent change in supply due to a one percent change in price, was 1.31, the elasticity with respect to growing stock was 1.10, and the elasticity with respect to forest area was -0.17 (Turner and others 2006), the negative value reflecting the higher cost of harvesting a given volume from a larger area.

For the United States, the price elasticity and rate of shift of wood supply and the rate of forest area change were exogenous and the same as in the United States Forest Products Module (USFPM) (table 3). The rates of shift of timber supply reflect in part future climate changes.

For the other countries, parameters of the Kuznets curve describing forest area change as a function of GDP per capita, and the parameters of the relationship between forest growth and forest stock on the residual forest were taken from Turner and others (2006), updated with more recent data. The constants of the forest area change equation and of the forest growth equation were calibrated so that the predicted values in the base year (2006) were equal to the most recent observed values in each country.

The calibration methods used to estimate the input-output coefficients and the corresponding manufacturing costs were those described in Buongiorno and others (2001), and updated in Buongiorno and Zhu (2011b). The main databases are the FAOSTAT (FAO 2009) and the WDI data bank (World Bank 2008). The calibration is done with goal programming. For each country, the method uses smoothed data on production, imports, exports, and prices from 1992 to 2007 to estimate input-output coefficients for the base year 2006 by minimizing the deviation of calculated from observed production for all products, given a-priori bounds on the input-output coefficients. Manufacturing costs are estimated as the difference between the price of a product and the cost of wood and fiber that go into it, under the assumption of equilibrium and thus zero net profit (beyond a normal return to capital).

Intergovernmental Panel on Climate Change Scenarios and Global Forest Products Model Drivers

Three scenarios (labeled A1B, A2, and B2) developed by the Intergovernmental Panel on Climate Change (IPCC) were initially selected to set the basic assumptions for the 2010 RPA Forest Assessment (USDA Forest Service, 2012). A fourth scenario (labeled A1B-Low Fuelwood) was added later, and makes the same assumptions as scenario A1B, except for the assumption about demand for fuelwood.

Each scenario is based on a separate IPCC storyline about the direction of global social, economic, technical, and policy developments. The storylines also reflect different directions possible for the interaction between developing and industrialized countries. The main characteristics of the three scenarios are presented in table 4.

Scenario A1B assumes continuing globalization that leads to high income growth and low population growth. The scenario implies the highest income per capita in 2060 among all scenarios, and assumes a rapid growth of biofuel demand, specifically, that global consumption of biofuels increased 5.5 times from 2006 to 2060.

Scenario A2 assumes a slowdown of globalization and the rise of more regional interests, leading to a lower income growth than scenario A1B, and higher population growth, and thus lower income per capita. In the scenario, biofuel production grows more slowly than in A1B but is still substantial, with global production by 2060 reaching 2.7 times that of 2006.

Scenario B2 has economic and demographic assumptions that fall between scenarios A1B and A2, and global fuelwood production reaches 2.9 times that of 2006 by 2060.

For the GFPM simulations, the exogenous variables taken from these scenarios are the growth of GDP, population, and global fuelwood demand.

National Gross Domestic Product Assumptions

Assumptions about Gross Domestic Product (GDP) growth in individual countries were obtained by first projecting national GDP per capita and then multiplying by national population, except for the United States, for which future GDP growth rates were established separately (USDA Forest Service, 2012). For the other countries, the main assumption was that the GDP per capita of the different countries would converge between 2006 and 2060 (Sala-i-Martin 2006), and specifically that, by the year 2100, the GDP per capita of all the countries within a region would be the same as well as equal to the average regional GDP per capita predicted by each IPCC scenario.

A secondary assumption was that the ratio of the GDP per capita of a particular country to the GDP per capita of its region would evolve from its initial value in 2006 to 1.0 in 2100 according to the logarithmic difference equation described in Appendix B. Tables 5 and 6 summarize the rate of growth of GDP and the level of GDP per capita obtained with this procedure for selected countries and world regions.

Fuelwood Demand Assumptions

For scenarios A1B, A2, and B2, it was assumed that, between 2006 and 2060, the world fuelwood consumption would grow as the world biofuel consumption predicted by the IPCC (i.e., approximately 5.5 times for scenario A1B, 2.7 times for scenario A2, and 2.9 times for scenario B2).

Another assumption was the convergence of the consumption per capita of fuelwood (energy wood) across countries, analogous to the past convergence observed for other products (Buongiorno 2009). Specifically, the assumption was that, by 2060, the ratio of national to world fuelwood consumption would be equal to the ratio of national to world GDP.

From these two assumptions, we computed the national fuelwood consumption in 2060 and the corresponding national annual growth rate of demand that would be needed between 2006 and 2060, at constant price, to achieve the level consumption in 2060. The demand growth rate applied to the GFPM gave projections of demand that differed from the desired level due to the endogenous change in price. The demand growth rate was then adjusted iteratively until the desired level of global consumption was achieved (appendix C).

For scenario A1B-Low Fuelwood, the demand for fuelwood was entirely defined by econometric demand equations. For high-income countries, the price elasticity was -0.1 and the GDP elasticity was 0.2 (Simangunsong and Buongiorno 2001). For low-income countries, the same price elasticity was used with a GDP elasticity of 0.05 to continue past trends.

Technical Change Assumptions

Technology for manufacture of wood products is mature but not static. Marginal improvements in techniques and equipment were made between 1961 and 2005, with less wood use per unit of output and more recycled paper used in making paper and paperboard (Kando and Buongiorno 2009).

Information about improvements in technology, in our view, is incorporated at the rate any necessary equipment changes are made, and because the state of the art in a mature industry is increasing slowly, inefficient producers have an opportunity to catch up with the best available technology. In this application, the assumption was made that the least cost techniques observed in 2006 would improve further by 2060. Furthermore, the assumption was made, too, that technology would become more similar across countries, using less wood per unit of output and more waste paper instead of pulp (appendix D).

4

Observed and Projected Evolutions of the Forest Economy

In this section, we present results of four scenarios run with the Global Forest Products Model (GFPM) for the following aspects of the world forest economy: forest area and forest stock; and prices, consumption, production, and trade of wood, wood products, and other papermaking fibers. We also offer global projections for the main regions and for selected individual countries in each region. We preface the projections with findings from an observed history (1992 to 2006, unless otherwise noted) of each aspect. The projections for each aspect cover the years 2006 to 2060, unless otherwise noted.

Forest Area

Figure 2 shows the observed and projected forest area by world region. Table 7 shows data for the main countries in each region. The data from 1992 to 2006 are interpolations and extrapolations of the data in the Global Forest Resources Assessment 2005 (FAO 2006) and earlier assessments. The data from 2007 to 2060 are projections obtained with the Global Forest Products Model (GPFM). As indicated above in the description of the dynamics of the GFPM, the evolution of forest area depends on the historical rate of change and the projected level of Gross Domestic Product (GDP) per capita.

Observed forest area evolution
Between 1992 and 2006, the world forest area decreased by 111 million ha. In developing countries, forest area decreased by 123 million ha and increased by 12 million ha in developed countries. The largest reductions were in Africa (-57 million ha, with -6 million in Nigeria) and in South America (-55 million, with -40 million ha in Brazil).[2] In Europe, the forest area increased by 12 million ha.

Projected forest area evolution
Scenario A1B—Under scenario A1B, the world forest area increases by 63 million ha, almost equally in developed and developing countries. The largest regional increases are in Asia (+96 million ha in China, and 28 million ha in India) and Europe (+49 million ha, spread over several countries). The largest regional reductions are in South America (-28 million ha, due mostly to a loss of 52 million ha in Brazil), Africa (-20 million ha), and North/Central America (-19 million ha, largely due to the -29 million ha in the United States).

Scenario A2—Under scenario A2, the world forest area declines by 628 million ha, with 431 million ha in developing

countries and 198 million ha in developed countries. The largest regional decrease is in South America (-217 million ha, of which -163 million ha in Brazil). In Europe, the decrease of 175 million ha is due mostly to -197 million ha in the Russian Federation. There are declines in Africa (by 127 million ha) and Asia (by 62 million ha, due mostly to -54 million ha in Indonesia). In North/Central America, there is little change except for decreases of 6 million ha in Mexico and 25 million ha in the United States, adding up to a regional decrease of 39 million ha. There is a decrease of 7 million ha in Oceania.

Scenario B2—Under scenario B2, the world forest area declines by 305 million ha, with most of the decline in developing countries (-287 million ha). The largest regional declines are in South America (-161 million ha, with -132 million ha in Brazil) and Africa (-93 million ha). There is more reduction in North/Central America (-26 million ha, with -19 million ha in the United States) than in Asia, where the increase in China (+43 million ha) and India (+14 million ha) compensates for the decrease in Indonesia (-51 million ha). There is a decrease in Europe of 6 million ha, due mostly to the 48 million ha decrease in the Russian Federation.

Scenario A1B-Low Fuelwood—Scenario A1B-Low Fuelwood led to the same projections as scenario A1B because the assumptions for GDP per capita were the same.

Forest Stock

Figure 3 shows the observed and projected forest stock (standing volume of trees) by world region. Table 8 shows data for the stock levels in the main countries in each region. The data from 1992 to 2006 are interpolations and extrapolations of the data in the Global Forest Resources Assessment 2005 (FAO 2006) and earlier assessments. The data from 2007 to 2060 are GFPM projections.

The evolution of the forest stock depends on the evolution of forest area, the periodic harvest, and the growth rate of the residual stock, which is inversely related to the stock density (stock per unit area). Due to this relationship, and depending on the initial growth rate of forest stock on nonharvested areas, the forest stock could increase while the forest area decreased in some countries, and vice-versa.

Observed forest stock evolution
Between 1992 and 2006, the forest stock decreased in developing countries by 14 billion m³ and increased in developed countries by 10 billion m³. The largest regional decrease was in South America (-7 billion m³, with -6 billion in Brazil). In Asia, the forest stock decreased by 3 billion m³ due principally to a 7 billion m³ decrease in Indonesia, partly compensated by a 2 billion m³ increase

---

[2] Here and in the remainder of the paper, a "-" sign in the text refers to a reduction, and a "+" sign to an increase. The data in the tables are in levels.

Forest area, scenario A1B

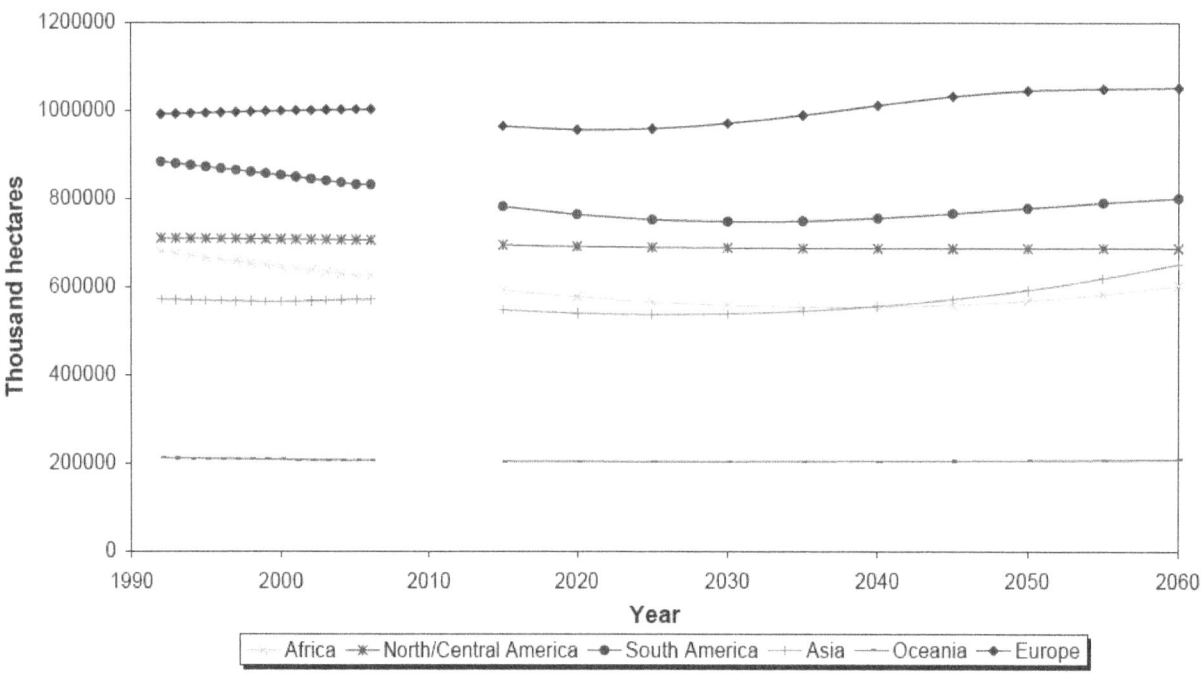

Forest area, scenario A2

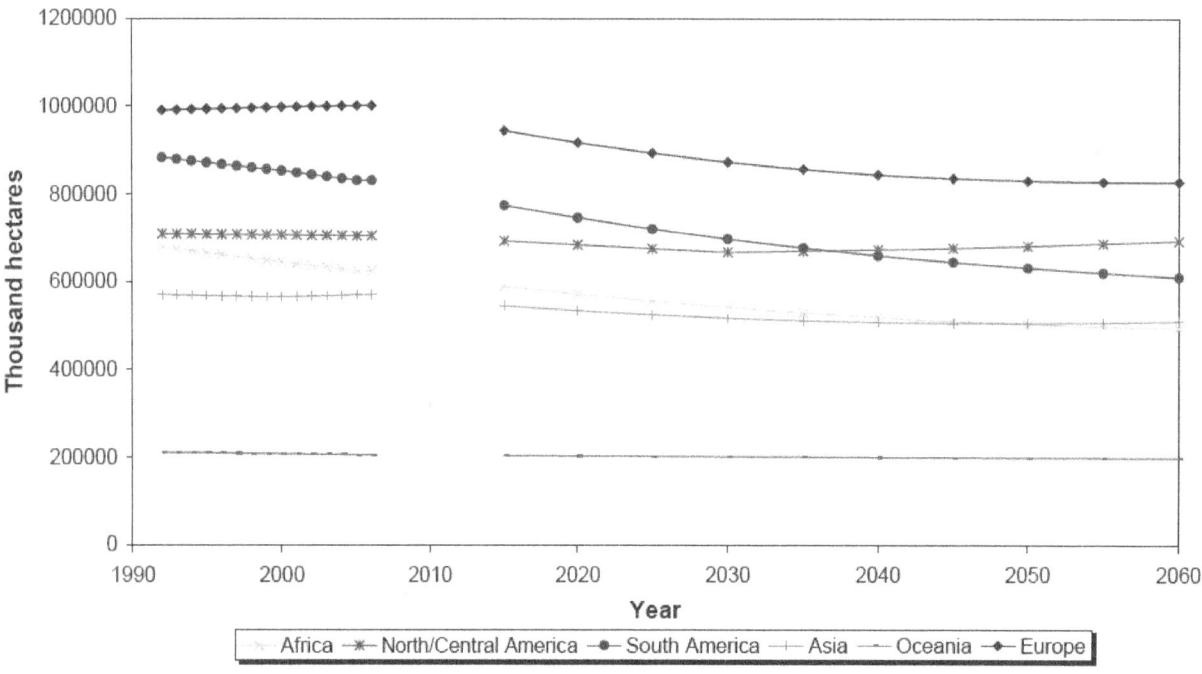

Figure 2—Forest area by world region, observed and projected with the Global Forest Products Model. (continued on next page)

Forest area, scenario B2

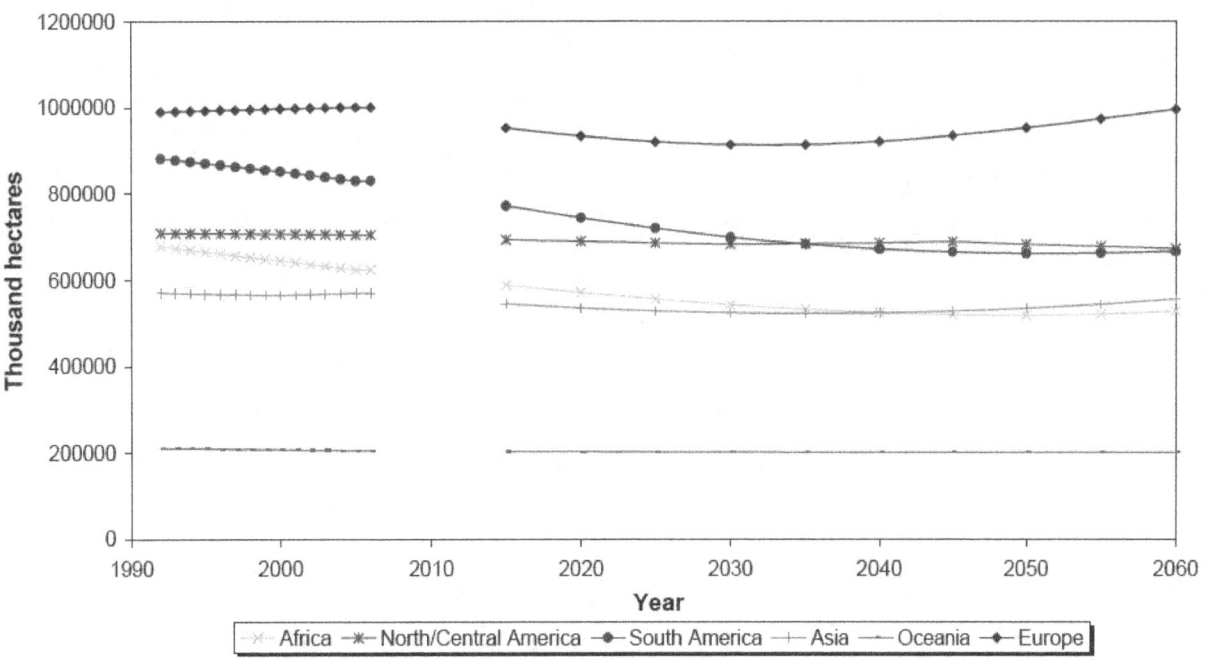

Forest area, scenario A1B-Low Fuelwood

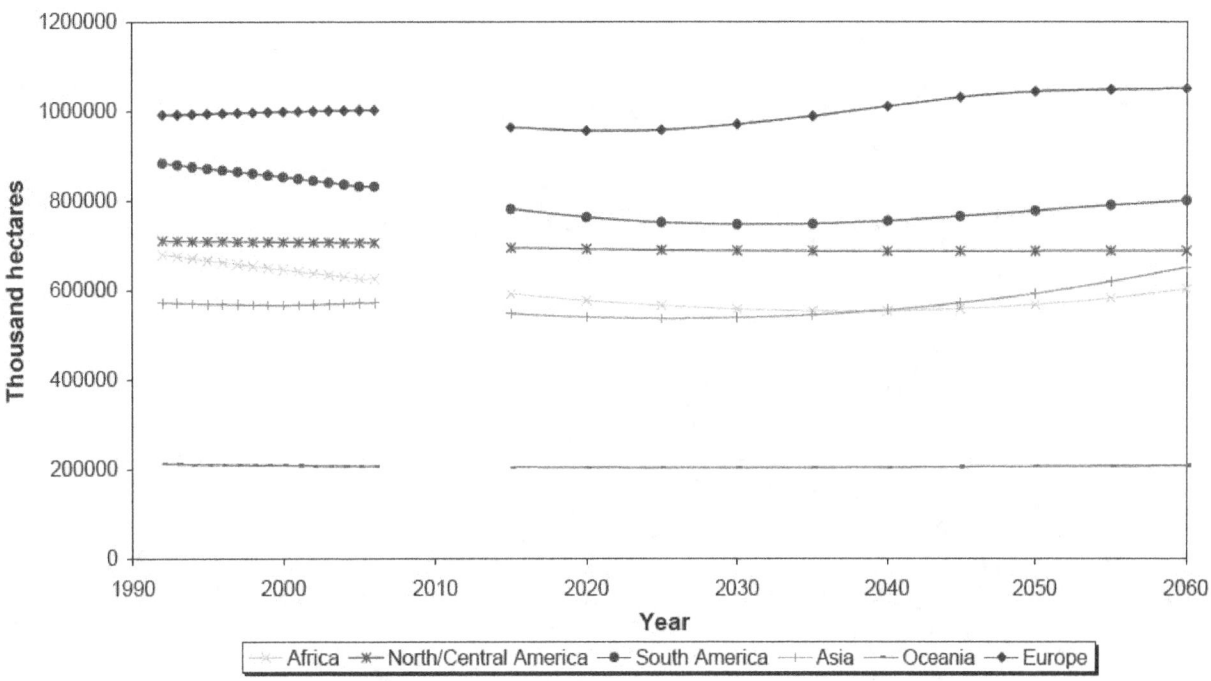

Figure 2 (continued)— Forest area by world region, observed and projected with the Global Forest Products Model.

Forest stock, scenario A1B

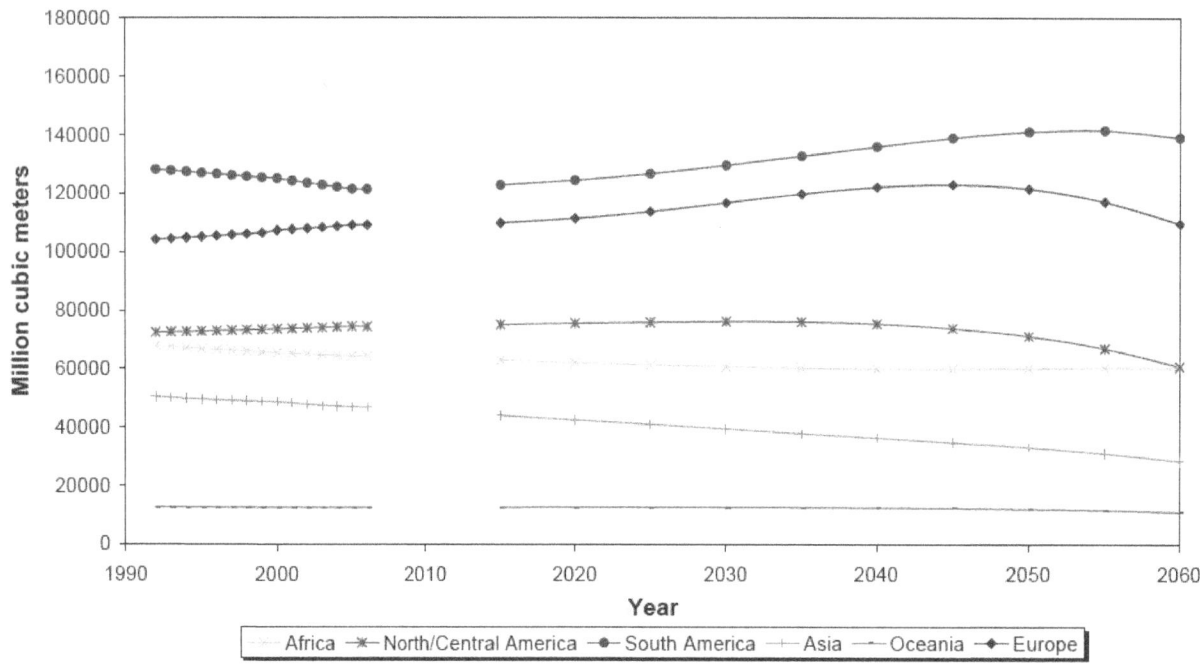

Forest stock, scenario A2

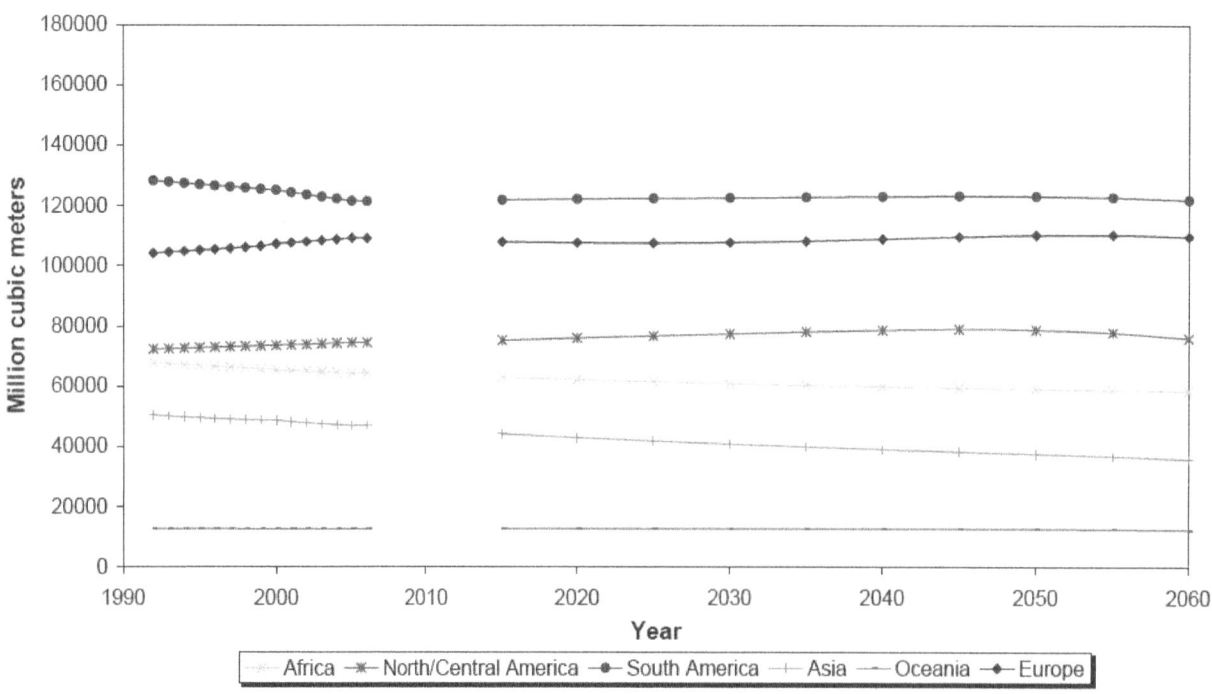

Figure 3—Forest stock by world region, observed and projected with the Global Forest Products Model. (continued on next page)

Forest stock, scenario B2

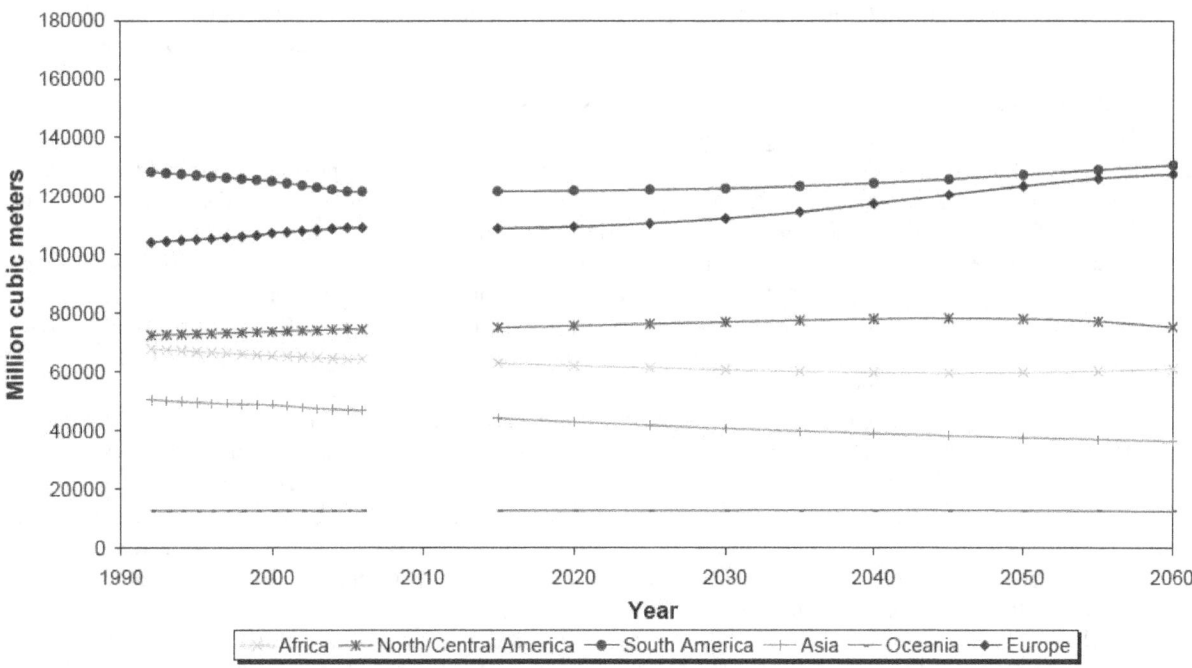

Forest stock, scenario A1B-Low Fuelwood

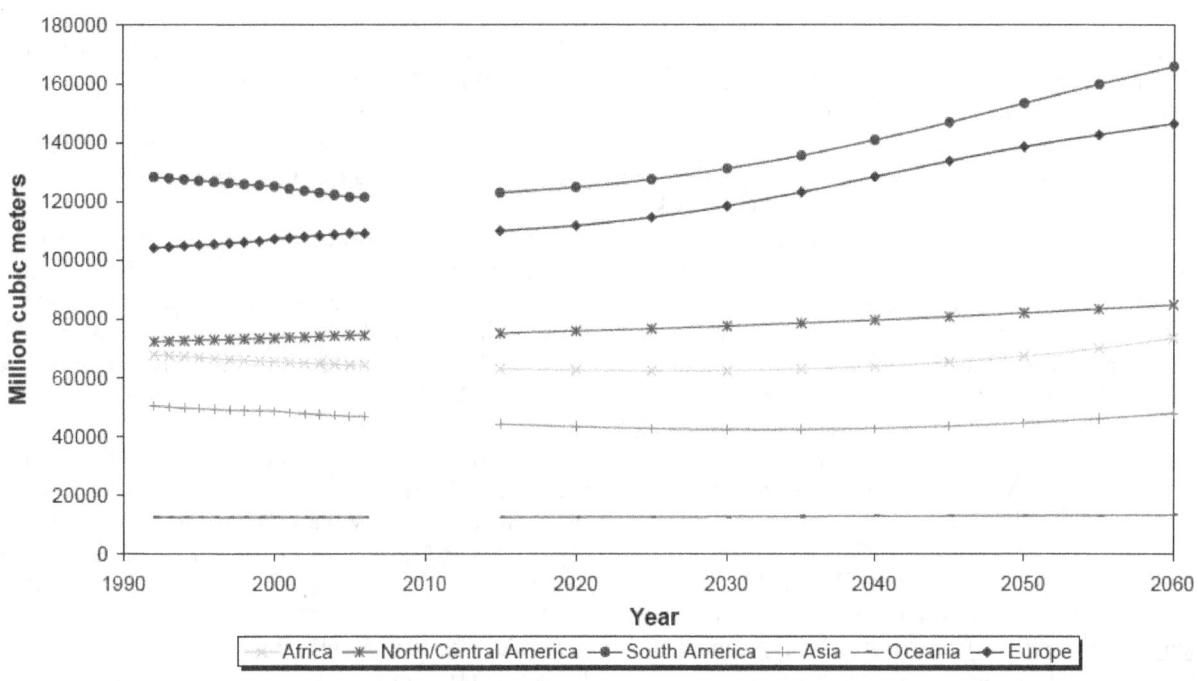

Figure 3 (continued)—Forest stock by world region, observed and projected with the Global Forest Products Model.

in China. The stock declined in Africa by 3 billion m³ but increased in Europe by 5 million m³ (spread out over many countries) and in North America (mostly in the United States) by 3 billion m³.

Projected forest stock evolution

Scenario A1B—Under scenario A1B, the world growing stock decreases by 22 billion m³, with 14 million m³ in developing countries. The largest regional decrease is in Asia (-18 billion m³, of which -10 billion m³ were in China). There is a projected decrease also for North/Central America (by 15 billion m³, spread among Canada, the United States, and Mexico) but an increase in South America (+18 billion m³, with +13 billion m³ in Brazil). Thus, it appears that the growth rate of stock, notably high in Brazilian new forests, more than compensates for the decrease in forest area observed above. There is a decrease in Oceania of 2 billion m³ and little change in Europe.

Scenario A2—Under scenario A2, the world growing stock decreases by 17 billion m³. This is larger than under scenario A1B in total but with a larger decrease in developing countries (-26 billion m³) and an increase in developed countries (+9 billion m³). The largest regional declines are in Asia (-11 billion m³, with -7 billion m³ in China) and Africa (-7 billion m³). In South America, where the stock is projected under A1B to increase, the stock changes little. Meanwhile, the stock of North/Central America (where the stock is projected under A1B to decrease) increases by 4 billion m³ in the United States. There is little overall change in growing stock in Europe, where the 13 billion m³ decrease in the Russian Federation is compensated by increases in several other countries.

Scenario B2—Under scenario B2, the world growing stock increases modestly, by 12 billion m³, although the stock decreases by 15 billion m³ in developing countries. As under scenario A2, the largest regional decline in growing stock is in Asia (-11 billion m³, with -8 billion m³ in China and -4 billion m³ in India and Indonesia). There are also declines in Africa (-4 billion m³) and North/Central America, although, globally, these declines are more than compensated by increases for Europe (+18 billion m³, with 3 billion m³ in the Russian Federation) and South America (+9 billion m³, with +6 billion m³ in Brazil).

Scenario A1B-Low Fuelwood—Under scenario A1B-Low Fuelwood, the world growing stock increases by 101 billion m³, with more than half of that increase in developing countries. The largest regional increases are in South America (+44 billion m³, with 32 billion m³ in Brazil) and Europe (+37 billion m³, with 12 billion m³ in the Russian Federation). In North/Central America, the growing stock increases by

9 billion m³, mostly due to the 11 billion m³ increase in the United States. There are modest positive changes in Asia (with declines in Indonesia, China, and India compensated in part by a combined 6 billion m³ increase in Japan and Oceania).

Solid Wood Prices

Figure 4 shows the past and projected world real prices of fuelwood, industrial roundwood, and sawnwood, measured by the unit value of exports expressed in 1997 U.S. dollars. Tables 9, 10, and 11 show the prices of the same commodities in the major countries within each world region. The data from 1961 to 2006 came from the FAOSTAT database (FAO 2009). The projections to 2060 were obtained with the GFPM.

Observed evolution of solid wood prices

Between 1961 and 2006, the real prices of fuelwood, industrial roundwood, and sawnwood fluctuated considerably. Prices were highest in the 1970s. Compared to the real world prices in 1992, fuelwood was $13 lower, industrial roundwood was $43 lower, and sawnwood was $10 lower in 2006.

Projected evolution of solid wood prices

Scenario A1B—Scenario A1B implies a very high increase in fuelwood demand. Under scenario A1B, the price of fuelwood more than doubles. The price of fuelwood rises rapidly and approaches the price of industrial roundwood by 2030. The real world price of industrial roundwood rises little until 2030, but thereafter, the prices of fuelwood and industrial roundwood increase in concert and reach $256/m³ by 2060. The price of sawnwood follows the trend of the price of industrial roundwood, hardly changing between 2006 and 2030 and then sharply rising to reach $392/m³ in 2060, for an overall rise of 72 percent above its 2006 level.

Scenario A2—Under scenario A2, the prices of fuelwood and industrial roundwood rise much less than under scenario A1B. The two prices converge 10 years later than under scenario A1B and reach $118/m³ in 2060. The real price of sawnwood declines until 2035 and then rises slightly to reach $250/m³ in 2060.

Scenario B2—Under scenario B2, the future real prices of fuelwood, industrial roundwood, and sawnwood are very similar to those under scenario A2, except for a slightly earlier convergence of the prices of fuelwood and industrial roundwood.

Scenario A1B-Low Fuelwood—Under scenario A1B-Low Fuelwood, prices of solid wood products are the lowest among all the scenarios. Even though the fuelwood price rises faster than the price of industrial roundwood, convergence of the two prices occurs only towards 2050. Compared to 2006, in

2060 the world price of fuelwood is $24 higher, but the world price of industrial roundwood is $9 lower, and the world price of sawnwood is $50 lower.

Fuelwood

Fuelwood consumption
Figure 5 shows the historic and projected data for fuelwood consumption (production plus imports minus exports), including industrial roundwood that is used for energy, and table 12 shows the corresponding data for major countries in each region.

Observed evolution of fuelwood consumption
Between 1992 and 2006, the annual consumption of fuelwood increased by 243 million m^3 in developing countries but declined by 10 million in developed countries. The largest regional increases were in Africa (208 million m^3 spread over many countries) and Europe (39 million m^3, the growth in France, Germany, and other countries compensating in part for the 18 million m^3 decline in the annual consumption of the Russian Federation). In South America, annual fuelwood consumption increased by 26 million m^3, of which more than half was in Brazil. In Asia, the increase of consumption in India and China was offset by a decrease of 45 million m^3 in Indonesia, resulting in no net change at the regional level. In North/Central America, annual fuelwood consumption decreased by 40 million m^3, mostly due to the decrease in the United States.

Projected evolution of fuelwood consumption
Scenario A1B—Under scenario A1B, the world annual consumption of fuelwood increases by 8 billion m^3 (i.e., at more than five times the average annual growth observed between 1992 and 2006). Almost half of this world increase of consumption occurs in Asia (850 million m^3 in China, 721 million m^3 in India, and 351 million m^3 in Japan). In Europe, consumption grows by 1.4 billion m^3 from 2006 to 2060, with especially strong growth in France, Germany, the Russian Federation, and the United Kingdom. The 1.6 billion m^3 increase of annual consumption in North America is due mostly to growth in the United States (+1.2 billion m^3). In South America, consumption grows more modestly (+481 million m^3, with 184 million m^3 in Brazil).

Scenario A2—Under scenario A2, the world annual fuelwood consumption increases by less than half than that under A1B, by 3 billion m^3. In contrast to scenario A1B, under scenario A2, two-thirds of this growth is in developed countries. Annual consumption grows the most in North America (+1.2 billion m^3, mostly in the United States), Asia (+936 million m^3, with 285 million m^3 in Japan and 117 million m^3 in China), and Europe (+800 million m^3, with strong growth in France and Germany). In South America, annual consumption

increases by 152 million m^3, largely in Argentina and Brazil. In Oceania, fuelwood consumption grows somewhat less than under scenario A1B. Africa is the only region where fuelwood consumption decreases.

Scenario B2—Under scenario B2, the world annual fuelwood consumption rises somewhat more than under scenario A2 but much less than under scenario A1B. As under scenario A2, about two-thirds of the growth is in developed countries. The main difference between scenarios B2 and A2 is the projection under scenario B2 of almost double the growth of consumption in Asia. Between 2006 and 2060, annual fuelwood consumption increases by 473 million m^3 in China and 232 million m^3 in India.

Scenario A1B-Low Fuelwood—Under scenario A1B-Low Fuelwood, the increase in world fuelwood consumption between 2006 and 2060 is approximately the same as the increase observed between 1992 and 2006. The growth of consumption in developing countries is triple that in developed countries. Annual consumption grows by 111 million m^3 in Asia, with 44 million m^3 in India and 28 million m^3 in China. Fuelwood consumption increases by 66 million m^3 in Africa and 38 million m^3 in Europe, with 28 million m^3 in the Russian Federation. In North/Central America, consumption increases by 19 million m^3, mostly due to an increase in the United States. Most of the 13 million m^3 increase in South America is in Brazil.

Fuelwood trade
Figure 6 shows the net trade (exports minus imports) of fuelwood by major world region, from 1961 to 2060, and table 13 shows the data for selected years and principal countries within each region.

Observed evolution of fuelwood trade
The main changes in fuelwood trade between 1992 and 2006 were increases in exports from Europe and North/Central America and a corresponding increase in imports in Asia.

Projected evolution of fuelwood trade
Under all scenarios, Asia is the main region of net imports, while South America and Europe are regions with net exports. However, the magnitude of the trade differed greatly among scenarios, from scenario A1B with the largest net trade to scenario to A1B-Low Fuelwood with the lowest, and B2 and A2 in between (fig. 6).

Scenario A1B—Under scenario A1B, the annual net exports of fuelwood from developed to developing countries increases by 819 million m^3 (table 13). More than 2 billion m^3 of the increase originates in South America, with nearly all of the increase coming from Brazil. Europe increases annual net

Solid wood prices, scenario A1B

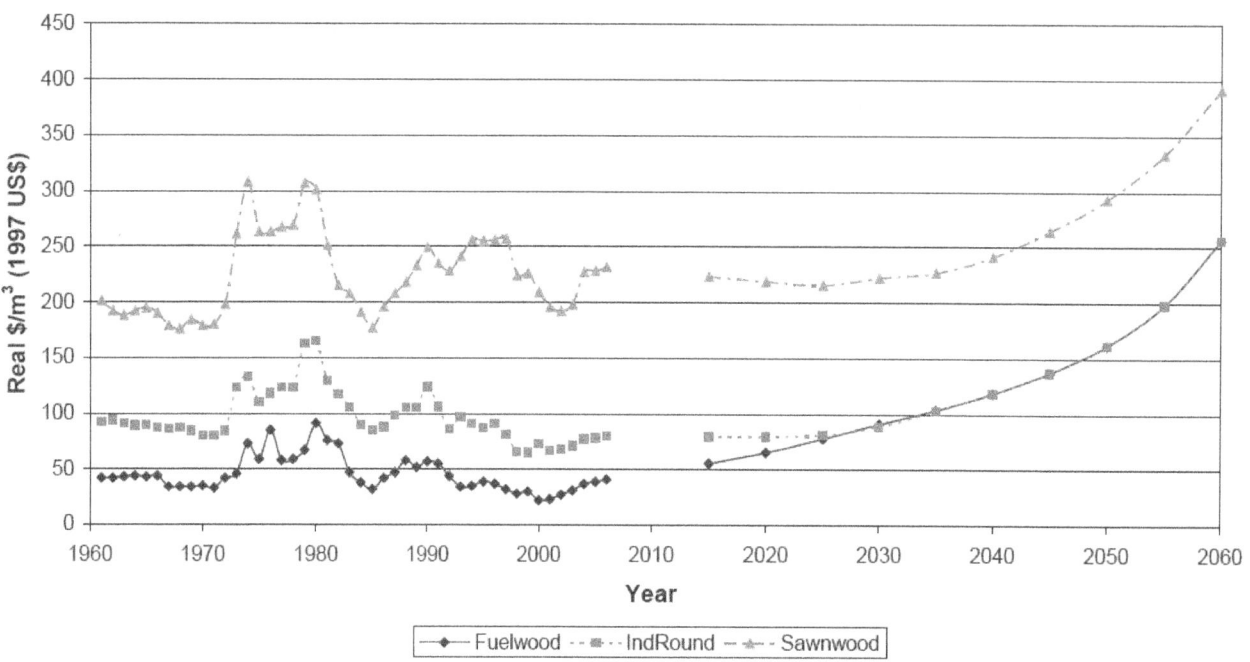

Solid wood prices, scenario A2

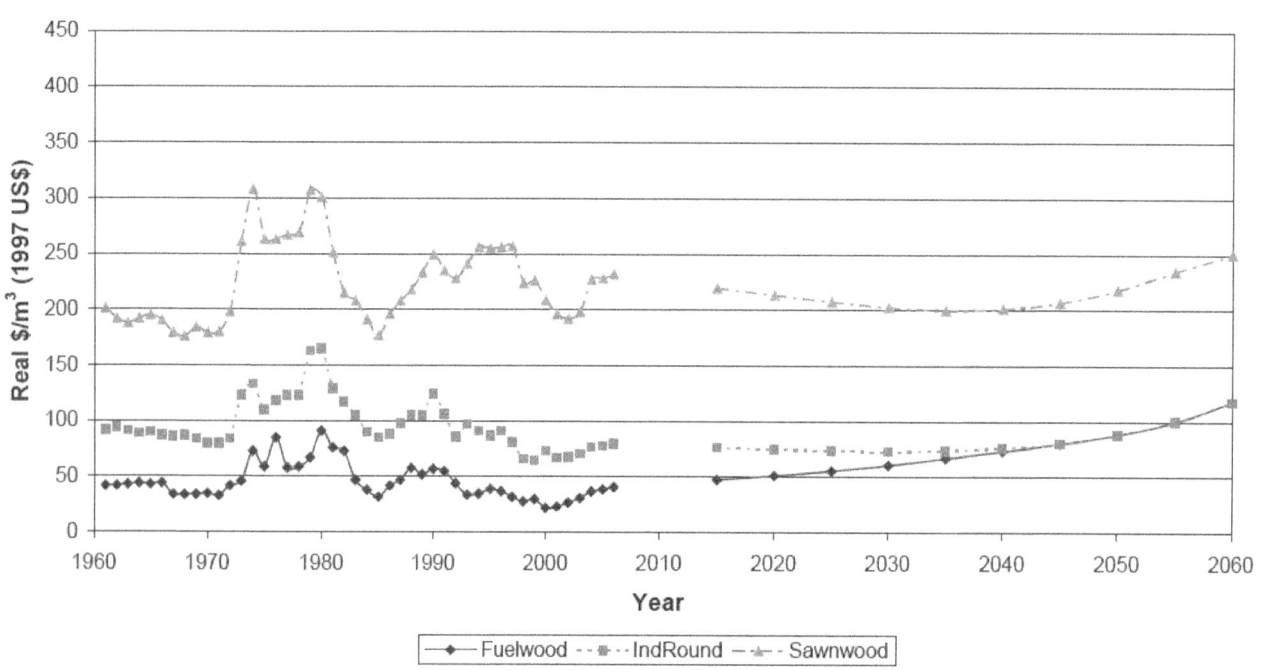

Figure 4—World prices of fuelwood, industrial roundwood, and sawnwood, observed and projected with the Global Forest Products Model. (continued on next page)

Solid wood prices, scenario B2

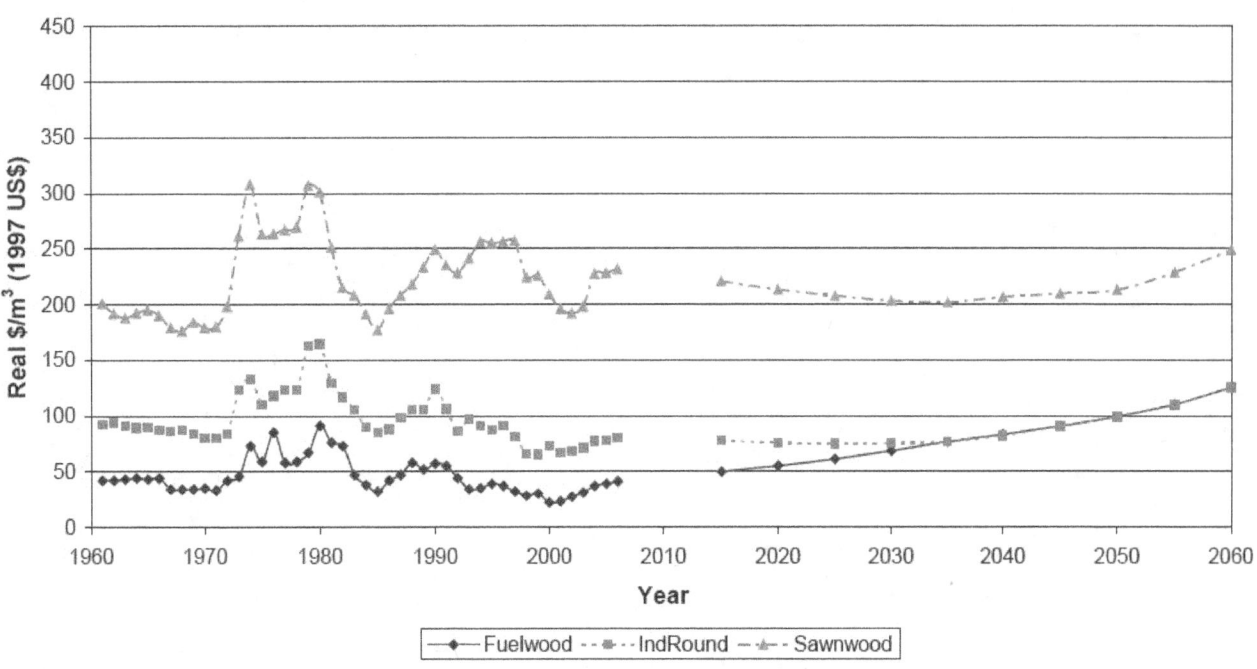

Solid wood prices, scenario A1B-Low Fuelwood

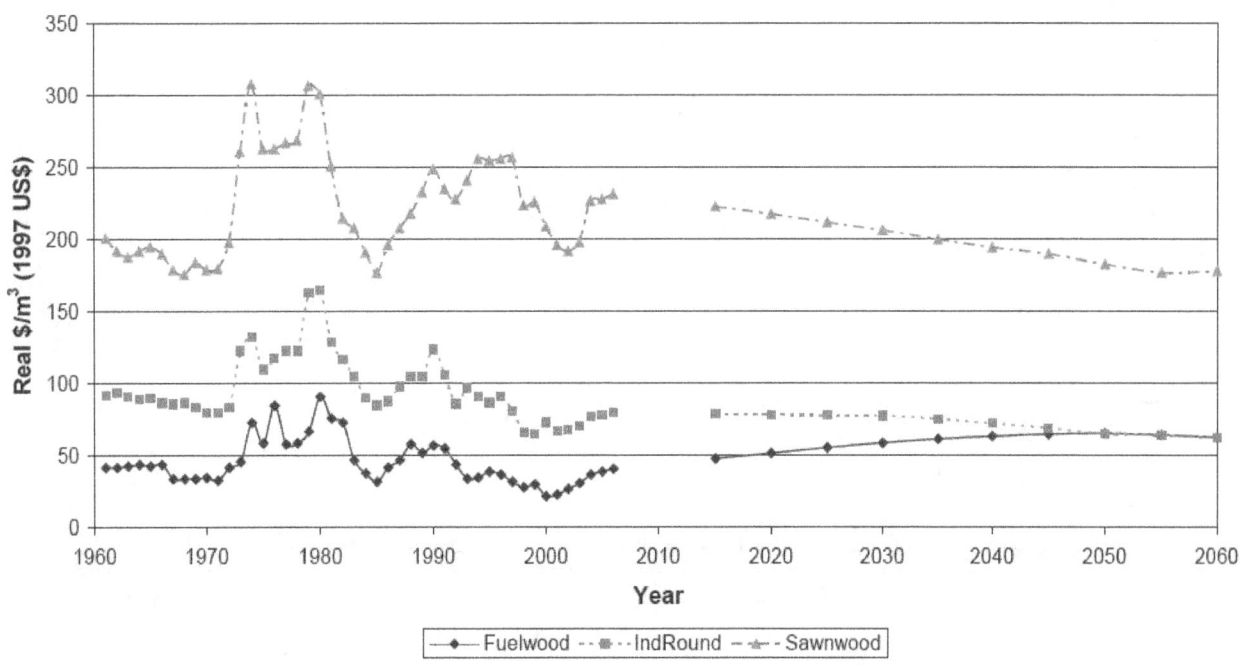

Figure 4 (continued)—World prices of fuelwood, industrial roundwood, and sawnwood, observed and projected with the Global Forest Products Model.

Fuelwood consumption, scenario A1B

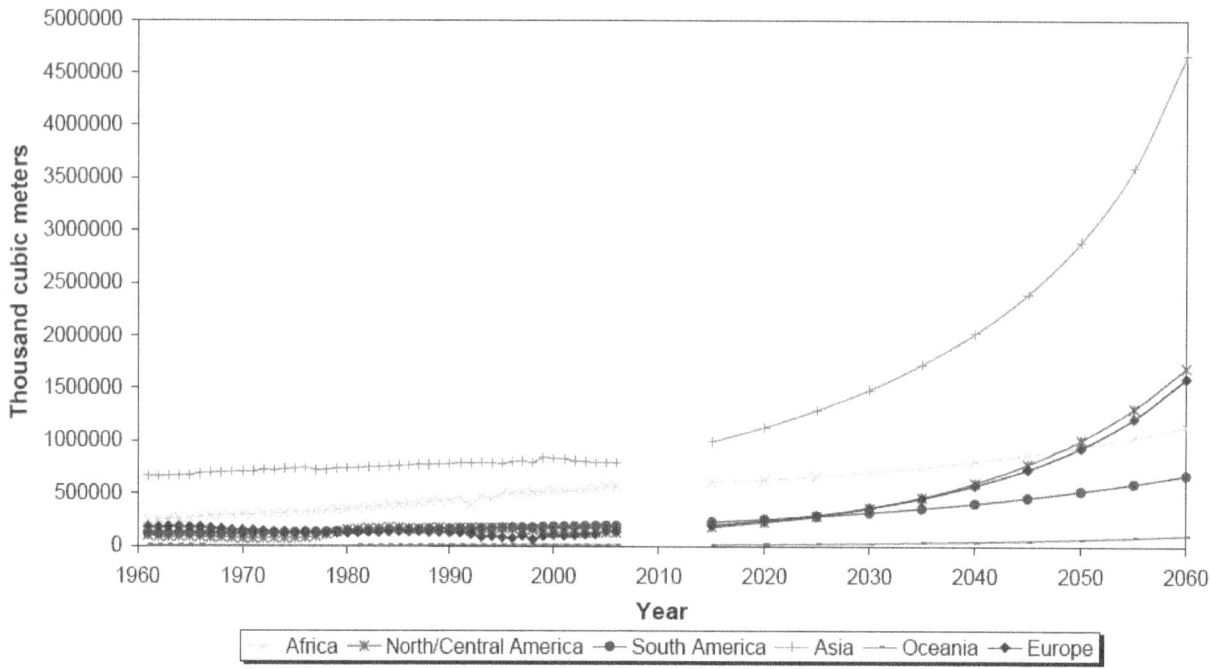

Fuelwood consumption, scenario A2

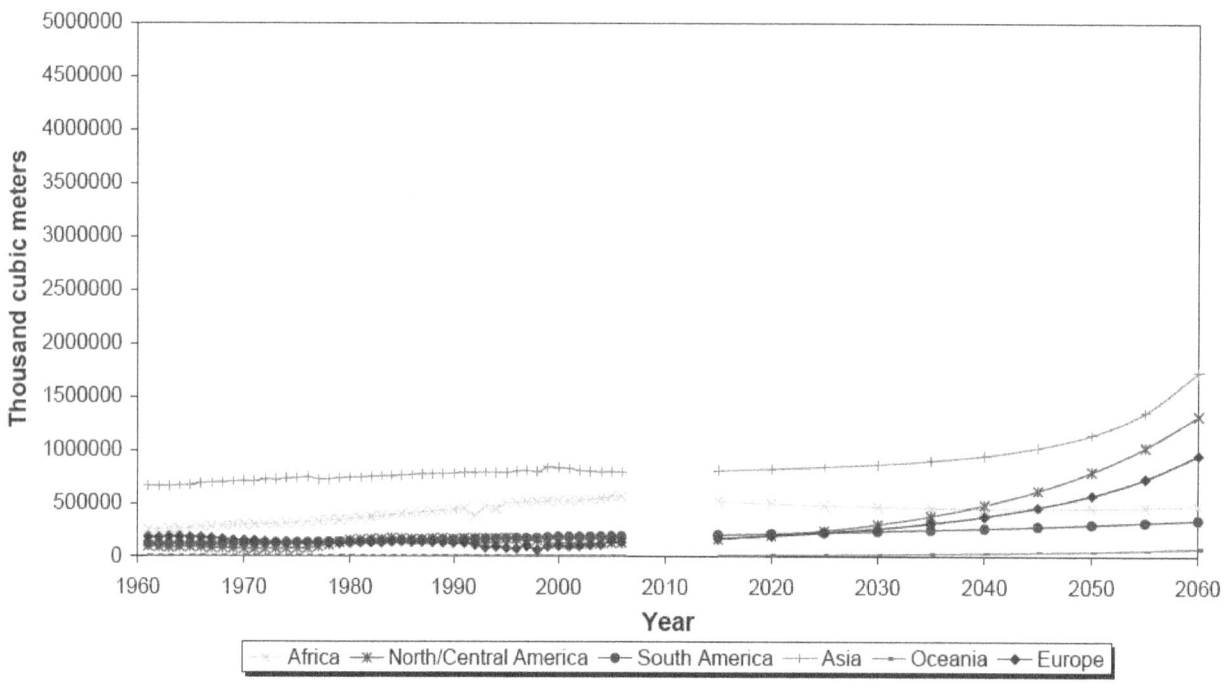

Figure 5—Fuelwood consumption by world region, observed and projected with the Global Forest Products Model. (continued on next page)

Fuelwood consumption, scenario B2

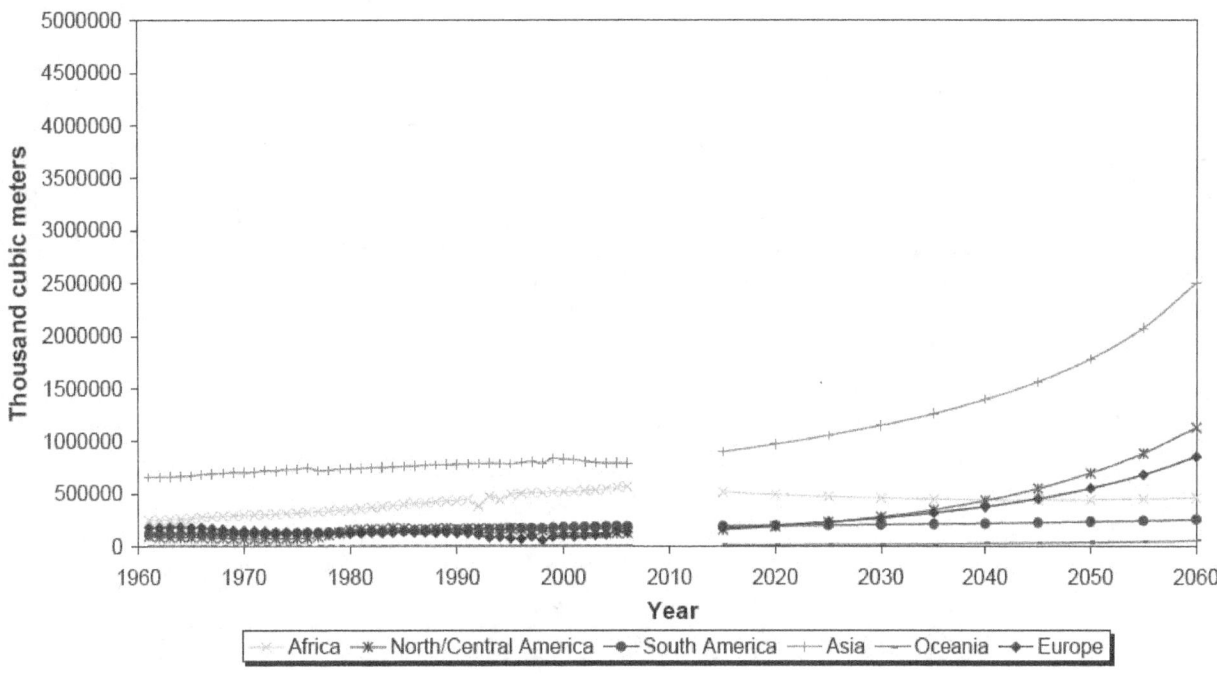

Fuelwood consumption, scenario A1B-Low Fuelwood

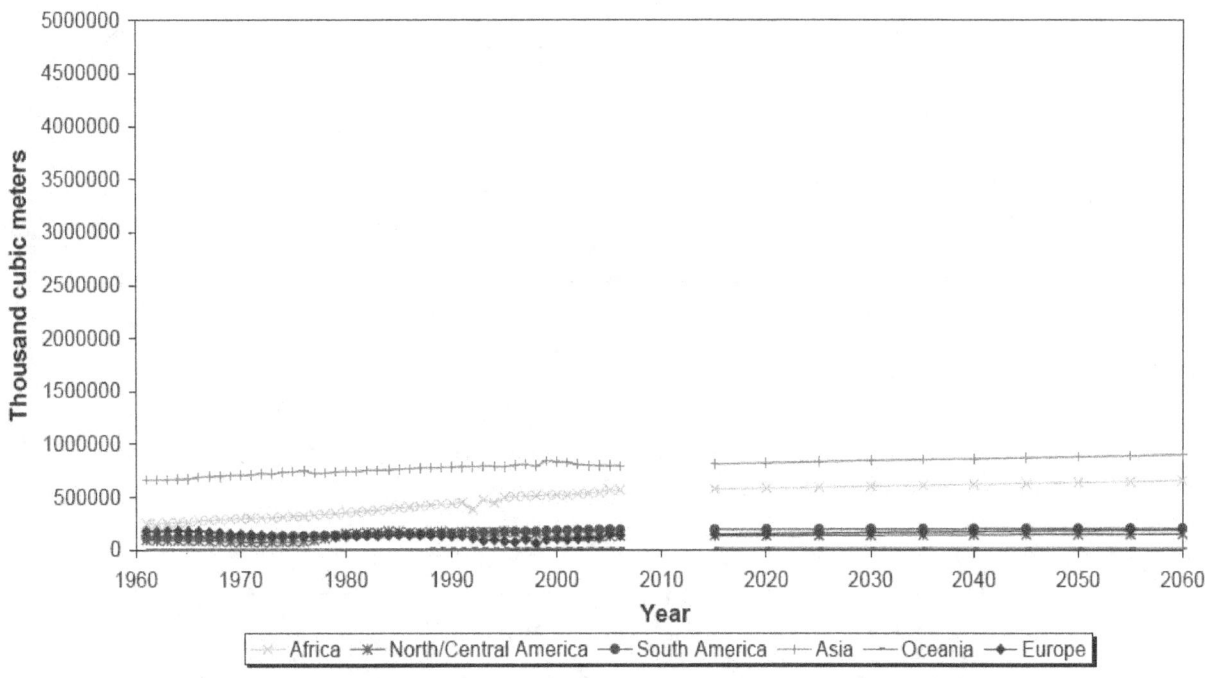

Figure 5 (continued)—Fuelwood consumption by world region, observed and projected with the Global Forest Products Model.

Fuelwood net trade, scenario A1B

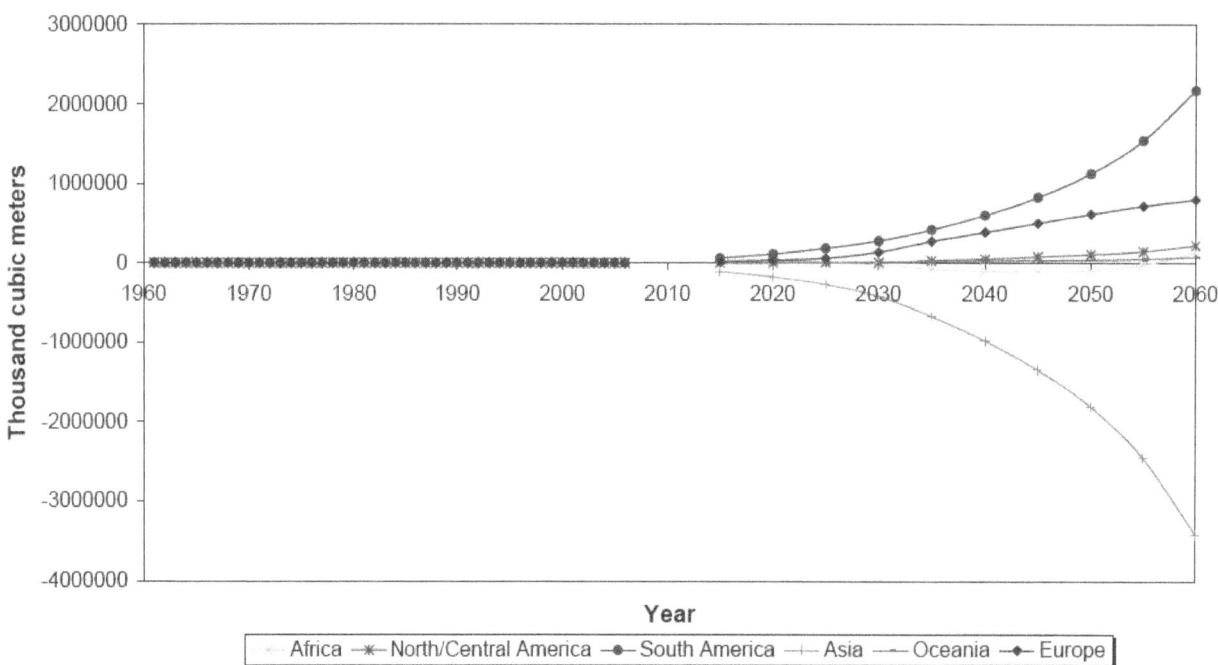

Fuelwood net trade, scenario A2

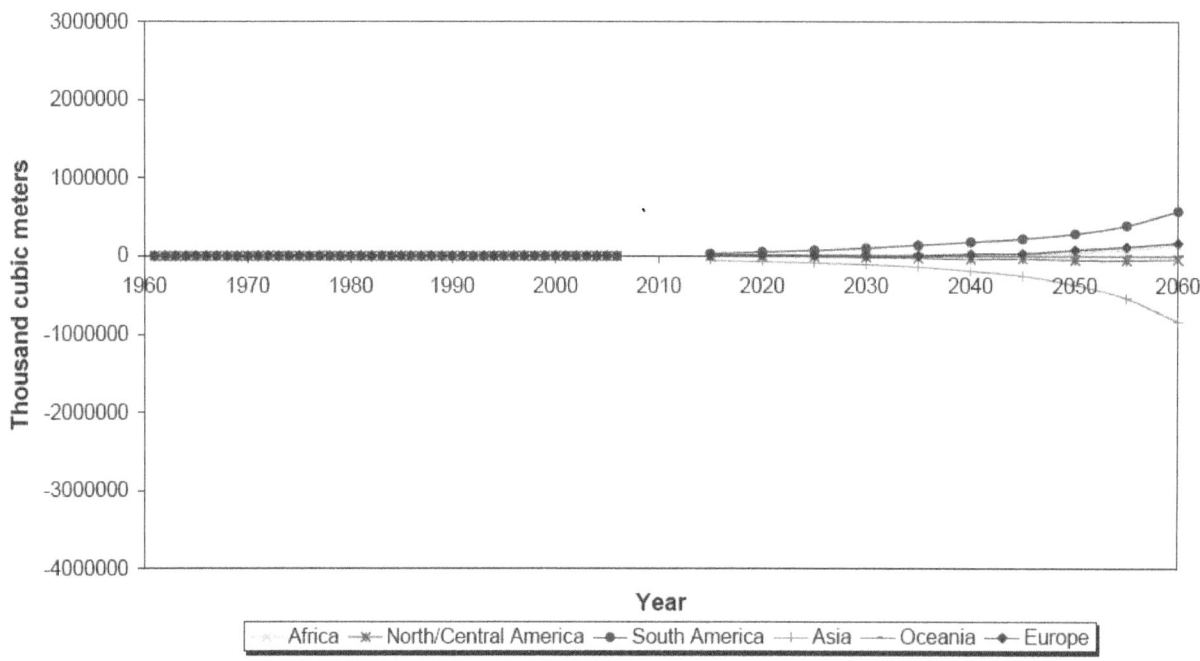

Figure 6—Fuelwood net trade by world region, observed and projected with the Global Forest Products Model. (continued on next page)

Fuelwood net trade, scenario B2

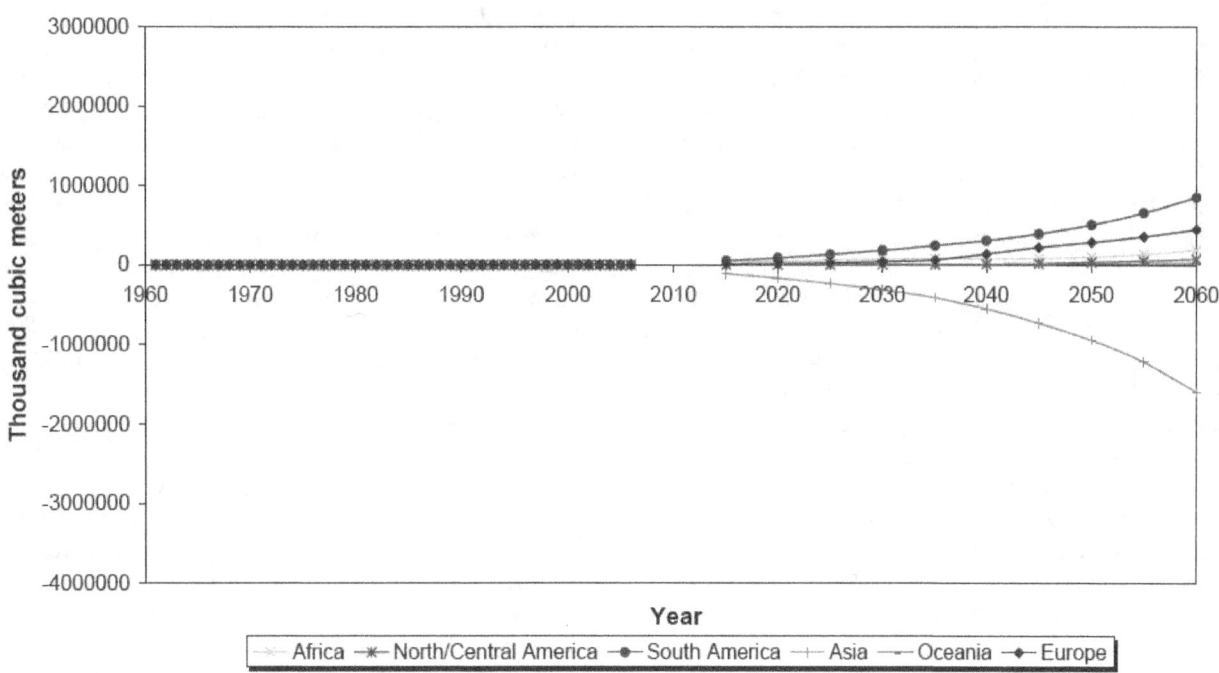

Fuelwood net trade, scenario A1B-Low Fuelwood

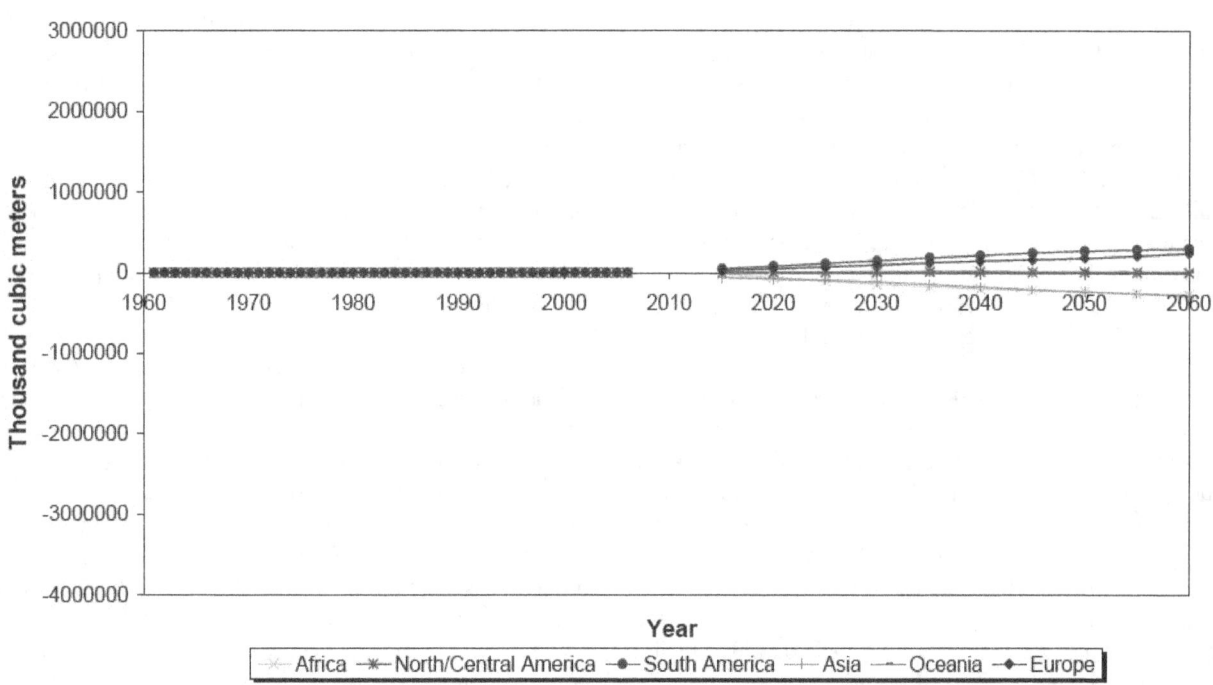

Figure 6 (continued)—Fuelwood net trade by world region, observed and projected with the Global Forest Products Model.

exports by 801 million m³, mostly from the Russian Federation. North/Central America increases its annual net exports by 222 million m³, with a 372 million m³ increase in net exports emerging from Canada, which is partially offset by 125 million m³ more net imports by Mexico. Asia is the main negative change of net trade, with India increasing its annual net imports by 929 million m³ and China by 694 million m³.

Scenario A2—Under scenario A2, the net trade of developed countries falls by 151 million m³, an event that turns developed countries from net exporters into net importers. The largest regional negative change in annual net trade is in Asia (-837 million m³, principally in Japan and India). The net trade of North/Central America also falls (-44 million m³, with -55 million m³ in Mexico and -29 million m³ in the United States offset by a 35 million m³ increase in Canada). The other regions experience an increase in annual net trade, mostly from South America (+576 million m³, with 449 million m³ from Brazil and 108 million m³ from Chile). In Europe, annual net trade increases by 165 million m³, mostly from the Russian Federation. Africa increases its annual net trade of fuelwood by 138 million m³, despite decreases in Egypt, Nigeria, and South Africa.

Scenario B2—Under scenario B2, as in scenario A1B but in contrast to scenario A2, the annual net trade of fuelwood increases in developed countries and decreases in developing countries by 320 million m³. The direction of changes in net trade is similar to that of scenario A1B but different in magnitudes. The increase in deficit of Asia is about half that of scenario A1B, and still occurs in China, India, Japan, and Indonesia. The annual net trade increases in all other regions: by 854 million m³ in South America (mostly Brazil and Chile), 447 million m³ in Europe (with 203 million m³ in the Russian Federation), and 192 million m³ in Africa. In North/Central America, annual net trade increases by 77 million m³, with a 93 million m³ increase in Canada more than compensating for a projected decrease of 31 million m³ in the United States. In Oceania, annual net trade increases by 25 million m³, mostly from Australia.

Scenario A1B-Low Fuelwood—Under scenario A1B-Low Fuelwood, the annual net trade of fuelwood decreases in developing countries and increases in developed countries, as in B2 but by a lesser amount. Asia and Africa were the two regions with negative changes of net trade. India is the country with the main negative change (-182 million m³). Net trade decreases also in Nigeria (by 62 million m³), and China's net trade is unchanged. The largest regional positive changes of annual net trade are in South America (+297 million m³, with 213 million m³ in Brazil) and Europe (+243 million m³, spread over several countries, including the Russian Federation and France).

Industrial Roundwood

Industrial roundwood consumption
Figure 7 shows the data of past and projected industrial roundwood consumption (production plus imports minus exports), except energy wood, between 1961 and 2060 in world regions.[3] Table 14 shows the same data for selected years and countries.

Projected evolution of industrial roundwood consumption
Under all four scenarios, the world annual industrial roundwood consumption decreases—especially under scenarios A2 and B2, less so under scenario A1B, and least so under scenario A1B-Low Fuelwood. There are substantial differences between scenarios, with scenario A1B aligning closest to A1B-Low Fuelwood, and scenario A2 with B2.

Scenario A1B—Under scenario A1B, the world annual consumption of industrial roundwood decreases by 341 million m³, despite a modest increase of 16 million m³ in developing countries. The largest decreases of consumption are in North/Central America (-245 million m³, with -167 million m³ in the United States), and Europe (-109 million m³, with -44 million m³ in the Russian Federation and -30 million m³ in Finland). Annual consumption also decreases in South America (-67 million m³, with -41 million m³ in Brazil and -21 million m³ in Chile), Africa (-17 million m³), and Oceania (-6 million m³). The annual consumption of industrial roundwood only increases in Asia (+103 million m³ by 2060, with +63 million m³ in China and +12 million m³ in Japan). In other regions, the decrease of industrial roundwood consumption is due mainly to the decrease of wood pulp in paper and paperboard manufacture, with its fiber needs provided by increased use of waste paper. Other causes include the increasing use of industrial roundwood for energy and, to a lesser extent, improvements in technology that decrease the amount of wood use in sawnwood, panels, and pulp production.

Scenario A2—Among all the scenarios, scenario A2 implies the largest decrease in world industrial roundwood consumption (-504 million m³, with -455 million m³ in developed countries). As in scenario A1B, the largest decline is in North/Central America (-390 million m³, with -345 million m³ in the United States and -49 million m³ in Canada). The decrease of annual consumption in Europe is more modest than under scenario A1B (the projected decrease under scenario A2 is -43 million m³, with -45 million in the Russian Federation and -23 million m³ in Finland). Annual consumption also decreases in Oceania (-14 million m³) and

[3] The large drop of consumption in Europe from 1990 to 1991 reflects the collapse of the former USSR and corresponding data changes. Beginning in 1991, Europe includes the data for the Russian Federation only.

Africa (-13 million m³). Annual consumption increases only in Asia, by a modest 18 million m³ due to an increase of 24 million m³ in China that is partly offset by decreases of 14 and 9 million m³ in Indonesia and Malaysia, respectively.

Scenario B2—Projections under scenario B2 are similar to projections under scenario A2, with somewhat lower decreases of annual industrial roundwood consumption in developed and developing countries. The decrease of consumption in North/Central America is lower than under scenario A2 but the projected decrease in Europe is about double that under A2. On the other hand, the increase of annual consumption in Asia is about double the increase under scenario A2, due in part to a 34 million m³ increase of annual consumption in China. The projections for Africa and Oceania are similar to those under scenario A2.

Scenario A1B-Low Fuelwood—Under scenario A1B-Low Fuelwood, the decrease of world annual industrial roundwood consumption is less than half the decrease under scenario A1B. Annual consumption decreases by 245 million m³ in developed countries and increases by 93 million m³ in developing countries. As under the other scenarios, Asia is the only region with an increase (+142 million m³, with 92 million m³ in China, 11 million m³ in India, and 10 million m³ in Japan). The largest regional decrease of annual consumption is in North/Central America (-158 million m³, with -87 million m³ in the United States and -77 million m³ in Canada). The annual consumption in Europe decreases by 74 million m³, mostly in the Russian Federation (-39 million m³), Finland (-23 million m³), and Sweden (-18 million m³). Consumption decreases in Oceania and Africa by 11 and 3 million m³, respectively.

Industrial roundwood trade

Figure 8 shows the annual net trade (exports minus imports) of total industrial roundwood between 1961 and 2060 by world region. Table 15 shows the same data for selected years and countries. The GFPM projections between 2007 and 2060 may include energy wood after the prices of fuelwood and industrial roundwood converge (fig. 4).

Observed evolution of industrial roundwood trade

A major change occurred between 1992 and 2006 as developed countries went from net importers to net exporters, increasing their annual net trade of industrial roundwood by 38 million m³, while developing countries went from net exporters to net importers. Net trade in Europe increased by 32 million m³, with +40 million m³ in the Russian Federation. Meanwhile, the largest decrease in net trade was in Asia (-13 million m³, with -25 million m³ in China) and North/Central America (-17 million m³, mostly in the United States).

Projected evolution of industrial roundwood trade

Under scenario A1B, the annual net trade of developed countries increases by 176 million m³. The primary growth in annual net trade is in Europe (+195 million m³, principally from Finland, Sweden, and Austria, but with a decrease of 48 million m³ in the Russian Federation). An almost symmetric growth of imports occurs in Asia, where annual net trade declines by 182 million m³. Net trade also decreases in Africa (-18 million m³) and Oceania (-9 million m³), but increases by in North/Central America (+2 million m³).

Scenario A2—Under scenario A2, the annual net trade of developed countries increases by about one-fourth of the increase projected under scenario A1B. The largest growths of net trade are in South America (+87 million m³, mostly from Brazil and Chile) and Europe (+58 million m³, with 43 million m³ from the Russian Federation). As under scenario A1B, the decrease in annual net trade is in Asia (-103 million m³, of which 66 million m³ in China and 15 million m³ in India), but net trade also decreases in North/Central America (-16 million m³, mostly in Mexico and the United States), Africa (-18 million m³), and Oceania (-10 million m³).

Scenario B2—Under scenario B2, the change in annual net trade of developed and developing countries falls between the changes projected under scenarios A1B and A2, with trade rising by 114 million m³ for developed countries. As under scenario A1B, the largest positive change is in Europe (+133 million m³, with 35 million m³ in Sweden and 30 million m³ equally in Finland and the Russian Federation). A symmetric change occurs in Asia, where annual net trade decreases by 131 million m³, with 76 million m³ in China and 21 million m³ in India. Annual net trade also decreases in Africa by 23 million m³, Oceania by 10 million m³, and North/Central America by 8 million m³ (with 6 million m³ in the United States).

Scenario A1B-Low Fuelwood—Among all the scenarios, scenario A1B-Low Fuelwood projects the largest positive change of annual net trade for developed countries with an increase of 179 million m³ between 2006 and 2030. The corresponding decline in developing countries centered in Asia, where net trade declined by 196 million m³ with 134 million m³ in China and 28 million m³ in India. Net trade also decreases in Africa and Oceania, by 29 and 10 million m³, respectively. These declines are matched by the increase in annual net trade principally in North/Central America (93 million m³, with 96 million m³ in the United States), Europe (76 million m³, with 20 million m³ in Finland), and South America (63 million m³, with 39 million m³ in Brazil and 28 million m³ in Chile).

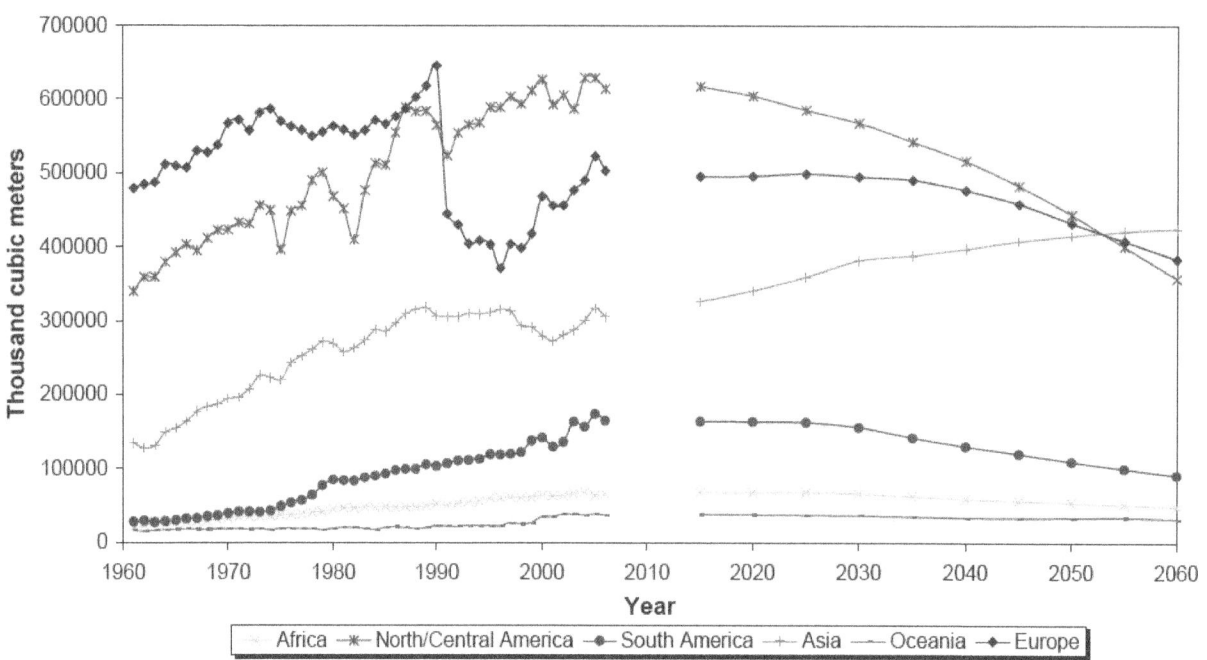

Industrial roundwood consumption except energy wood, scenario A1B

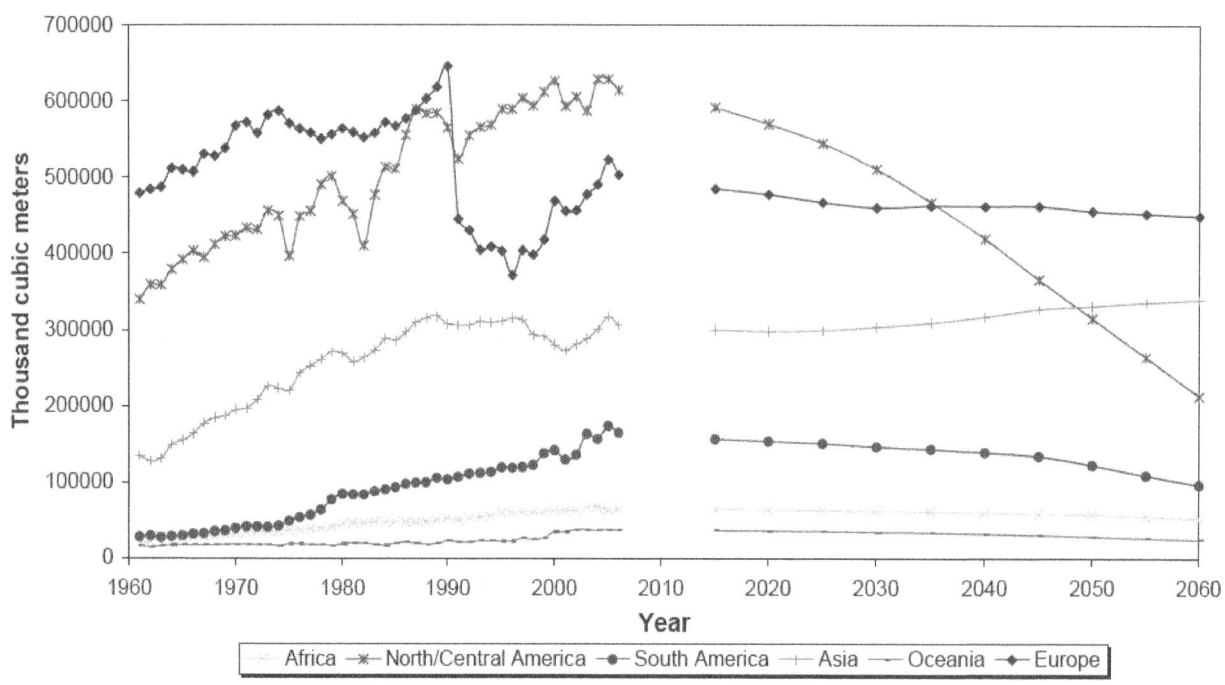

Industrial roundwood consumption except energy wood, scenario A2

Figure 7—Industrial roundwood consumption (except energy wood) by world region, observed and projected with the Global Forest Products Model. (continued on next page)

Industrial roundwood consumption except energy wood, scenario B2

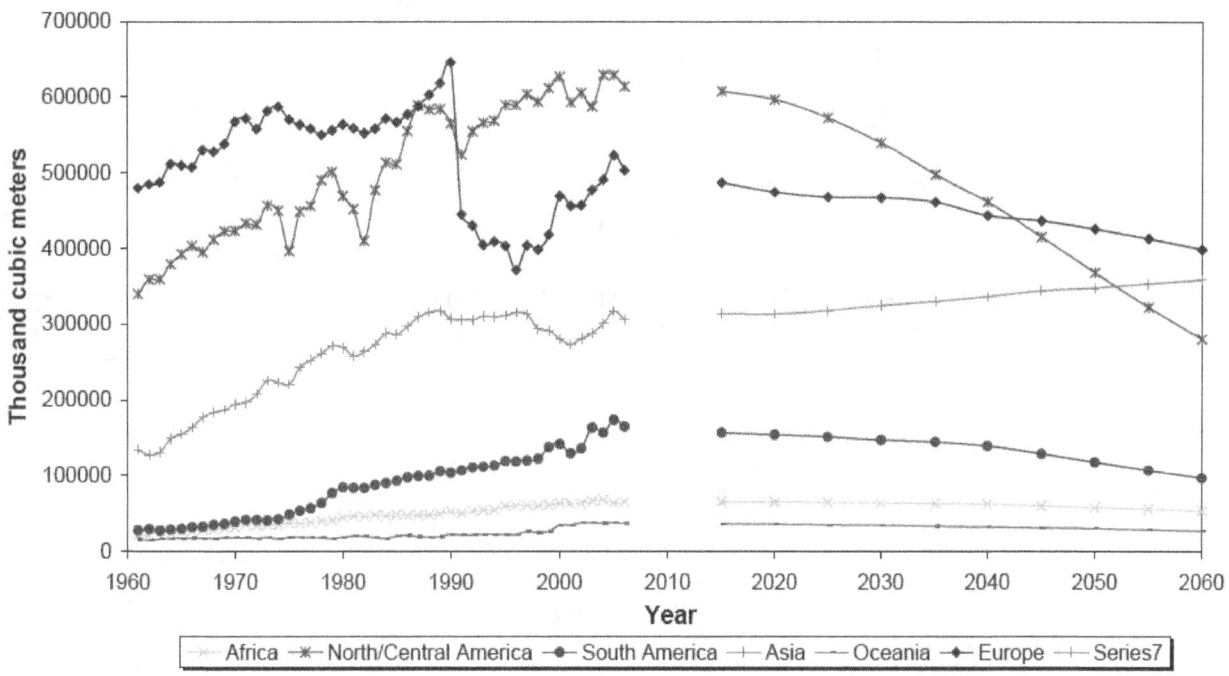

Industrial roundwood consumption except energy wood, scenario A1B-Low Fuelwood

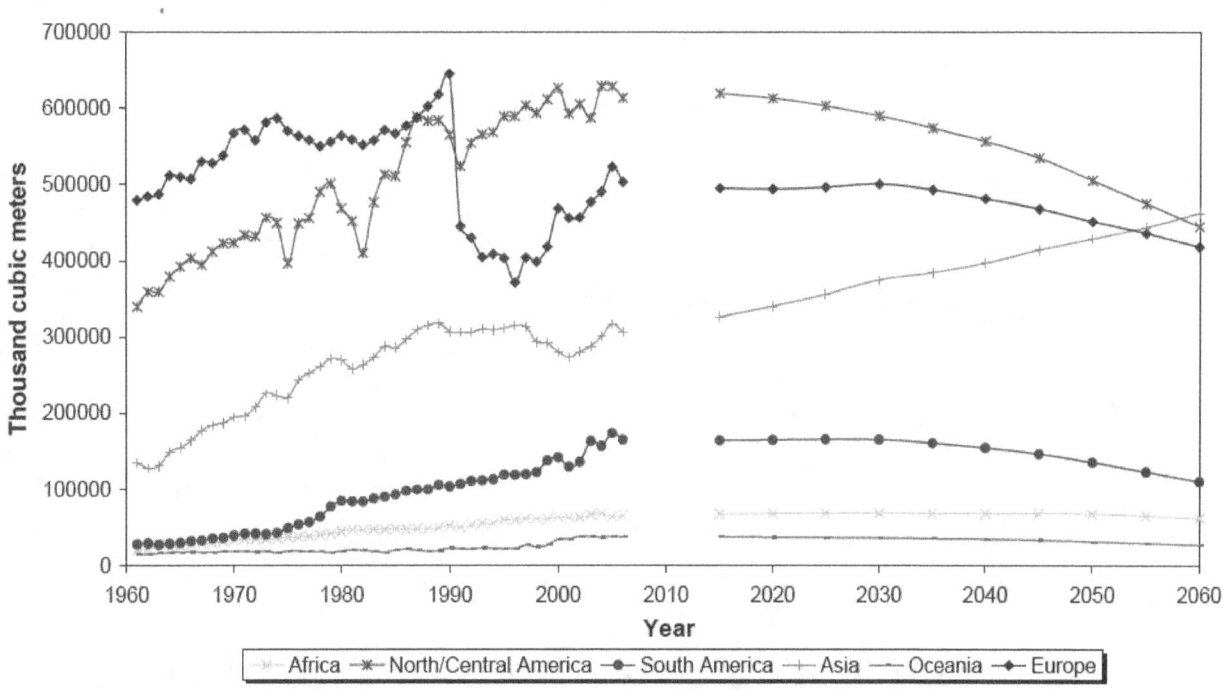

Figure 7 (continued)—Industrial roundwood consumption (except energy wood) by world region, observed and projected with the Global Forest Products Model.

Total industrial roundwood net trade, scenario A1B

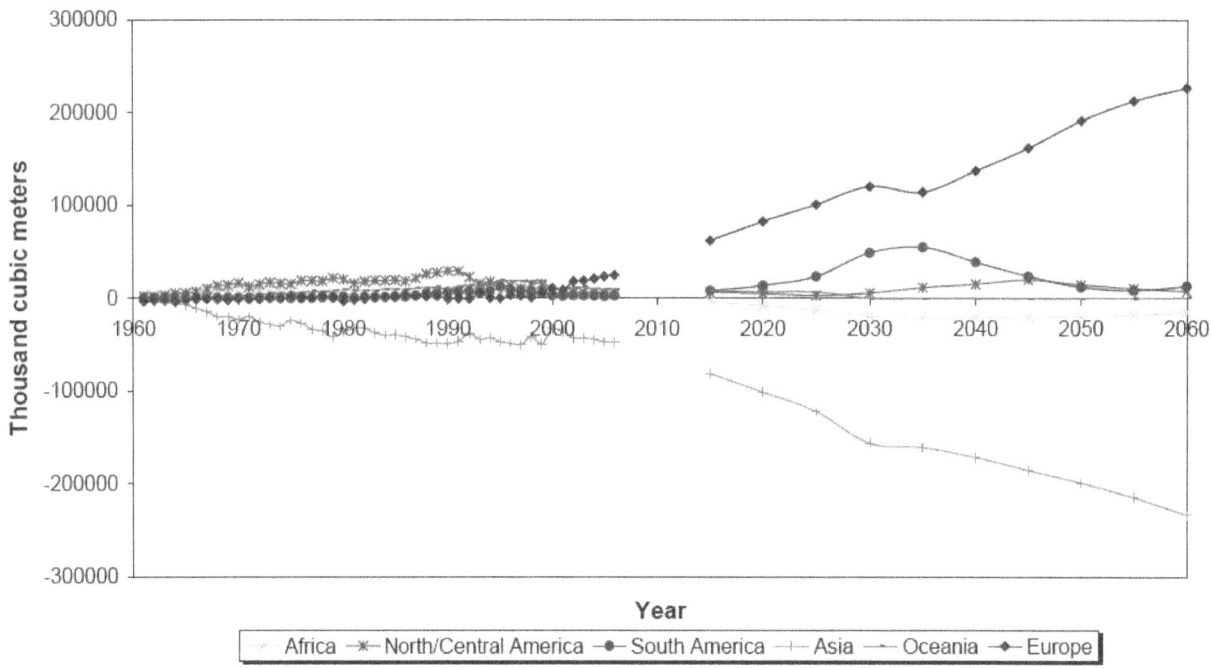

Total industrial roundwood net trade, scenario A2

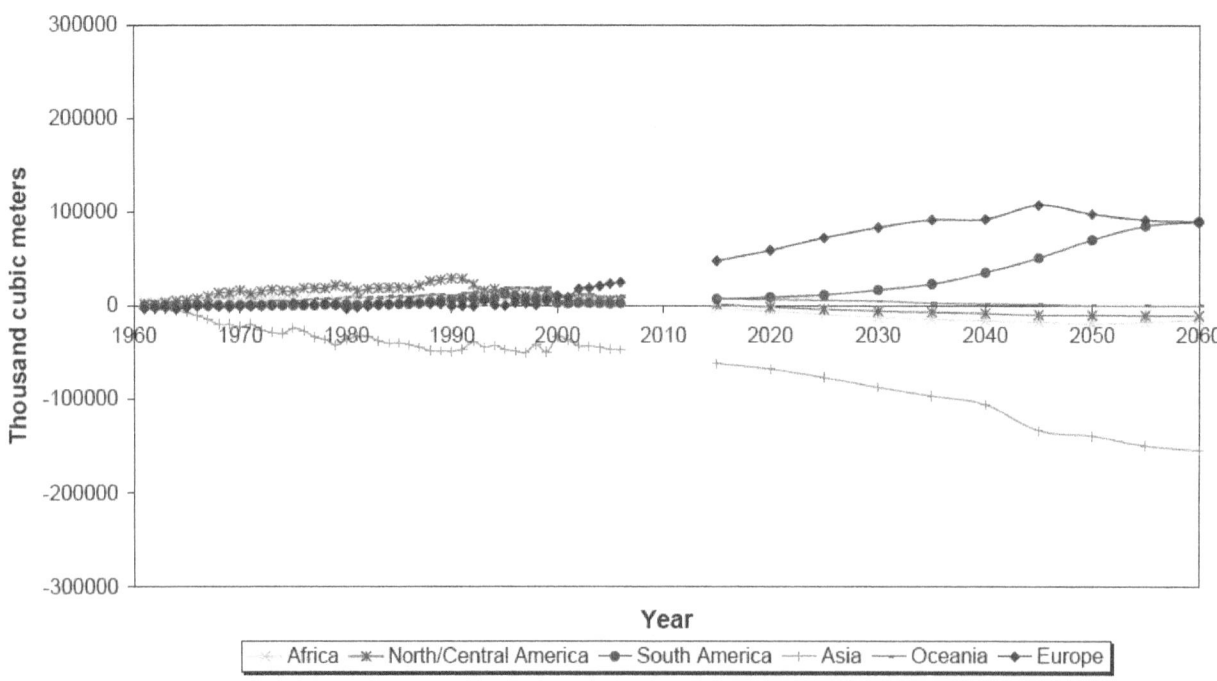

Figure 8—Total industrial roundwood net trade by world region, observed and projected with the Global Forest Products Model. (continued on next page)

Total industrial roundwood net trade, scenario B2

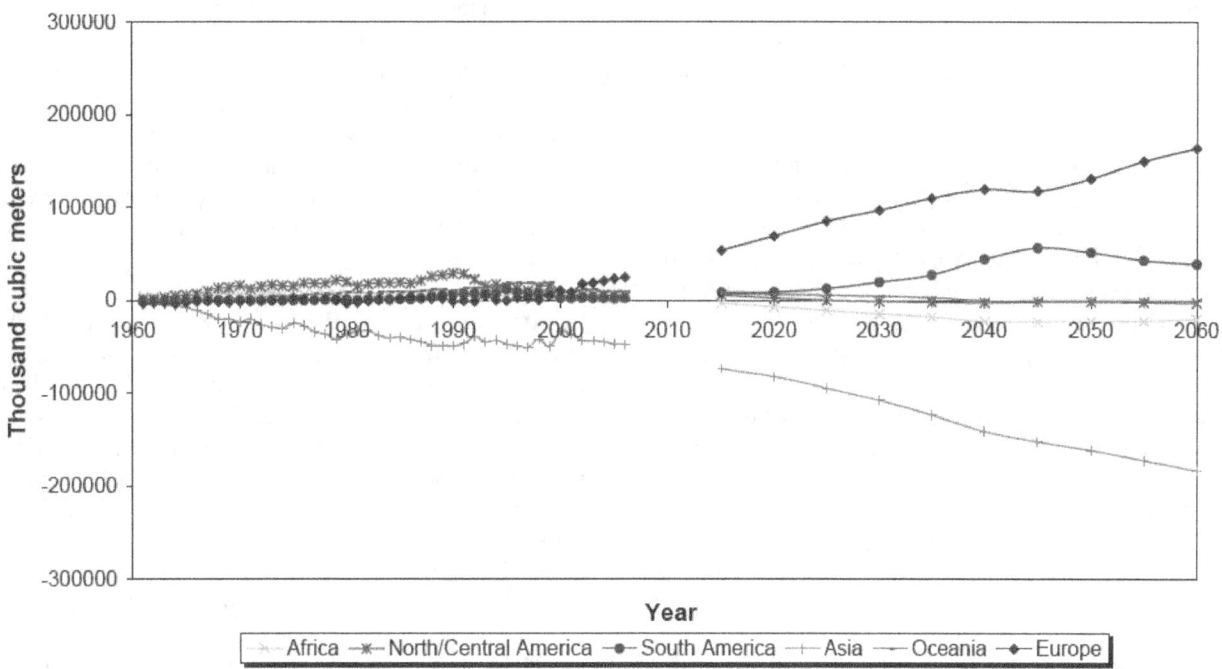

Total industrial roundwood net trade, scenario A1B-Low Fuelwood

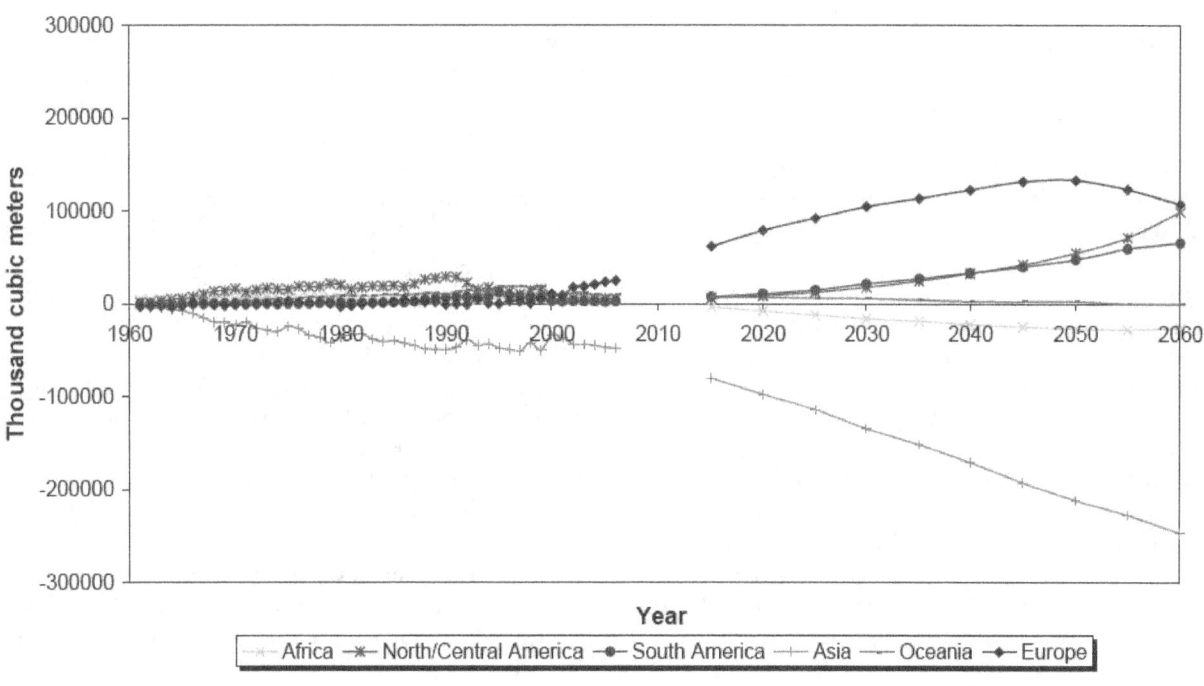

Figure 8 (continued)—Total industrial roundwood net trade by world region, observed and projected with the Global Forest Products Model.

Sawnwood

Sawnwood consumption
Figure 9 shows the past and projected annual sawnwood consumption in world regions between 1961 and 2060. Table 16 shows the same data for selected years and countries.

Observed evolution of sawnwood consumption
The world annual consumption of sawnwood increased by 31 million m^3 between 1992 and 2006, with 22 million m^3 of the increase taking place in developing countries and 9 million m^3 in developed countries. The largest regional increase was in North/Central America (41 million m^3, with 27 million m^3 in the United States). Annual consumption also increased in South America and Africa by 7 and 2 million m^3, respectively. The largest regional decrease in annual consumption was in Europe (-15 million m^3, with -41 million m^3 in the Russian Federation, but offset by small increases in other countries). Annual consumption also decreased in Asia by 6 million m^3, the cumulative result of an increase of 11 million m^3 in China offset by a decrease of 16 million m^3 in Japan and other smaller decreases in other countries.

Projected consumption of sawnwood
Scenario A1B—Under scenario A1B, the world annual consumption of sawnwood increases by 53 million m^3, mostly in developing countries. The largest growth is in Asia (+33 million m^3, with 10 million m^3 in India and 8 million m^3 in China). Annual consumption grows by 7 million m^3 in South America, with 5 million m^3 in Brazil, and by the same amount in Africa. In North/Central America, annual sawnwood consumption grows by 3 million m^3, with two-thirds of the projected increase taking place in the United States. The regional change is less in Europe (+2 million m^3, with +4 million m^3 in the Russian Federation and small declines in several other countries).

Scenario A2—Scenario A2 implies the smallest world increase of annual sawnwood consumption: 12 million m^3, the cumulative result of a 17 million m^3 increase in developing countries offset by a 5 million decrease in developed countries. The main decline is in Europe (-6 million m^3 originating in several countries, a decline that offsets a 2 million m^3 increase in the Russian Federation). Under scenario A2, Asia has an increase in annual consumption of 11 million m^3, with a 4 million m^3 increase in India. Consumption also increases in Africa by 3 million m^3, North/Central America by 2 million m^3 (mostly in the United States), and South America and Oceania by 1 million m^3 each.

Scenario B2—In scenario B2, the growth of the world sawnwood annual consumption falls between the growth projected in scenarios A1B and A2. As under A2, consumption increases in developing countries and decreases in developed countries, but to a greater degree. There is a world increase of 20 million m^3 in annual consumption that matches the increase in Asia, where the increase includes increases in India and China of 7 and 3 million m^3, respectively. Consumption also increases in Africa and South America, by 7 and 4 million m^3, respectively. However, annual consumption decreases in North/Central America by 6 million m^3, mostly in the United States, and Europe (-4 million m^3 with decreases in several countries not compensated by the 3 million m^3 increase in the Russian Federation).

Scenario A1B-Low Fuelwood—The scenario A1B-Low Fuelwood induces the highest world growth in annual sawnwood consumption: +95 million m^3, with +63 million m^3 in developing countries. As there is little competition between energy wood and logs for sawnwood under this scenario, the price of wood is lower than under scenario A1B, and this leads to cheaper sawnwood and more consumption in all regions. As under all the other scenarios, the largest growth is in Asia (+43 million m^3, with 11 million m^3 in China and 12 million m^3 in India). In North/Central America, annual consumption grows by 20 million m^3, with 16 million m^3 in the United States. In Europe, annual consumption increases by 12 million m^3, with 4 million m^3 in the Russian Federation. Consumption grows almost as much in South America (+10 million m^3, with 7 million m^3 in Brazil) and Africa (+9 million m^3).

Sawnwood trade
Figure 10 shows the historical data of annual sawnwood net trade (exports minus imports) by world region, and table 17 shows the data for selected years and countries.

Observed evolution of sawnwood trade
Between 1992 and 2006, the net trade of developed countries increased by 18 million m^3. Most of this increase took place in Europe where net trade increased by 26 million m^3, including increases of 10 million m^3 in the Russian Federation and 8 million m^3 in Germany. North/Central America passed from a surplus to a deficit region, with a decline in net trade of 14 million m^3 due largely to the 19 million m^3 decrease in the United States. Asia increased its annual deficit by 12 million m^3, with 5 million m^3 in China and 4 million m^3 in Malaysia.

Projected evolution of sawnwood trade
Scenario A1B—Under scenario A1B, there is a 3 million m^3 reduction in the annual net trade of developed countries. The annual deficit of Asia decreases by 15 million m^3, with 6 million m^3 in China and 8 million m^3 in Japan. Meanwhile, the annual deficit worsens in North/Central America by 9 million m^3 due to a 34 million decrease in the surplus of

Canada that is only partly offset by a 28 million m³ decrease in the annual deficit of the United States. The positive annual net trade of Europe decreases by 4 million m³ due to a 15 million m³ reduction in the Russian Federation surplus that is offset only in part by an increase of 11 million in Sweden's surplus. The annual trade deficit of Africa decreases by 3 million m³, while the surplus of Oceania decreases by 1 million m³.

Scenario A2—Under scenario A2, the annual net trade of sawnwood decreases by 20 million m³ in developed countries, traceable largely to the worsening trade deficit of North/Central America by 97 million m³, including a 25 million m³ reduction of the annual trade surplus of Canada, and a worsening of the United States annual deficit by 76 million m³. This regional deficit is met by improvements of the trade balance in all other regions, mostly in Europe, where annual net trade would increase by 73 million m³, with 72 million m³ in Sweden but declines in some other countries. The annual net trade also improves in Asia by 16 million m³, with 8 million m³ in Japan and 6 million m³ in China, and in Africa by 9 million m³.

Scenario B2—Under scenario B2, there is a reduction in the annual net trade of developed countries by 4 million m³, coming largely from a 32 million decrease in the net trade of North/Central America that stems from a 35 million reduction in the annual surplus of Canada, and despite a 6 million m³ decrease in the United States' deficit. The annual surplus of Europe increases by 18 million m³, largely from the 41 million m³ increase in Sweden's annual surplus, and despite the 15 million m³ reduction in the surplus of the Russian Federation. The annual sawnwood trade deficit of Africa is reduced by 4 million m³, while the annual surplus of Oceania is reduced by 1 million m³.

Scenario A1B-Low Fuelwood—Under scenario A1B-Low Fuelwood, the development of net trade is similar to that under scenario A1B but with an improvement of the net trade of developing countries, where the deficit is reduced by 6 million m³. As under scenario A1B, the main regional gains of annual net trade occur in Asia (+13 million m³, with 8 million m³ in Japan and 5 million m³ in China). Also as under scenario A1B, the annual trade surplus of Europe decreases by 15 million m³, stemming from the Russian Federation, Finland, and Austria. The annual trade surplus decreases also in South America, by 5 million m³, with 3 million m³ in both Brazil and Chile. As under scenarios A2 and B2, Africa goes from deficit in 2006 to surplus in 2060, improving net trade by 6 million m³, while the annual surplus of Oceania is reduced by 1 million m³.

Wood-Based Panels

Wood-based panels prices
Figure 11 shows the past and projected world real prices of veneer and plywood, particleboard, and fiberboard, measured by the unit value of exports expressed in 1997 U.S. dollars. Tables 18, 19, and 20 show the corresponding prices in the major countries within each world region.

Observed evolution of wood-based panels prices
From 1961 to 2006, the real prices of wood-based panels fluctuated considerably, especially for veneer and plywood, with peaks around 1980. The general tendency was of decreasing real prices. In 2006, the real world price of veneer and plywood was $49 lower than it had been in 1992, and $18 lower for particleboard and $38 lower for fiberboard.

Projected evolution of wood-based panels prices
Scenario A1B—Under scenario A1B, the prices of wood based panels remain approximately constant in real terms up to 2030. Then they increase rapidly and reach nearly $600/m³ for plywood, $400/m³ for particleboard, and $480/m³ for fiberboard.

Scenarios A2 and B2—Under scenarios A2 and B2, there is a slight decrease in prices of wood-based panels until 2030, followed by a rise that brings the prices in 2060 to approximately their level of 2006. There is also a convergence of the prices of fiberboard and particleboard towards the end of the projection period.

Scenario A1B-Low Fuelwood—Under scenario A1B-Low Fuelwood, the prices of veneer and plywood, particleboard, and fiberboard continue their historic negative and parallel trend to end lower in 2060 than in 2006.

Wood-based panels consumption
Figure 12 shows the past and projected annual wood-based panel consumption in world regions, from 1961 to 2060. Tables 21, 22, and 23 show the same data for selected years and countries and for each component, veneer and plywood, particleboard, and fiberboard.

Observed wood-based panels consumption
The world annual consumption of wood-based panels increased by 121 million m³ between 1992 and 2006, three times as much as for sawnwood. Consumption grew in all world regions, and more in developing than developed countries. The largest regional increase was in Asia (59 million m³, with 46 million m³ in China). Annual consumption increased by 28 million m³ in Europe, spread out in several countries. It grew nearly as much in North/Central America (27 million m³, with 23 million m³ in the United States). A large part of the 5 million m³ growth of

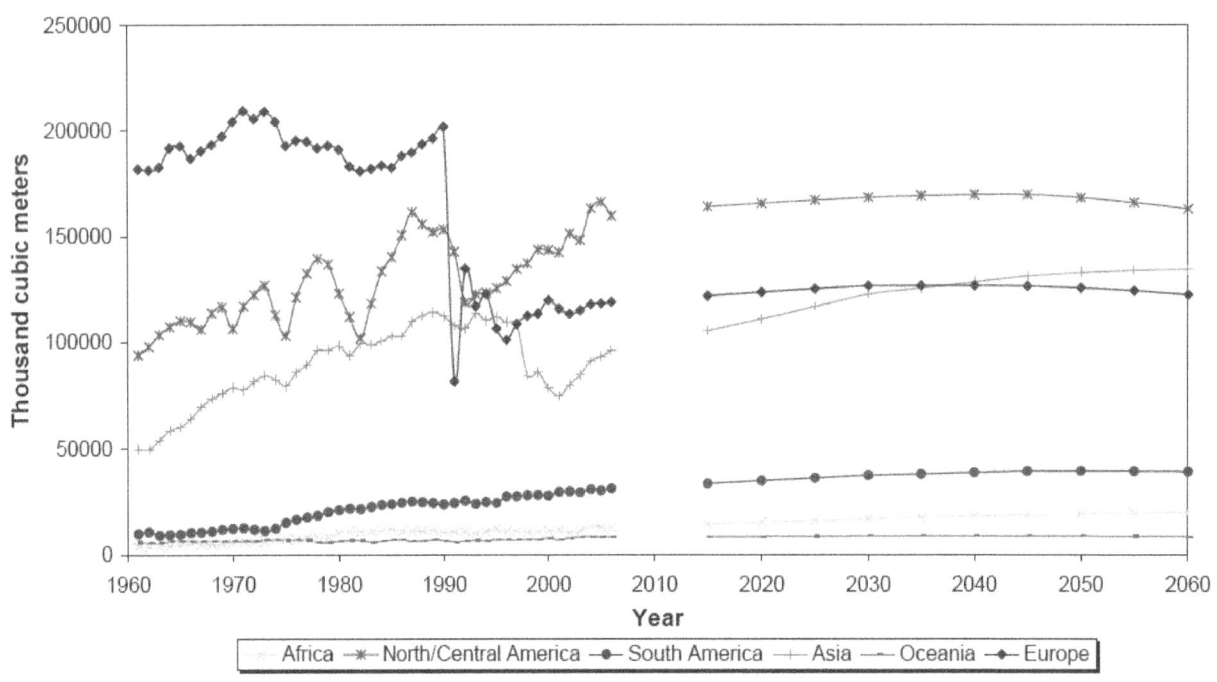

Sawnwood consumption, scenario A1B

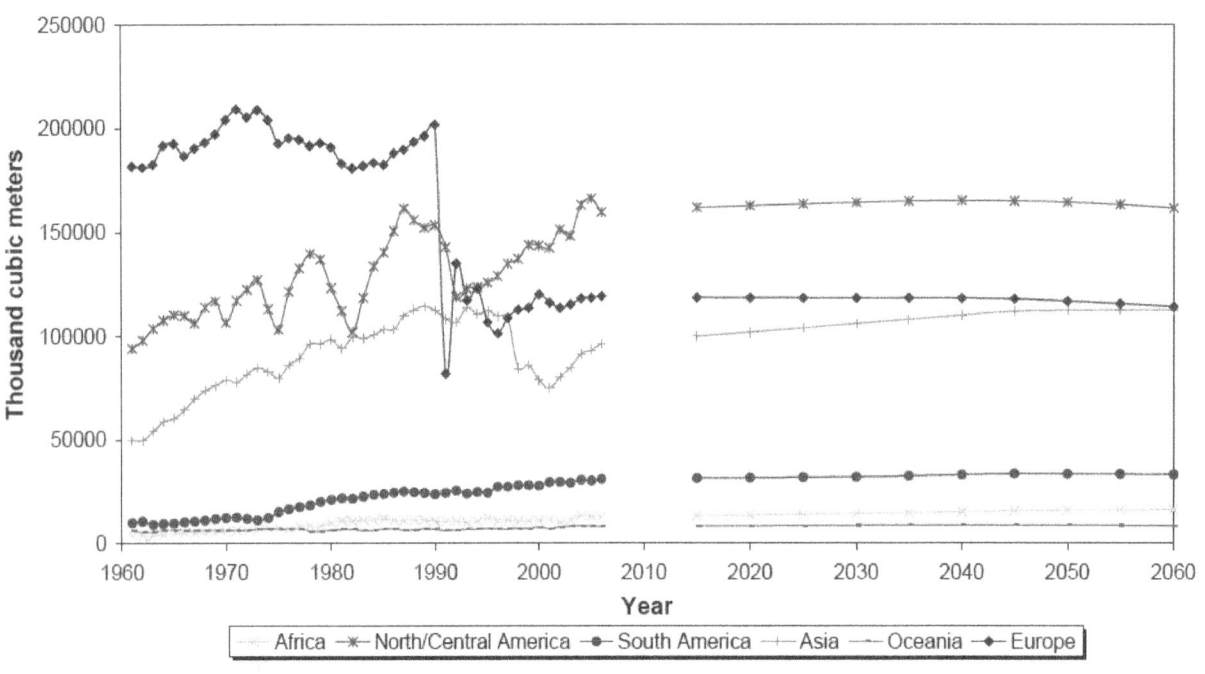

Sawnwood consumption, scenario A2

Figure 9—Sawnwood consumption by world region, observed and projected with the Global Forest Products Model. (continued on next page)

Sawnwood consumption, scenario B2

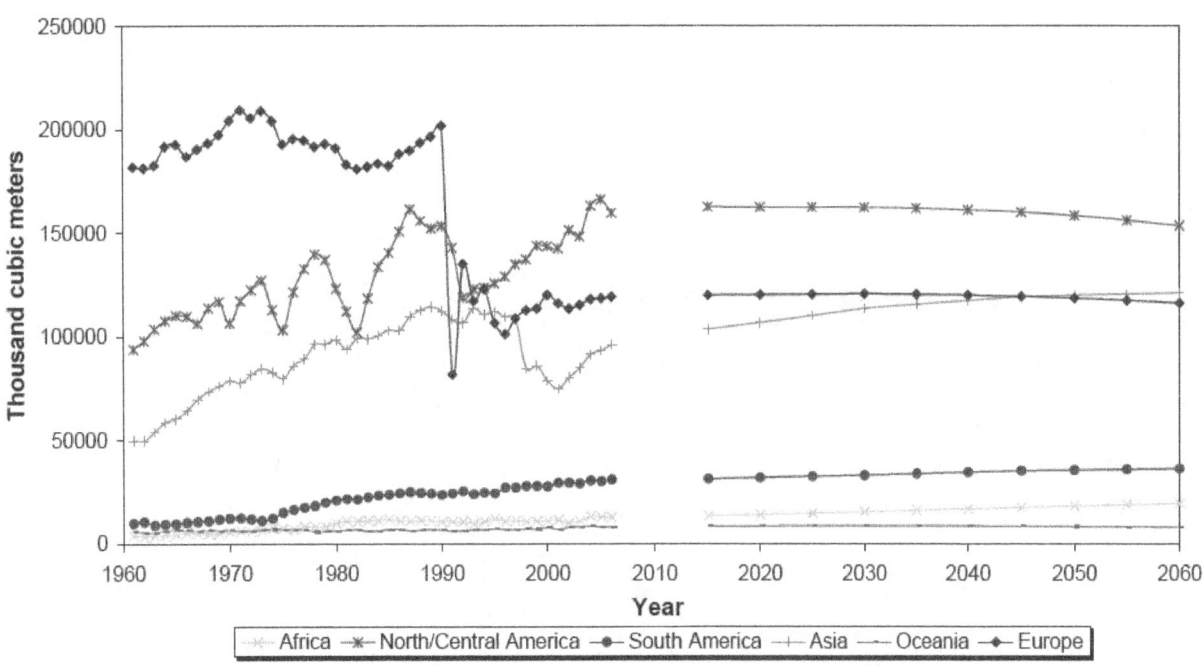

Sawnwood consumption, scenario A1B-Low Fuelwood

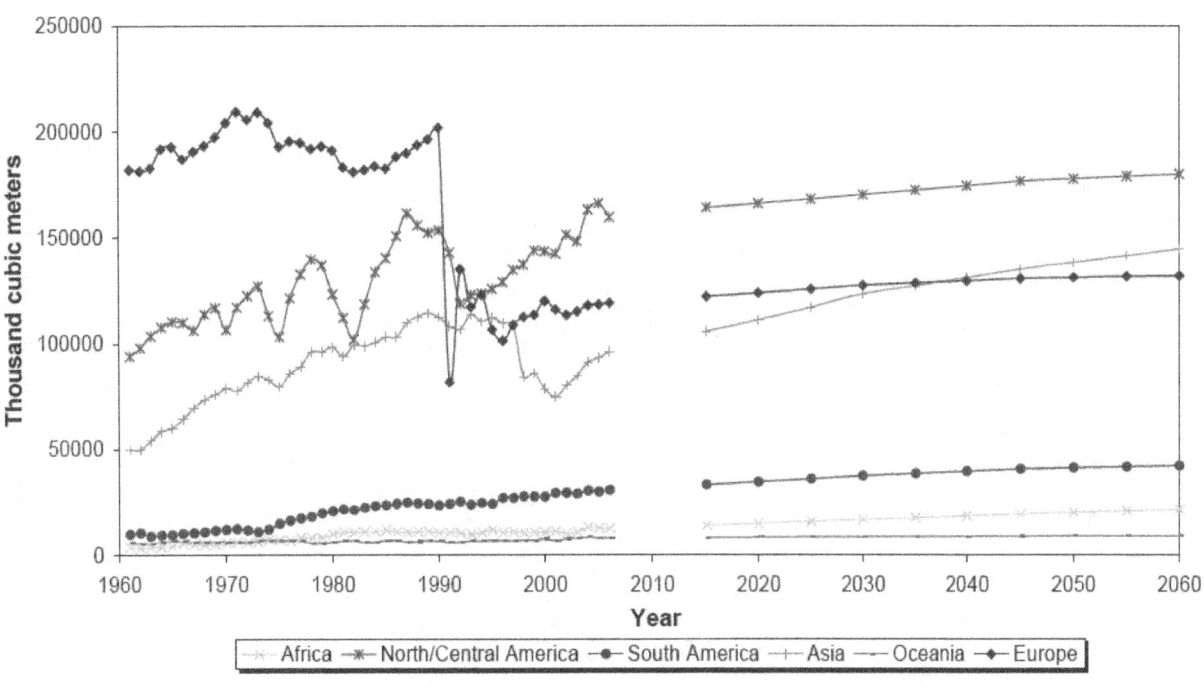

Figure 9 (continued)—Sawnwood consumption by world region, observed and projected with the Global Forest Products Model.

Sawnwood net trade, scenario A1B

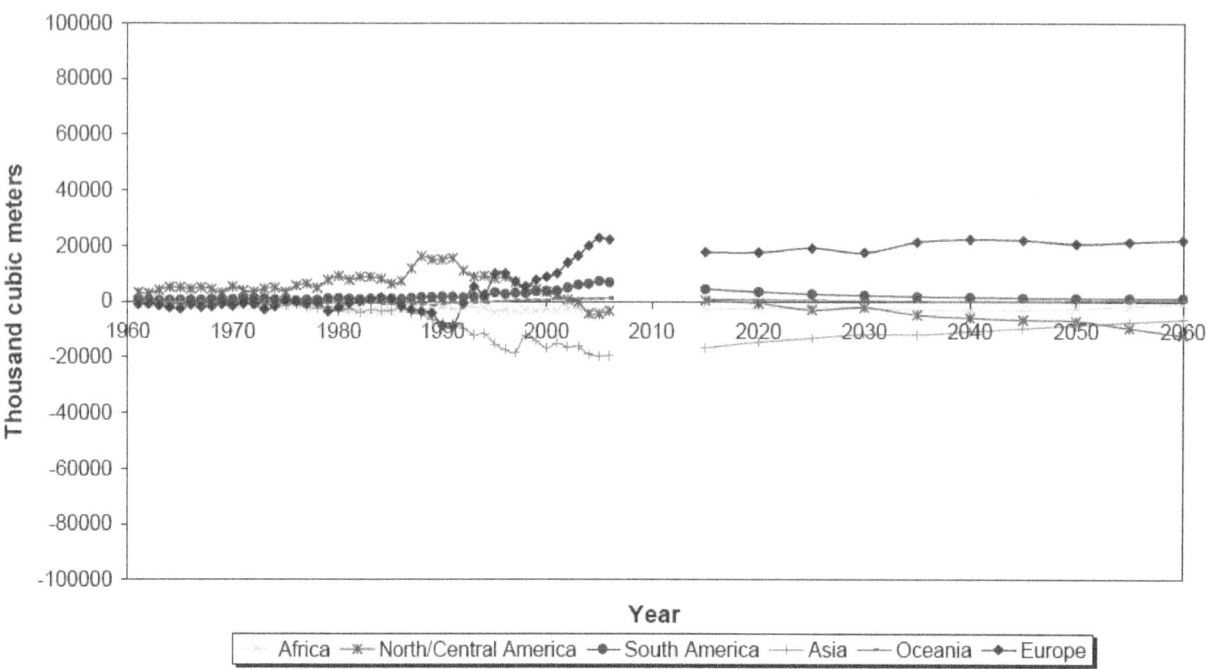

Sawnwood net trade, scenario A2

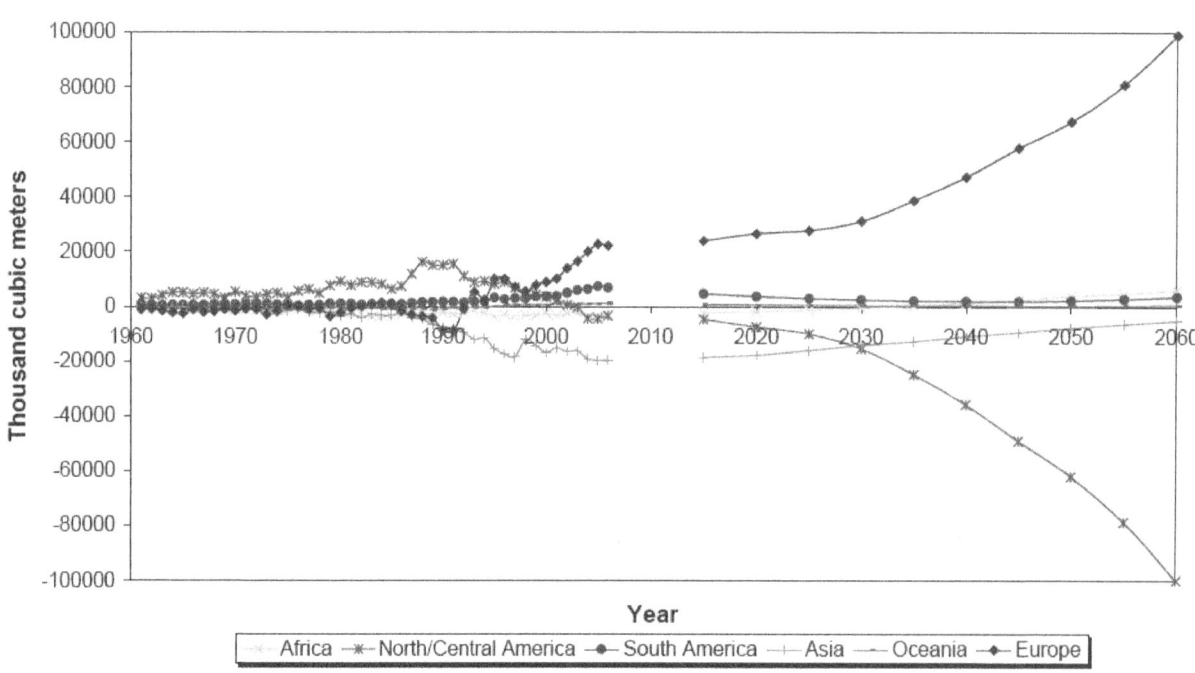

Figure 10—Sawnwood net trade by world region, observed and projected with the Global Forest Products Model. (continued on next page)

Sawnwood net trade, scenario B2

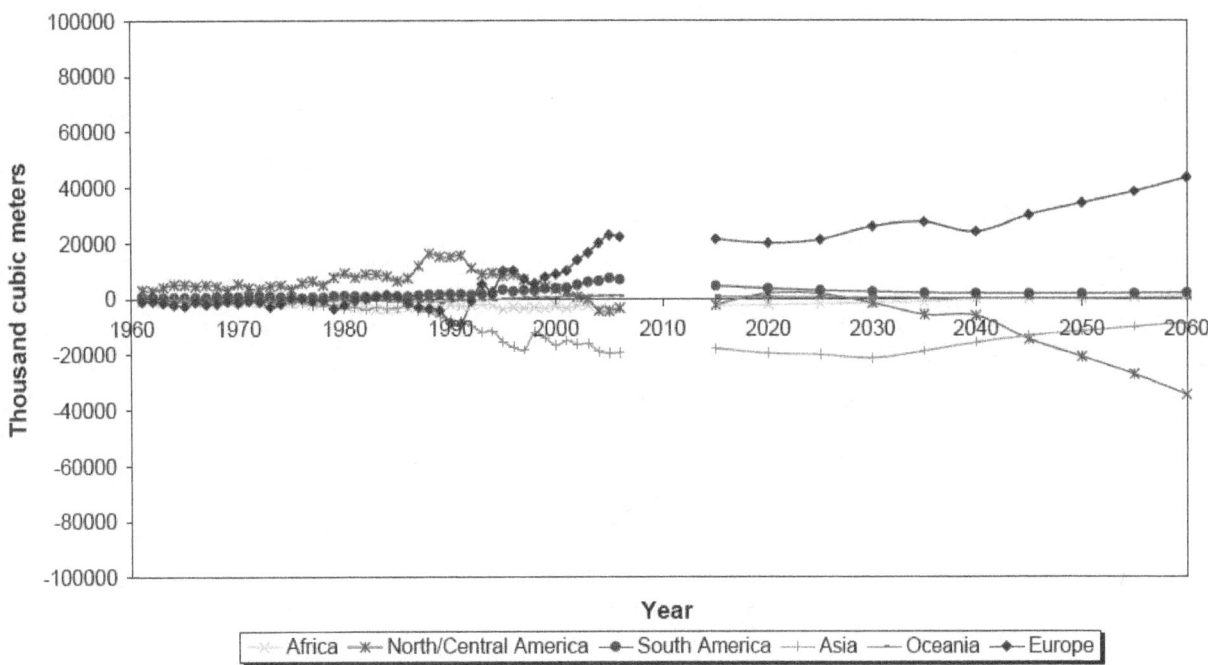

Sawnwood net trade, scenario A1B-Low Fuelwood

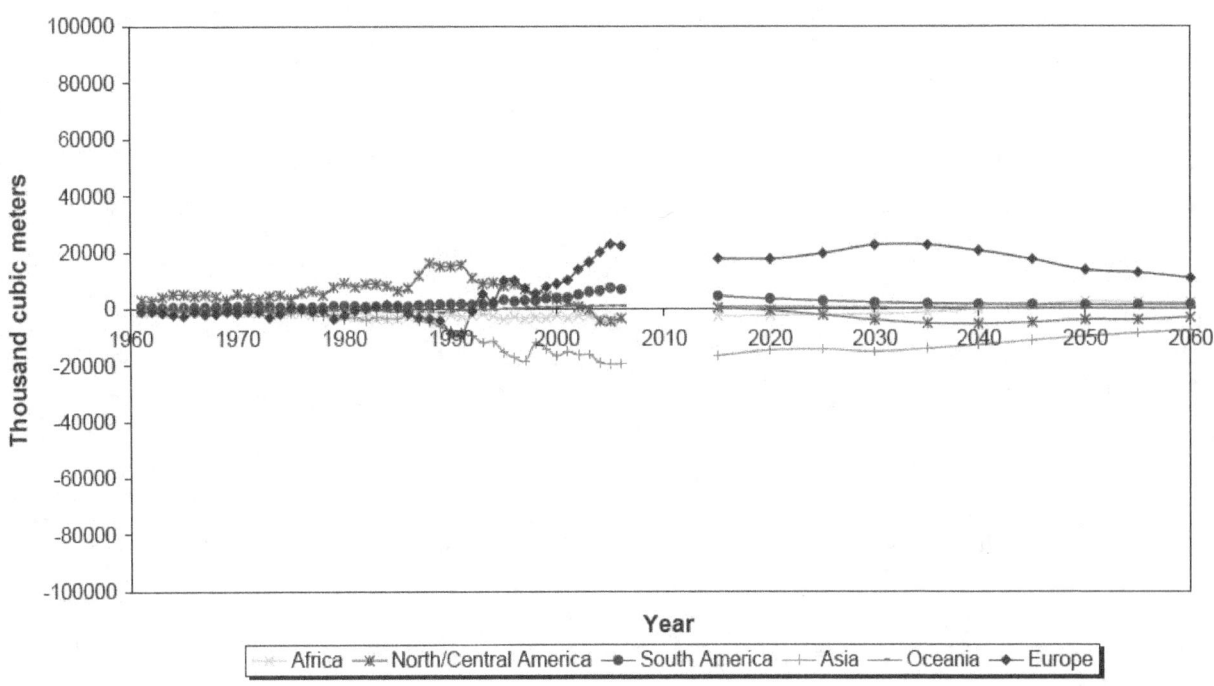

Figure 10 (continued) —Sawnwood net trade by world region, observed and projected with the Global Forest Products Model.

Wood-based panels prices, scenario A1B

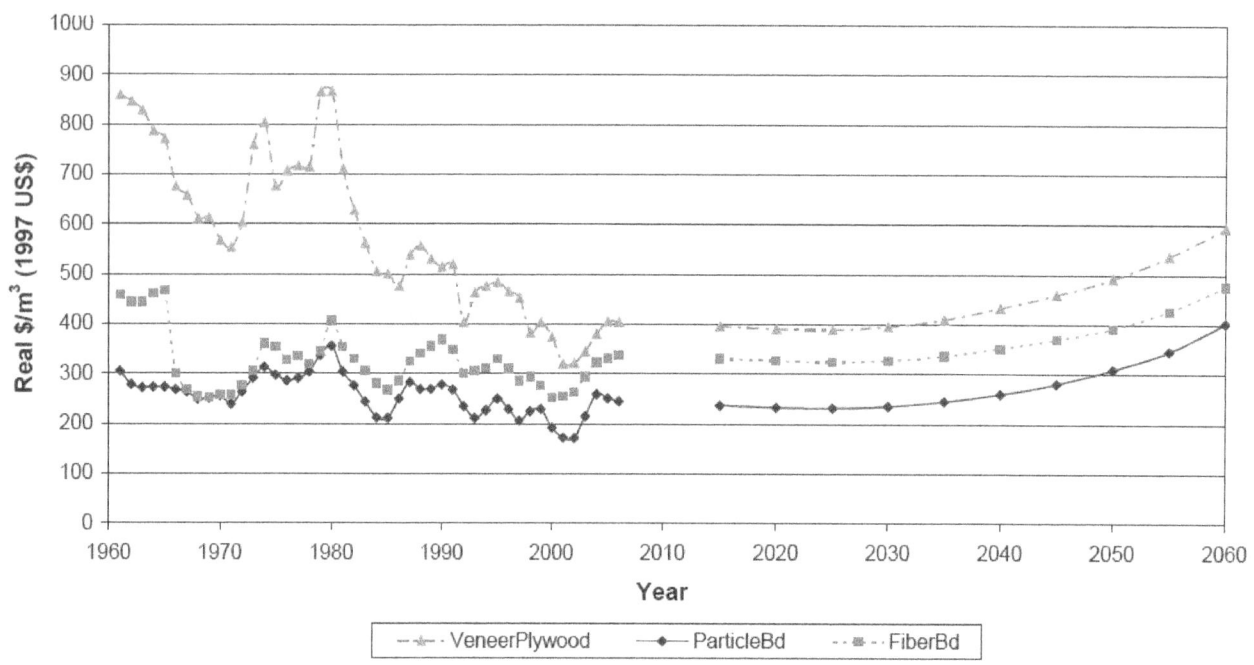

Wood-based panels prices, scenario A2

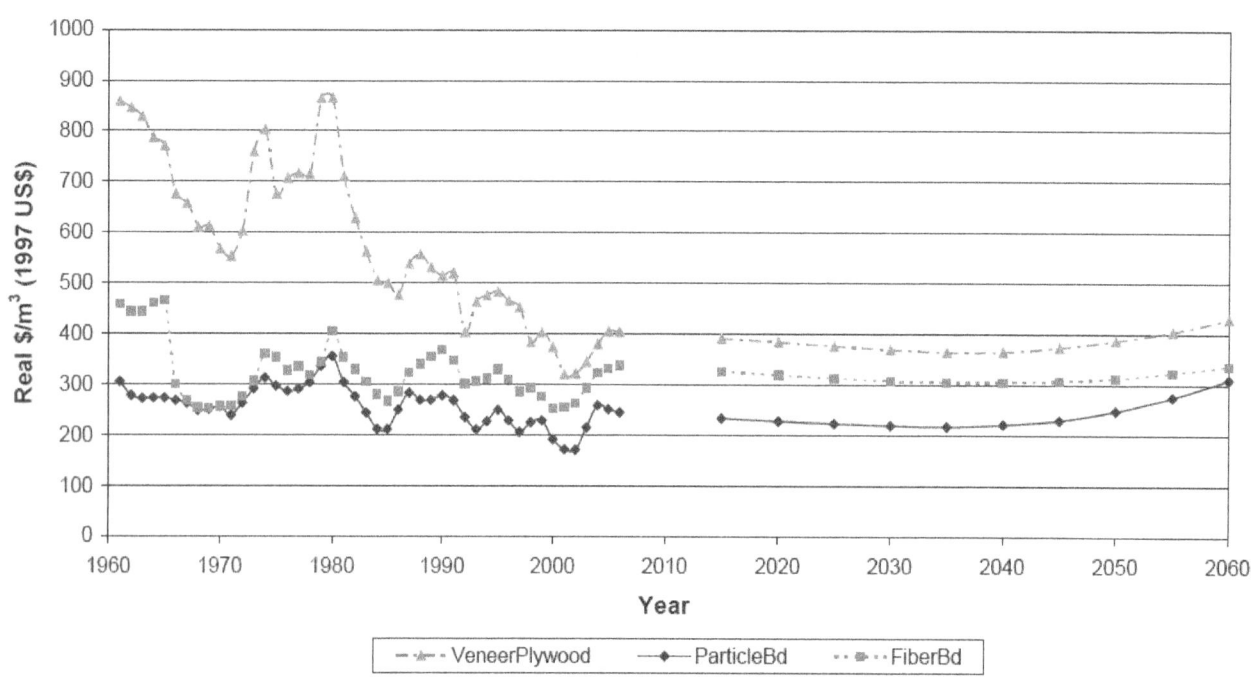

Figure 11—World prices of wood-based panels, observed and projected with the Global Forest Products Model. (continued on next page)

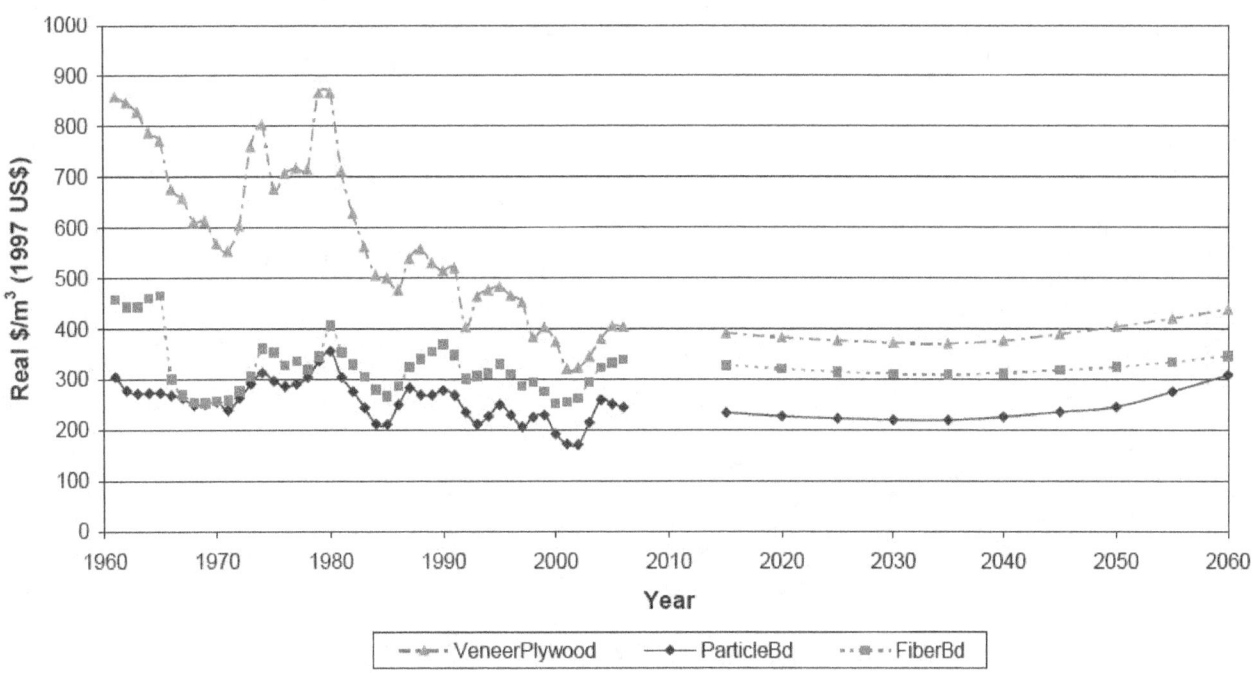

Wood-based panels prices, scenario B2

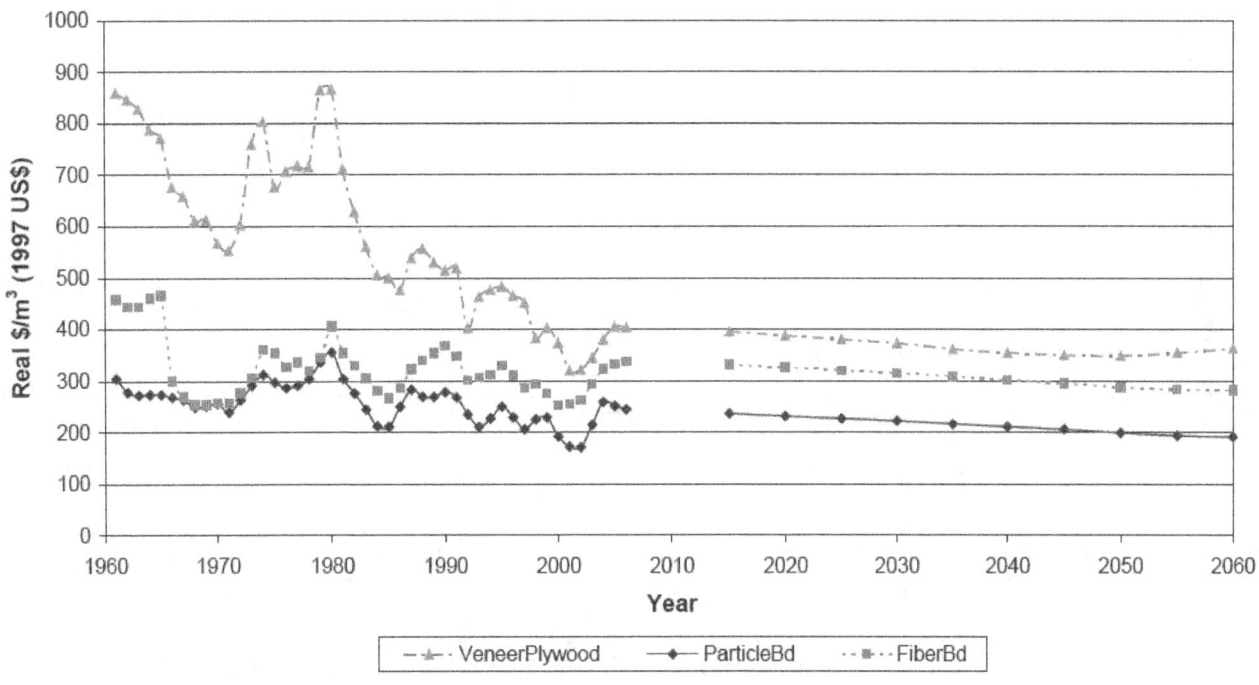

Wood-based panels prices, scenario A1B-Low Fuelwood

Figure 11 (continued)—World prices of wood-based panels, observed and projected with the Global Forest Products Model.

Wood-based panels consumption, scenario A1B

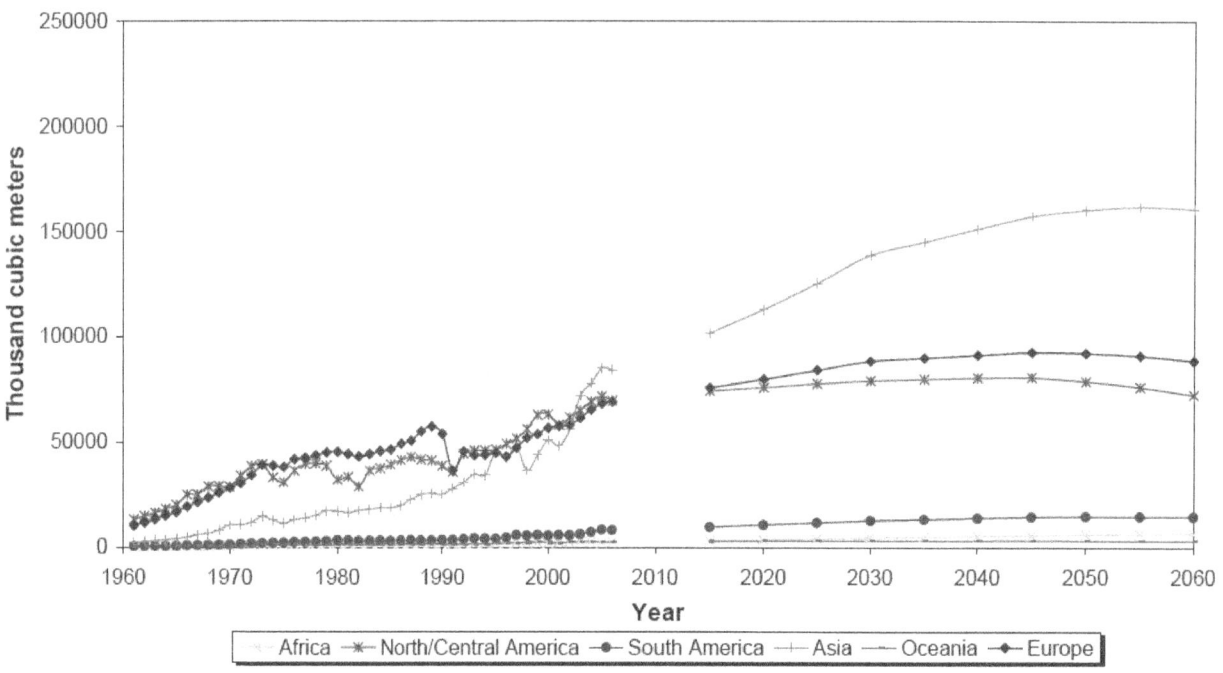

Wood-based panels consumption, scenario A2

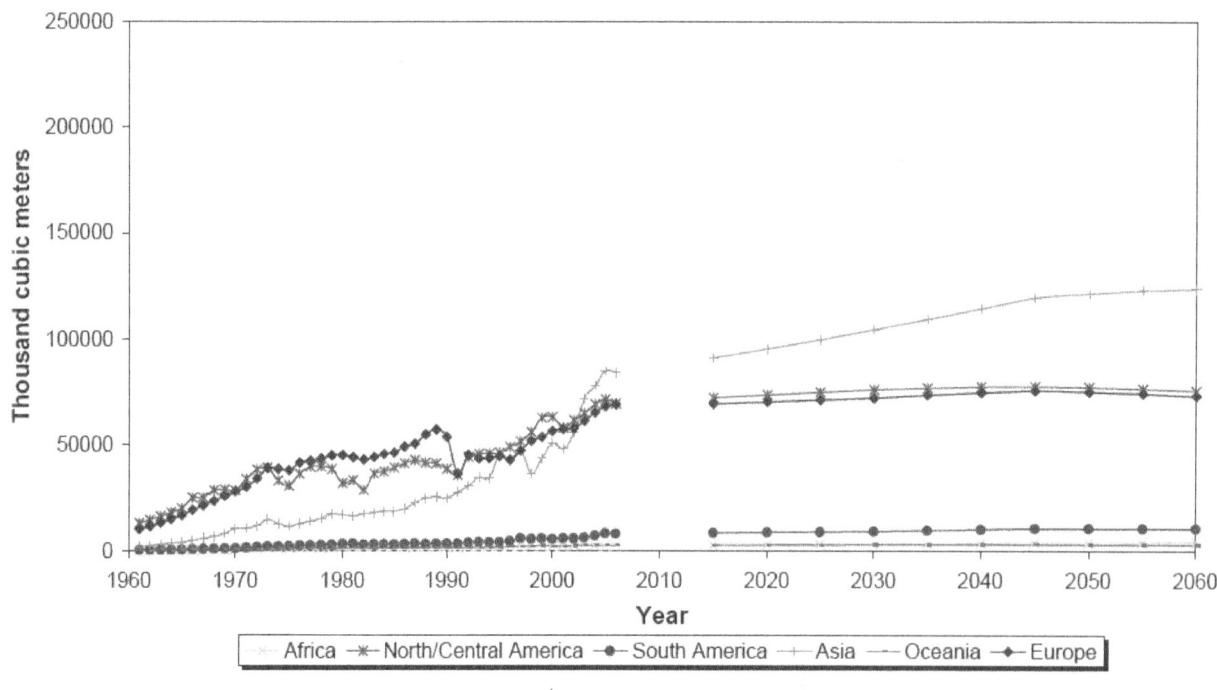

Figure 12—Wood-based panels consumption by world region, observed and projected with the Global Forest Products Model. (continued on next page)

Wood-based panels consumption, scenario B2

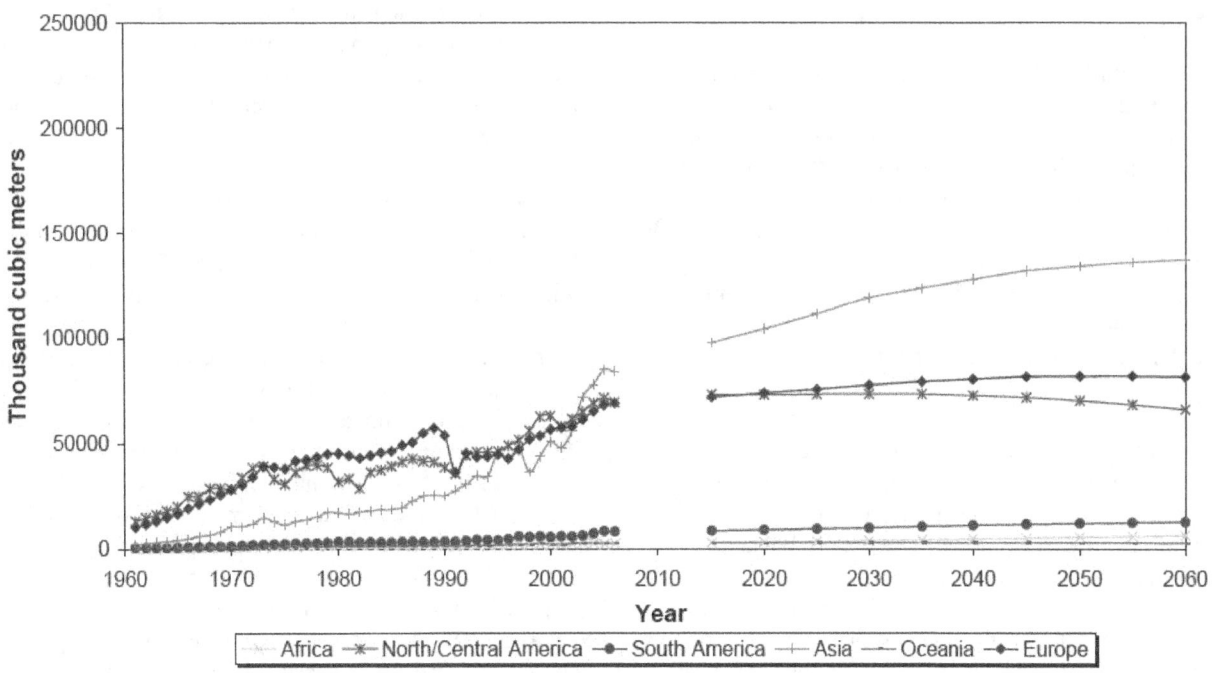

Wood-based panels consumption, scenario A1B-Low Fuelwood

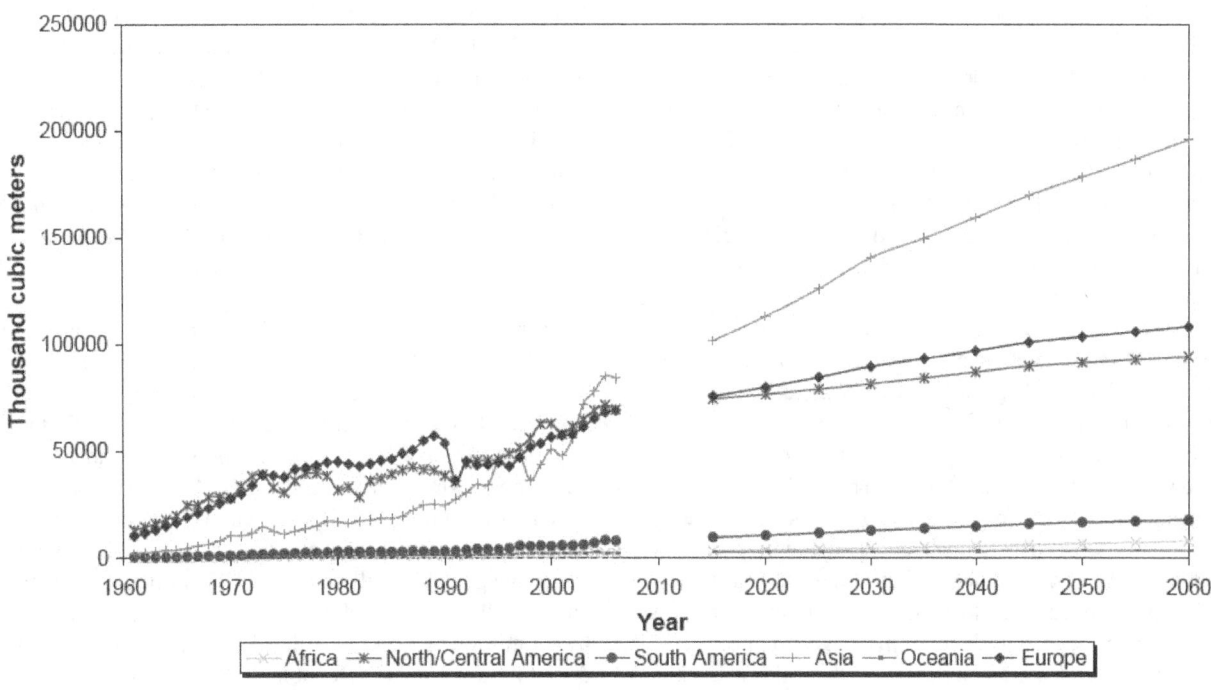

Figure 12 (continued) —Wood-based panels consumption by world region, observed and projected with the Global Forest Products Model.

annual consumption in South America took part in Brazil. Consumption also increased by about 1 million m³ in Africa and Oceania.

Projected evolution of wood-based panels consumption
Scenario A1B—Under scenario A1B, the world annual consumption of wood-based panels increases by 98 million m³. Eighty percent of this growth takes place in developing countries. The largest growths are in Asia (+72 million m³, with 51 million m³ in China and Europe (+16 million m³, with 6 million m³ in the Russian Federation). Annual consumption also grows by 6 million m³ in South America, with 4 million m³ in Brazil, and 4 million m³ in Africa. Growth in North/Central America is small (1 million m³), and there was hardly any change in Oceania.

Scenario A2—Scenario A2 implies the smallest world increase of annual wood-based panels consumption: 42 million m³, resulting from a 40 million m³ increase in developing countries. In contrast to scenario A1B, under scenario A2, Asia experiences a modest increase in annual consumption (+34 million m³, with a 26 million m³ increase in China, in particular). Consumption also increases in Africa by 2 million m³, North/Central America by 4 million m³ (mostly in the United States), and South America.

Scenario B2—Under scenario B2, the growth of the world wood-based panels annual consumption falls between the growth projected under scenarios A1B and A2. As under scenario A2, consumption increases most in developing countries, but more than under scenario A2. The world increase of 59 million m³ in annual consumption is mostly in Asia, which includes increases of 2 million m³ in India and 35 million m³ in China. Consumption increases in Africa by 3 million m³ and South America by 4 million m³. However, annual consumption decreases in North/Central America by 5 million m³, mostly in the United States, and Europe stagnates as in scenario A2.

Scenario A1B-Low Fuelwood—Scenario A1B-Low Fuelwood induces the highest world growth in annual wood-based panels consumption: +180 million m³, with +120 million m³ in developing countries. Consumption grows in all regions due to the lower panel prices (fig. 11) induced by the lower price of wood due to little diversion of industrial roundwood for energy. As under the other scenarios, the largest growth is in Asia (+106 million m³, with 74 million m³ in China and 4 million m³ in India). In North/Central America, annual consumption grows by 23 million m³, with 20 million m³ in the United States. In Europe, annual consumption increases by 35 million m³, with 10 million m³ in the Russian Federation. Consumption also grows in South America (+10 million m³ from 2006 to 2060, with 7 million m³ in Brazil) and Africa (+9 million m³).

Wood-based panels trade
Figure 13 shows the historical annual net trade of wood-based panels (exports minus imports) from 1961 to 2006, and the GFPM projections from 2006 to 2060, by world region. More detailed data for selected years, countries, and component products (veneer and plywood, particleboard, and fiberboard) are in tables 24, 25, and 26.

Observed wood-based panels trade
From 1992 to 2006, developing countries were net exporters of wood-based panels, and their net trade increased by 9 million m³. Annual trade grew by 4 million m³ in Asia (+11 million m³ in China, partly offset by -7 million m³ in Indonesia and -2 million m³ in Japan). The South American annual net trade grew by 4 million m³, with 3 million m³ in Brazil. In Europe, annual net trade also grew by 8 million m³, with 5 million m³ in Germany and 2 million m³ in France. Most of the decrease in annual net trade was in North/Central America (-11 million m³, with -17 million m³ in the United States offset in part by +7 million m³ in Canada).

Projected wood-based panels trade
Scenario A1B—Under scenario A1B, the developing countries turn from net exporters into net importers, their annual net trade decreasing by 18 million m³. The largest decrease is in Asia, which goes from net exporter in 2006 to net importer in 2060. In total, the Asian net trade decreases by 12 million m³, with 7 million m³ in China and 6 million m³ in Malaysia, and partly offset by an increase of 7 million m³ in Japan and the Republic of Korea. Annual net trade decreases in South America (-2 million m³), Europe (-1 million m³, with small unequal changes in various countries), and Oceania (-1 million m³). The change in North/Central America is almost the opposite of the change in Asia, as the region transitions from net importer to net exporter, with an increase in the Canadian annual surplus of 9 million m³ and a decrease of the United States' deficit by 6 million m³.

Scenario A2—Under scenario A2, there is little change in the trade balance of developed countries and developing countries as a whole, but there are large changes within regions and countries. In particular, the annual trade deficit of North/Central America worsens by 20 million m³, due to a 48 million m³ increase in the deficit of the United States, offset only in part by the 27 million m³ increase in the surplus of Canada. The trade surplus of Asia becomes a deficit with a net trade change of -12 million m³, with -7 million m³ in China and -6 million m³ in Malaysia, compensated only in part by a 4 million m³ and a 2 million m³ reduction of the trade deficit in Japan and the Republic of Korea, respectively. These changes are matched by increases in the surplus of Europe (+17 million m³, spread over several countries) and South America (+12 million m³, mostly in Brazil).

Scenario B2—Under scenario B2, the annual surplus in wood-panel trade of developing countries decreases by 8 million m³. This is due in large part to the passage of Asia from net exporter to net importer, with a reduction in net trade of 12 million m³, distributed in the same amounts as under scenario A2 between China, Malaysia, Japan, and the Republic of Korea. But the annual trade deficit of North America is much less than under scenario A2 (-5 million m³, with a 29 million m³ increase of the trade deficit of the United States matched in part by an improvement in the Canadian surplus of 24 million m³). Net exports increase less than under A2 in South America (+8 million m³, of which 7 million m³ in Brazil) and Europe (+7 million m³, distributed in several countries). As under scenario A2, the trade surplus of Oceania is reduced by 1 million m³ while the trade deficit of Africa is reduced by the same amount.

Scenario A1B-Low Fuelwood—Under scenario A1B-Low Fuelwood, the changes of net trade resemble those under scenario A1B for the developed and developing countries as a whole, but are more pronounced by region and country. In particular, the net trade of Asia decreases by 21 million m³, as the region changes from exporter to major importer, with the trade surplus of China, Malaysia, and Indonesia decreasing by 7 million m³, 6 million m³, and 3 million m³, respectively. This worsening of the trade balance of Asia is matched by a 21 million m³ improvement in the annual trade of North/Central America, where the annual deficit of the United States decreases by 19 million m³ and the surplus of Canada increases by 3 million m³. The trade balance would also improve in South America (+5 million m³, due in part to a 6 million m³ increase in Brazilian annual net exports). In contrast, the trade balance of Europe worsens by 8 million m³, changing the region from net exporter to net importer, with a decrease of 5 million m³ in net exports from Germany and France.

Wood Pulp and Other Fibers

Fiber prices
Figure 14 shows past and projected values of the world real prices of mechanical pulp, chemical and semi-chemical pulp, other fiber pulp, and waste paper measured by the unit value of exports expressed in 1997 U.S. dollars. Tables 27, 28, 29, and 30 show the same data for selected years and countries.

Observed evolution of the prices of wood pulp and other fibers
There was a slight negative trend in real prices of the three wood pulp grades and of waste paper from 1961 to 2006, and a positive trend for the price of other fibers, with strong annual fluctuations around this trend. For these four papermaking fibers, the world price was somewhat lower in 2006 than it had been in 1992.

Projected evolution of the prices of wood pulp and other fibers
Scenario A1B—Under scenario A1B, the world prices of mechanical and chemical wood pulp increase by about $300/mt, and the prices of waste paper by $130/mt. The price of other fiber pulp decreases by $60/mt.

Scenario A2—Under scenario A2 the price of mechanical pulp increases by about $20/mt and the price of chemical pulp by $60/mt from 2006 to 2060. The price of waste paper also increases by $34/mt while it decreases by $240/mt for other fiber pulp.

Scenario B2—Under scenario B2, the world prices trends are similar to those of scenario A2 (fig. 14), with a slightly higher price increase for wood pulps and waste paper, and a lower decrease for other fiber pulp.

Scenario A1B-Low Fuelwood—Scenario A1B-Low Fuelwood leads to prices in 2060 that are about $80/mt, $50/mt, and $170/mt lower than in 2006 for mechanical pulp, chemical pulp, and other fiber pulp, respectively. However, the price of waste paper is $140/ton higher in 2060 than in 2006.

Wood pulp consumption
Figure 15 shows the data on wood pulp consumption (mechanical and chemical pulp) from 1961 to 2006 and projections for world regions, according to the four scenarios. More detailed data for selected years and countries, and separated by mechanical and chemical pulp, are in tables 31 and 32.

Observed evolution of wood pulp consumption
From 1992 to 2006, the world annual consumption of wood pulp increased by 25 million mt, of which 16 million mt were in developing countries. World consumption increased or remained stable in all regions, except in North America where it decreased by 5 million mt, due mostly to the decrease of 6 million mt in the United States. Wood pulp consumption increased in Europe (+16 million mt, of which +4 million mt occurred in Finland and +2 million mt each in Sweden and Germany). In Asia, annual consumption increased by 12 million mt, mostly in China (+7 million mt), and Indonesia and the Republic of Korea (+2 million mt each). Annual consumption also increased in South America by 2 million mt, mostly in Brazil.

Projected evolution of wood pulp consumption
Scenario A1B—Under scenario A1B, the world annual wood pulp consumption increases by 12 million mt, rising by 41 million mt in developing countries while it declines by 29 million mt in developed countries. Much of this decrease is in North/Central America where it accelerates after 2030, with the United States annual consumption ending 23 million mt lower in 2060 than in 2006. Annual wood pulp consumption

Wood-based panels net trade, scenario A1B

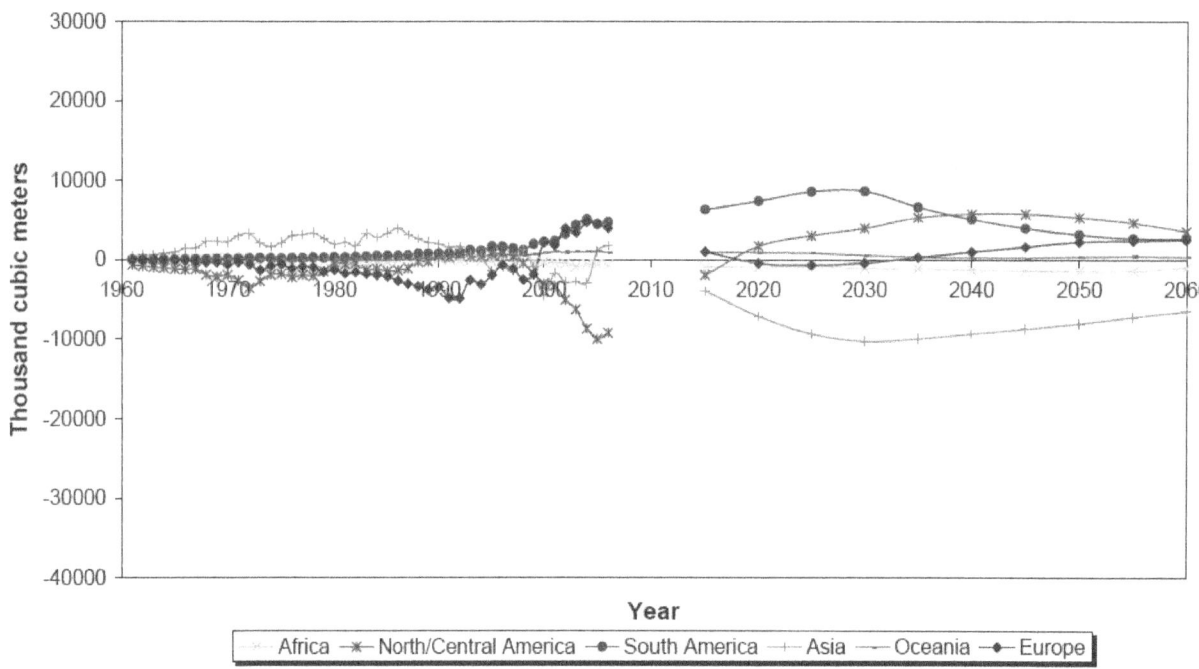

Wood-based panels net trade, scenario A2

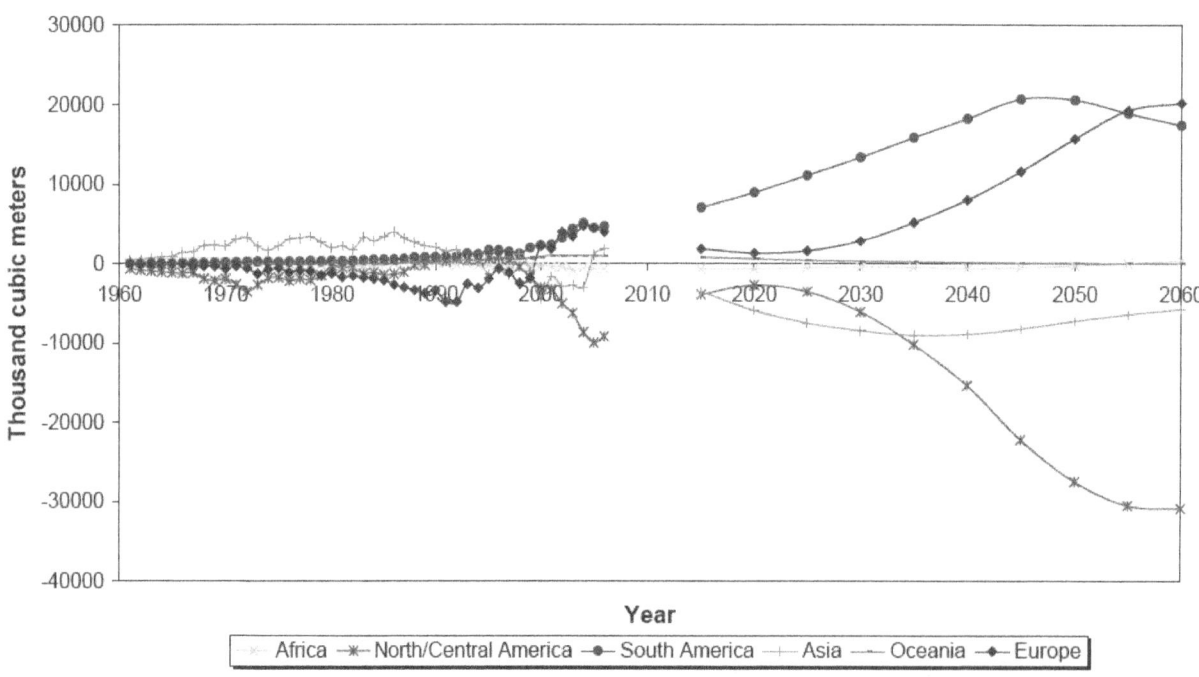

Figure 13—Wood-based panels net trade by world region, observed and projected with the Global Forest Products Model. (continued on next page)

Wood-based panels net trade, scenario B2

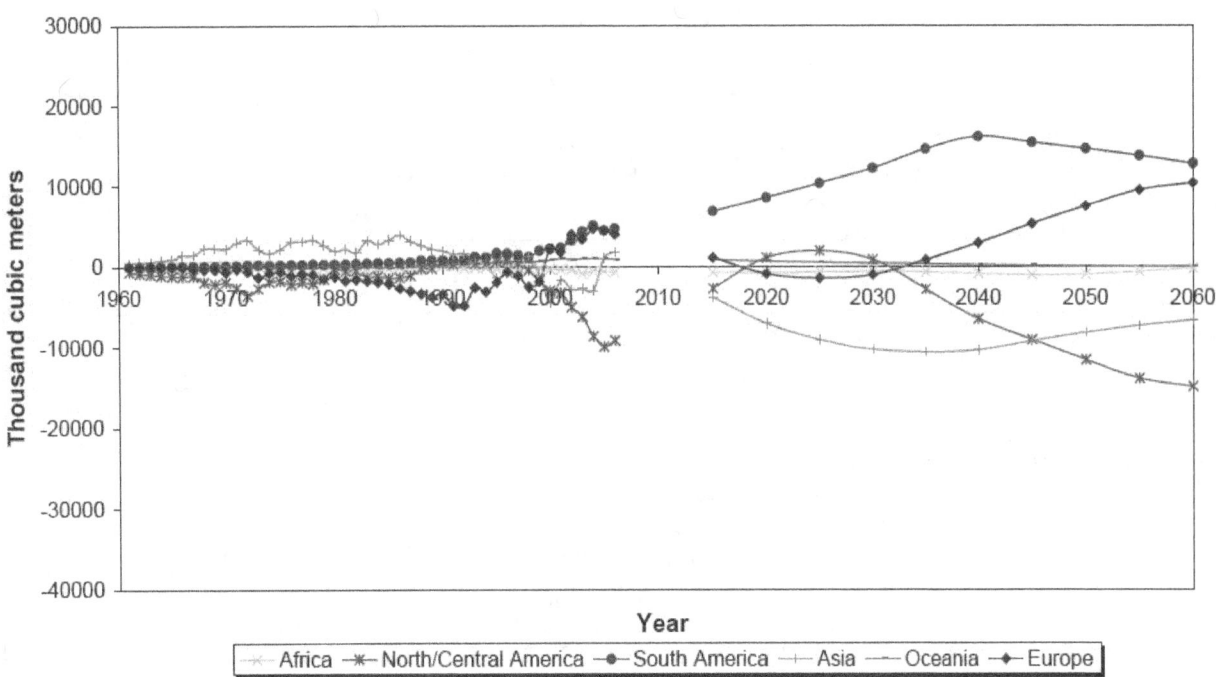

Wood-based panels net trade, scenario A1B-Low Fuelwood

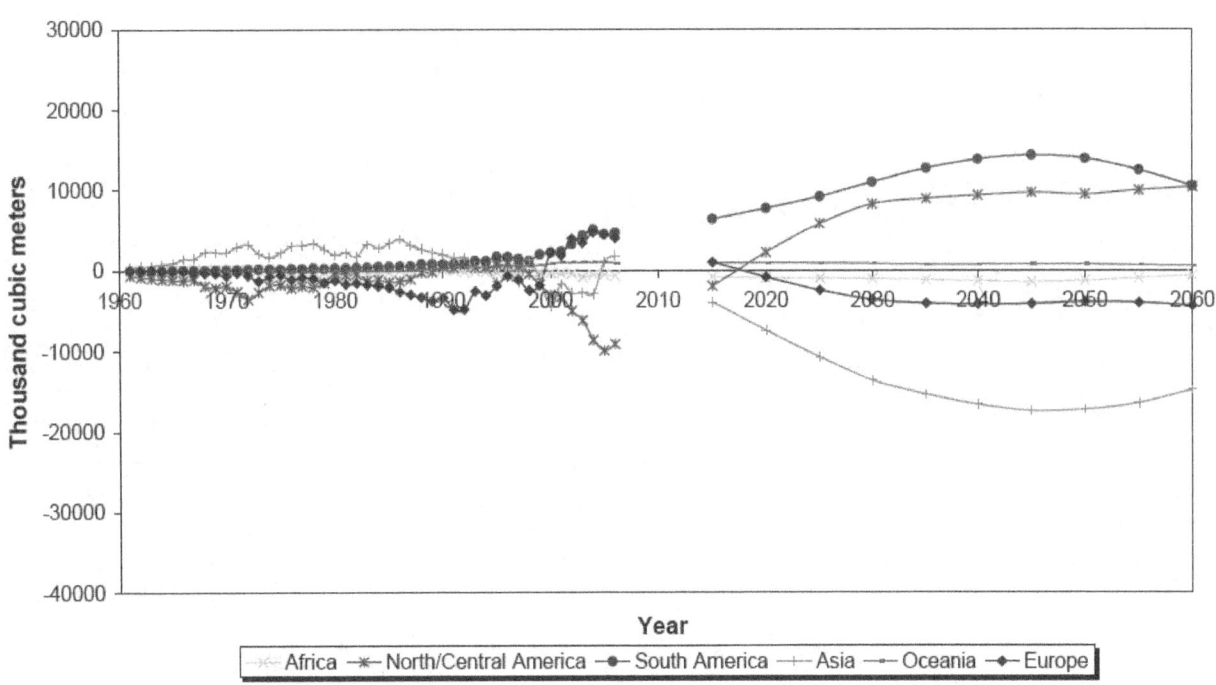

Figure 13 (continued)—Wood-based panels net trade by world region, observed and projected with the Global Forest Products Model.

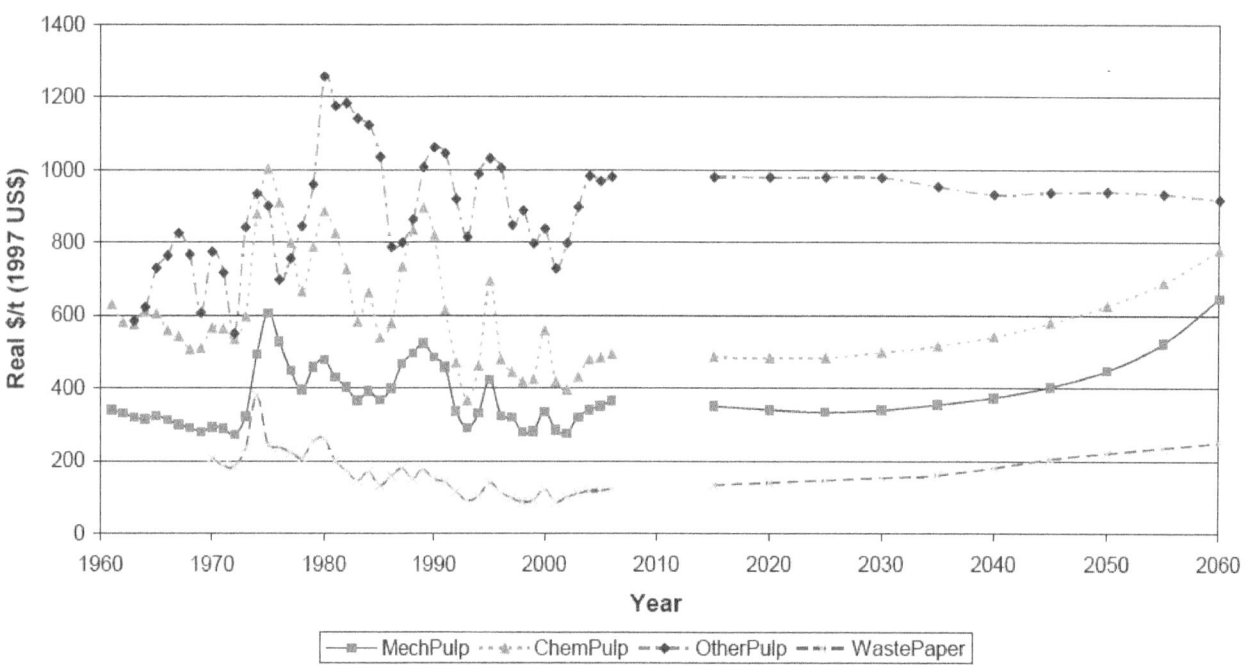

Fiber prices, scenario A1B

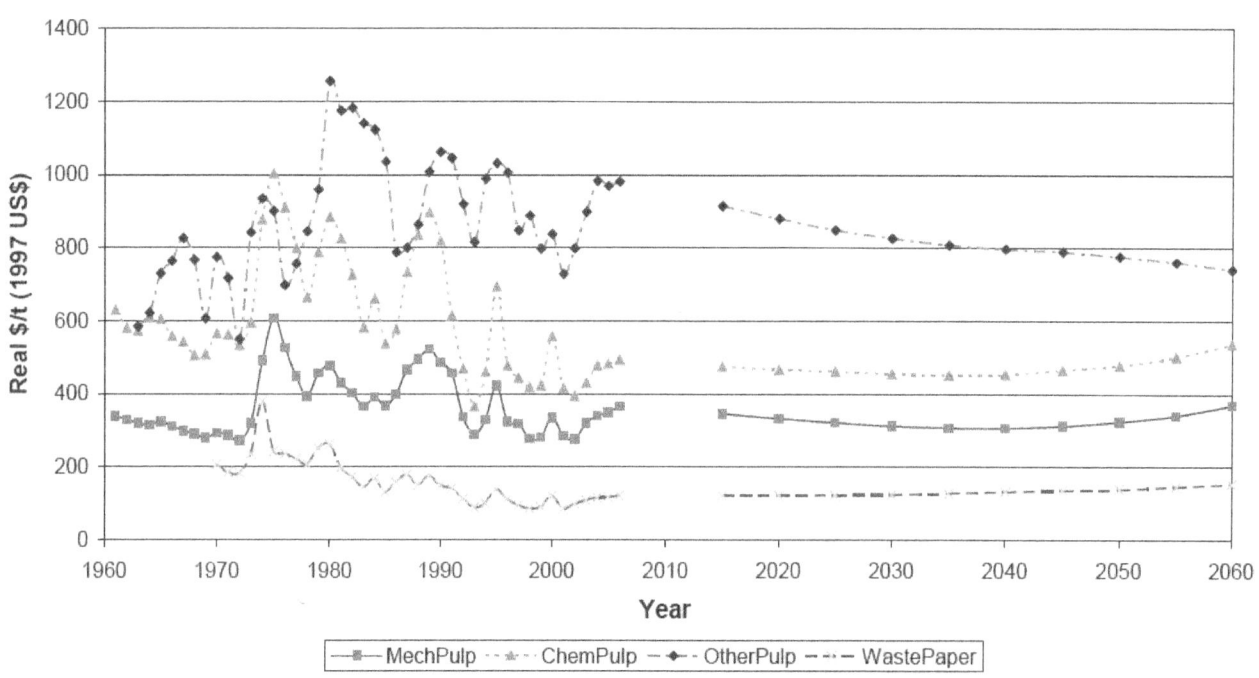

Fiber prices, scenario A2

Figure 14—World prices of papermaking fibers, observed and projected with the Global Forest Products Model. (continued on next page)

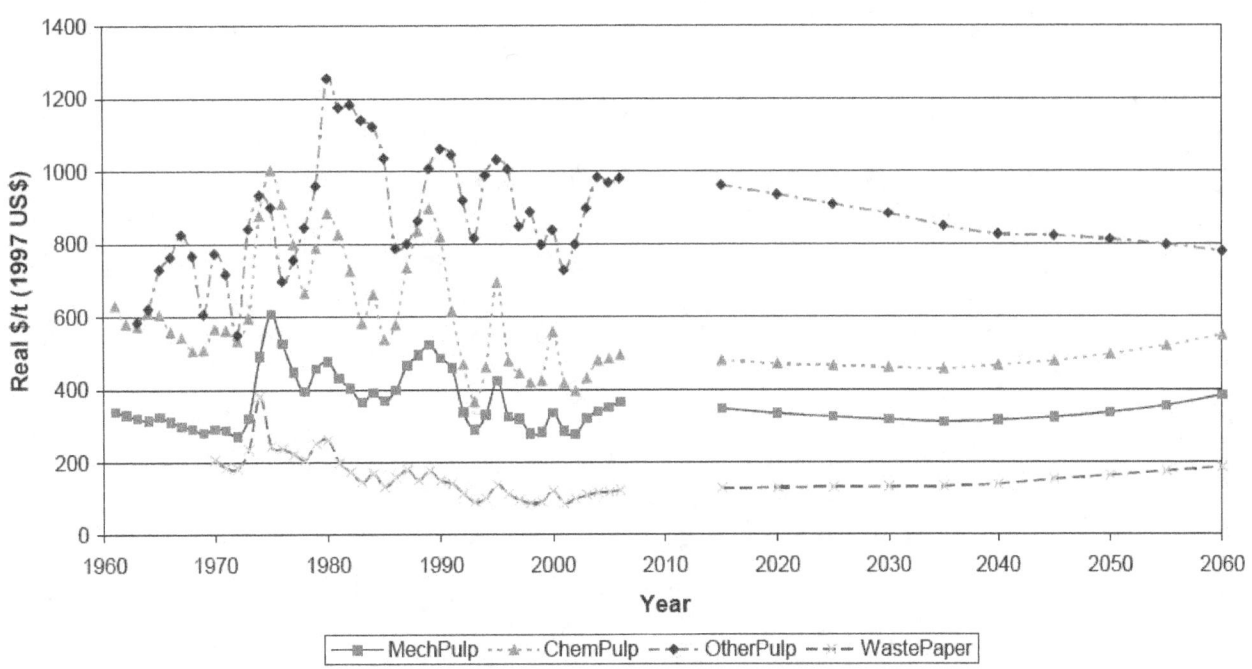

Fiber prices, scenario B2

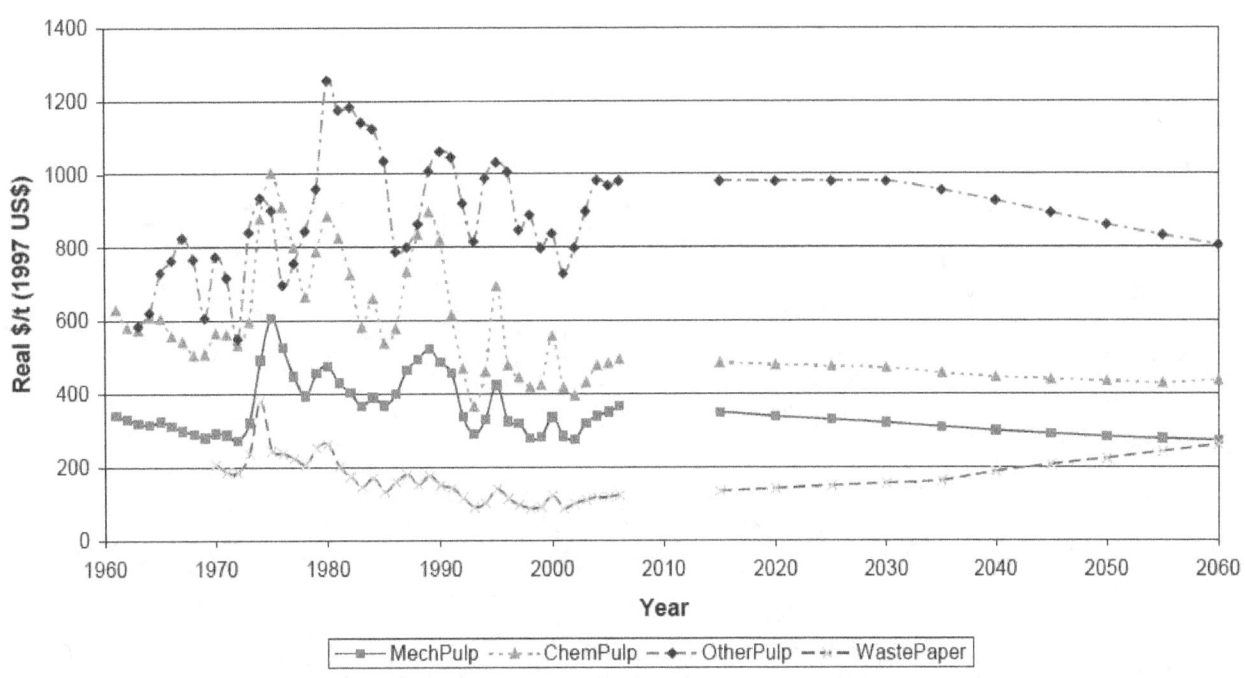

Fiber prices, scenario A1B-Low Fuelwood

Figure 14 (continued)—World prices of papermaking fibers, observed and projected with the Global Forest Products Model.

Wood pulp consumption, scenario A1B

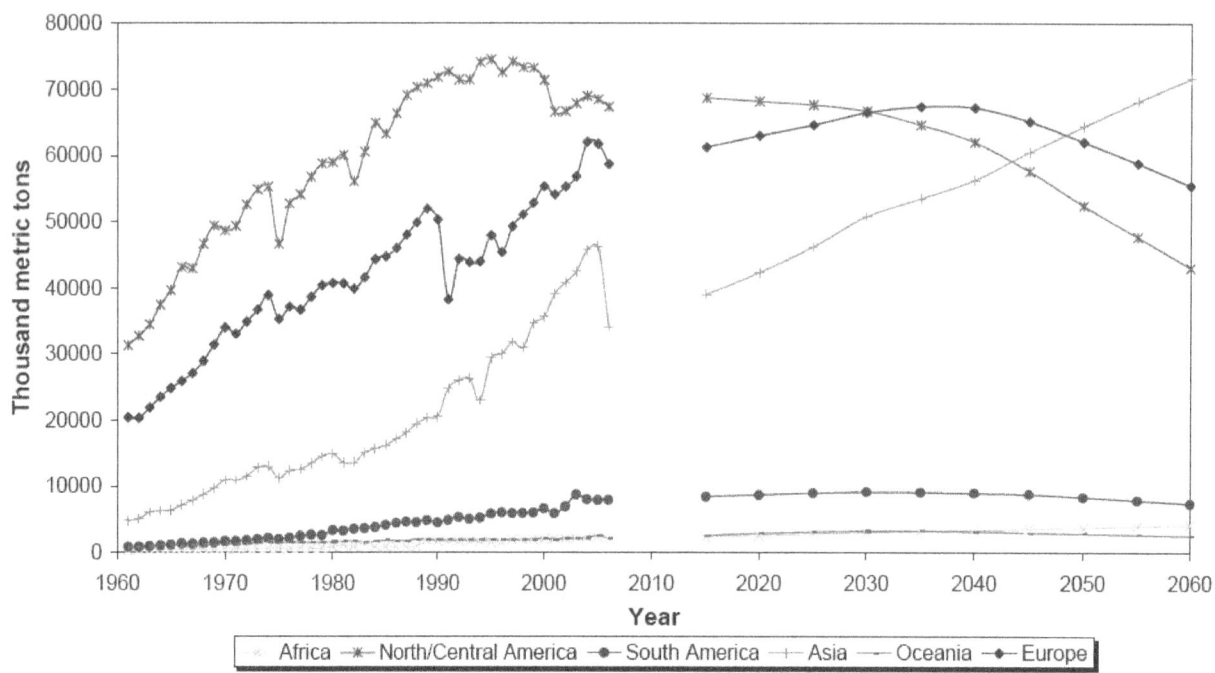

Wood pulp consumption, scenario A2

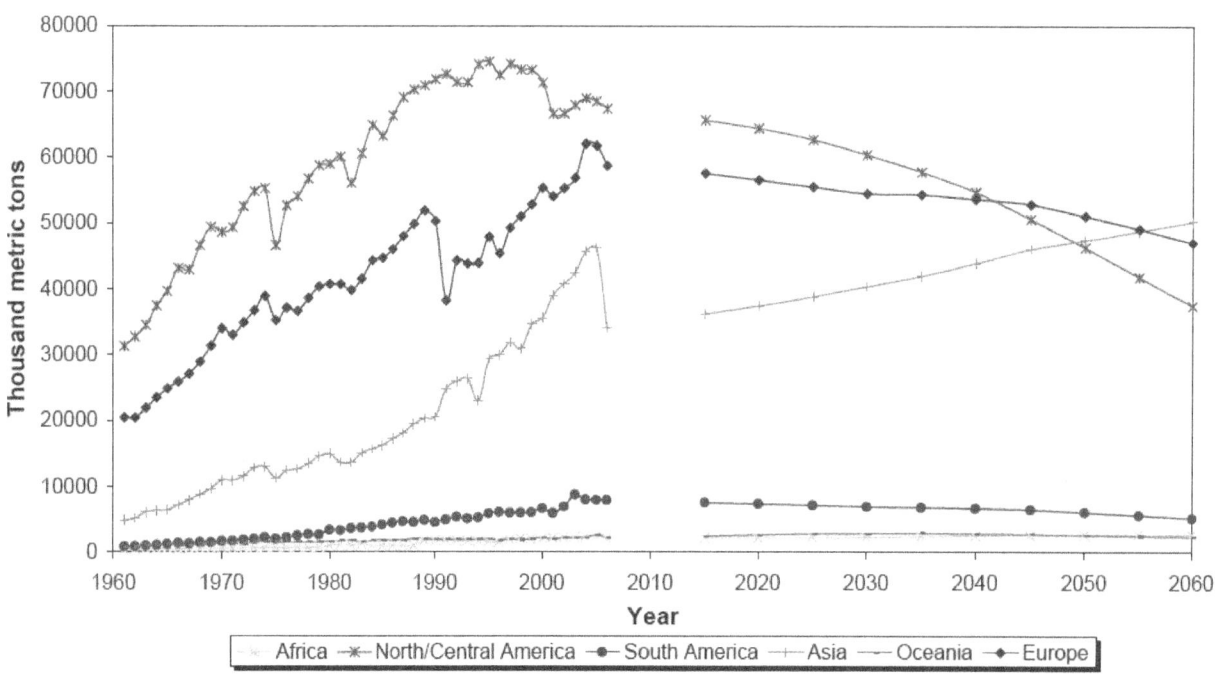

Figure 15—Wood pulp consumption by world region, observed and projected with the Global Forest Products Model. (continued on next page)

Wood pulp consumption, scenario B2

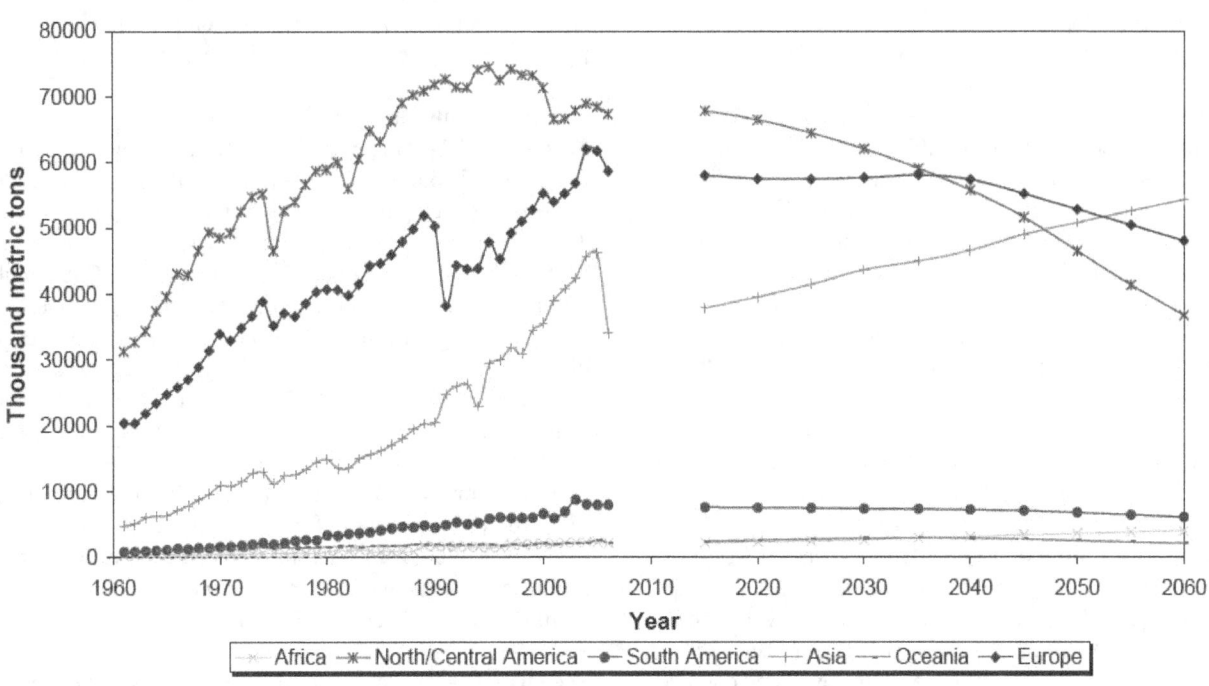

Wood pulp consumption, scenario A1B-Low Fuelwood

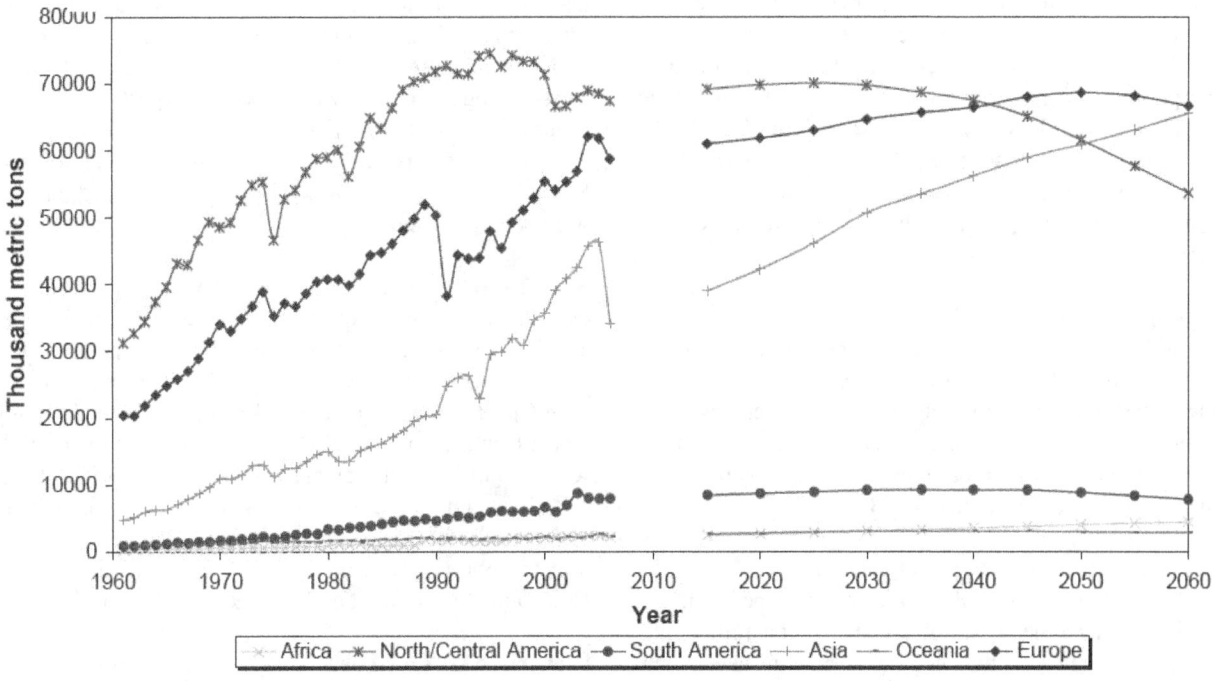

Figure 15 (continued)—Wood pulp consumption by world region, observed and projected with the Global Forest Products Model.

also decreases in Europe by 4 million mt, with -6 million mt in Finland and -8 million mt in Sweden. Meanwhile, annual wood pulp consumption increases by 37 million mt in Asia, with 24 million mt in China and 3 million mt in India.

Scenario A2—Scenario A2 implies a decrease in world wood pulp consumption of 27 million mt, with -44 million mt in developed countries. The main decrease is in North/Central America (-29 million mt, with -24 million mt in the United States and -5 million mt in Canada). Annual consumption also decreases in Europe by 13 million mt, including -8 million mt in Sweden and -7 million mt in Finland. The largest increase in annual wood pulp consumption is in Asia (+16 million mt from 2006 to 2060, with +14 million mt in China).

Scenario B2—The projections for scenario B2 are similar to A2, with small differences by region and country.

Scenario A1B-Low Fuelwood—Under scenario A1B-Low Fuelwood, the annual world consumption of wood pulp increases the most, compared to the other three scenarios, by 29 million mt, with a 35 million increase in developing countries and a 6 million mt decrease in developed countries. As was the case under the other scenarios, most of the growth is in Asia, where annual production increases by 31 million mt (with 18 million mt in China and 3 million mt in India). Annual consumption also increases in Europe (+7 million mt spread over several countries, and despite an 8 million mt decline in Sweden). The decrease in annual consumption in North America (-12 million mt due mainly to -18 million mt in the United States) is about half of what was obtained under the other scenarios. The better performance of wood pulp in this scenario than in A1B stems from the lower price of wood pulp (fig. 14) due to the lower use of industrial roundwood for energy.

Wood pulp net trade
Figure 16 shows the historical data of the net trade of wood pulp (mechanical pulp and chemical pulp), from 1961 to 2006, and the GFPM projections to 2060, for the world regions, according to each scenario. More detailed data for selected years and countries, and separated by mechanical pulp and chemical pulp, are presented in tables 33 and 34.

Observed evolution of wood pulp net trade
From 1992 to 2006, the annual net trade of developed and developing countries decreased by less than half a million mt, developed countries remaining net exporters while developing countries stayed net importers. The main regional change was in South America where annual net exports increased by 6 million mt, of which +4 million mt occurred in Brazil. Europe also improved its net trade by reducing net imports

by 1 million mt. Symmetrically, the annual deficit of Asia increased by 5 million mt, due largely to China increased annual net imports by 6 million mt, compensated in part by positive net trade changes of 2 million mt in Indonesia.

Projected evolution of wood pulp net trade
Scenario A1B—Under scenario A1B, the annual net exports of developed countries increase by 19 million mt, while the net imports of developing countries increase by a similar amount. The largest regional change is in Asia, where net imports increase by 13 million mt, with 11 million mt in China and 2 million mt each in India and Indonesia, partly compensated by decreases of 2 million mt each in Japan and the Republic of Korea. This rise in net imports is met by an increase in annual net exports in North/Central America (+8 million mt, primarily due to +9 million mt in Canada) that compensate for the decrease in annual net exports of South America (-5 million mt, with 3 million mt in Brazil and 2 million mt in Chile). Europe changes from net importer in 2006 to net exporter in 2060, with a net trade change of 5 million mt stemming from an increase in the surplus of Finland of 4 million mt and Sweden of 3 million mt.

Scenario A2—Under scenario A2, the annual net exports of developed countries (net imports of developing countries) changes by about half of the change in A1B. As under scenario A1B, the main regional change is an increase in the annual net imports of Asia (7 million mt due largely to a 5 million mt increase in China). As under A1B, annual net exports of South America decrease by 5 million mt, from Brazil and Chile. These changes are met by increased net exports from North/Central America (+5 million mt, with +11 million mt in Canada and notwithstanding -6 million mt in the United States) and Europe (+5 million mt, of which +4 million mt occurred in Finland).

Scenario B2—Under scenario B2, the wood pulp annual net exports of developed countries increase by 16 million mt. The increase occurs primarily in Europe, which goes from net importer to net exporter, adding 8 million mt to net trade, with 4 million mt in Finland and 3 million mt in Germany. North/Central America also adds 4 million mt to net trade, with a 10 million mt increase in Canada's surplus and despite a 5 million mt increase in the U.S. deficit. Annual net exports also increase in Oceania by 3 million mt to meet an increase of net imports of 11 million mt in Asia, with 8 million mt in China and 2 million mt each in India and Indonesia.

Scenario A1B-Low Fuelwood—Scenario A1B-Low Fuelwood gives the same increase as scenario B2 for the changes in net annual exports of developed countries, with variations in regional and country effects. The annual exports of North/Central America grow more than in the other scenarios

(+13 million mt, due mostly to increases of 8 million mt in the United States, which goes from net importer to net exporter, and a 4 million mt increase in Canada's net exports). Another positive change of net trade is in Europe (+3 million mt due to lower imports in particular in France and Germany). On the other hand, Asia increases its annual deficit by 13 million mt, of which 7 million mt are due to increased net imports of China and 2 million mt of India.

Other fiber consumption

In addition to wood pulp, the GFPM projects production, consumption, prices, and net trade of waste paper and other fiber pulp. The past world consumption of other fiber pulp was approximately 5 percent of the world consumption of total papermaking fiber, and it is expected to change little until 2060 (table 35). On the other hand, waste paper constituted 46 percent of the world fiber consumption for papermaking in 2006, and this share is projected to increase to about 70 percent by 2060, a level that seems achievable given 2006 shares of 68 percent in the United Kingdom, 61 percent in Germany, 71 percent in Spain, and 66 percent in China. This increase is made possible by the rise of waste paper recovery rate, the ratio of waste paper production to paper and paperboard consumption, which reaches 75 percent in Europe and North America, and above 60 percent in Asia by 2060, with a faster increase in scenario A1B due to more rapid economic growth (fig. 17).

Figure 18 shows the historical data and projections of waste paper consumption in the main world regions. Table 36 shows the same data for selected years and countries within each region.

Observed evolution of waste paper consumption

From 1992 to 2006, the world annual consumption of waste paper increased by 94 million mt, nearly four times the growth of wood pulp consumption. More than half of this growth was in developing countries. The main regional growth was in Asia (+54 million mt, with 42 million mt in China and 3 million mt in Indonesia), followed by Europe (+21 million mt, with +6 million mt in Germany), and in North/Central America (+17 million mt, with +13 million mt in the United States). Annual consumption also grew by 1 million mt each in Africa and Oceania, but by less than one half million ton in South America.

Scenario A1B

—According to scenario A1B, the world consumption of waste paper grows by 330 million mt, with 184 million mt in developing countries. Most of the regional growth is in Asia (+163 million mt, with 91 million mt in China, 14 million mt in India, and 11 million mt in Japan). Annual consumption grows by 69 million mt in North/Central America, with 40 million mt in the United States, 20 million mt in Canada, and 7 million mt in Mexico. An almost equal

growth occurs in Europe (+68 million mt, principally in the Russian Federation, the United Kingdom, Finland, Germany, and France). Annual consumption grows by 16 million mt in South America, with 9 million mt in Brazil and 3 million mt in Argentina, and by 11 million mt and 4 million mt in Africa and Oceania, respectively.

Scenario A2

—Under scenario A2, the world annual consumption of waste paper grows by 207 million mt, and more in developed countries (+114 million mt) than in developing countries. As under scenario A1B, the main regional change is in Asia, but smaller (+82 million mt, with 46 million in China, 6 million mt in India, and 9 million mt in Japan). Consumption also grows less in North/Central America (+56 million mt, with 36 million mt in the United States, 15 million mt in Canada, and 4 million mt in Mexico). Consumption grows by 49 million mt in Europe, mostly in Germany, Finland, and the United Kingdom; 10 million mt in South America (with 6 million mt in Brazil); 6 million mt in Africa; and 3 million mt in Oceania (mostly Australia).

Scenario B2

—Under scenario B2, the change of annual waste paper consumption, 231 million mt, is slightly higher than in scenario A2. The 118 million mt growth in developing countries is almost equal to that in developed countries. Consumption in Asia grows more than under scenario A2 (+99 million mt, with 55 million mt in China, 9 million mt in India, and 7 million mt in Japan). In North/Central America, annual consumption grows by 53 million mt, with 28 million mt in the United States, 18 million mt in Canada, and 5 million mt in Mexico. European consumption also grows by 53 million mt, principally in Finland, Germany, and the United Kingdom. In South America, annual waste paper consumption increases by 13 million mt, with 7 million mt in Brazil, while it grows by 10 million mt in Africa and 3 million mt in Oceania.

Scenario A1B-Low Fuelwood

—Scenario A1B-Low Fuelwood gives the highest increase in the world annual consumption of waste paper among the four scenarios, 348 million mt, with 195 million mt in developed countries. The growth in Asia (132 million mt, with 61 million mt in China, and 12 million each in India and Japan) is smaller than under scenario A1B. Instead, the North/Central American annual consumption grows more than under A1B (98 million mt, with 52 million mt in the United States, 36 million mt in Canada, and 6 million mt in Mexico). Annual consumption in Europe also grows more than under A1B (+86 million mt, with 17 million mt in Finland, 12 million mt in Germany, and 9 million mt in the United Kingdom). In Africa and Oceania, waste paper annual consumption increases by 11 million mt and 4 million mt respectively, the same as under scenario A1B.

Wood pulp net trade, scenario A1B

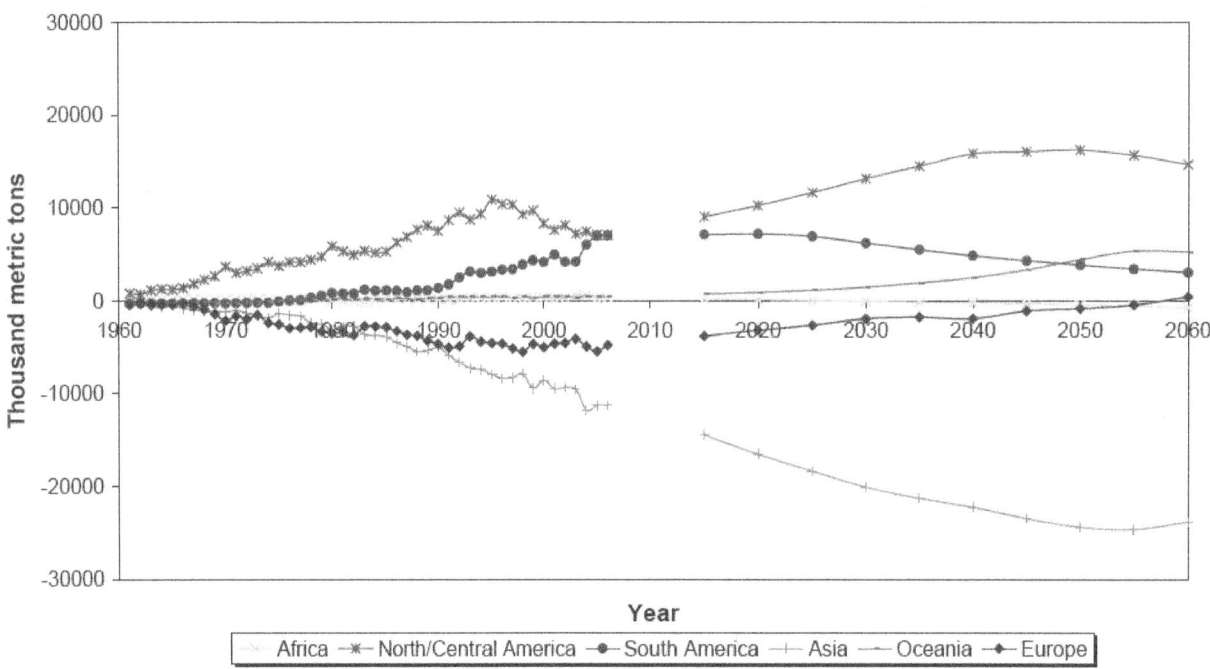

Wood pulp net trade, scenario A2

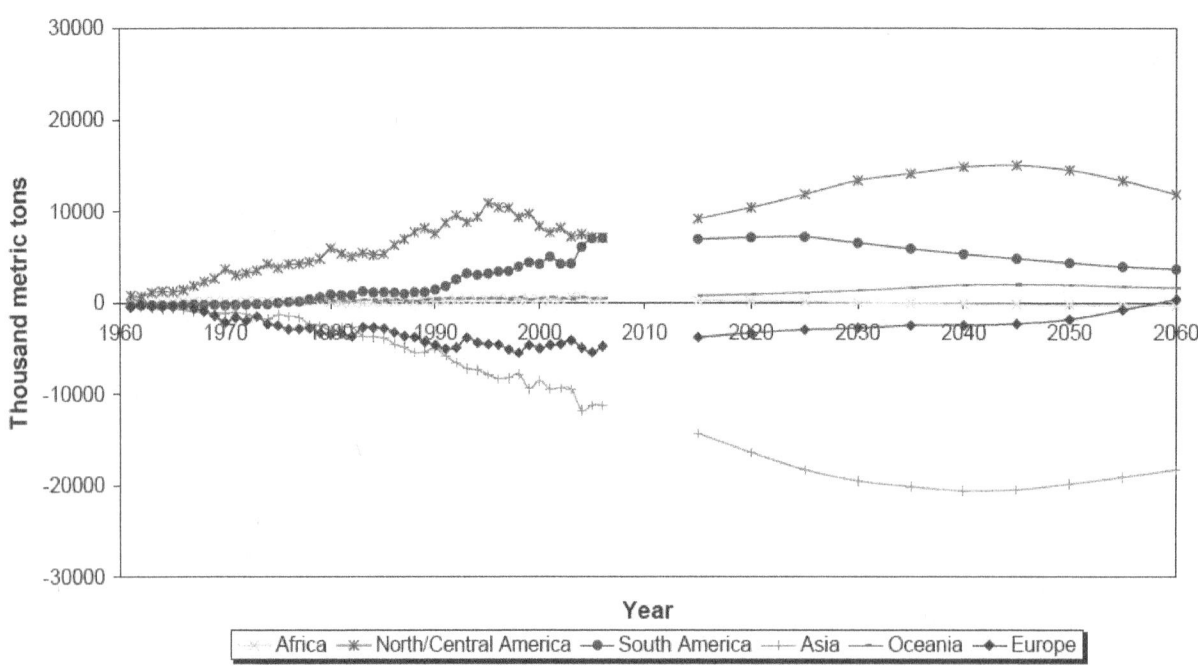

Figure 16—Wood pulp net trade by world region, observed and projected with the Global Forest Products Model. (continued on next page)

Wood pulp net trade, scenario B2

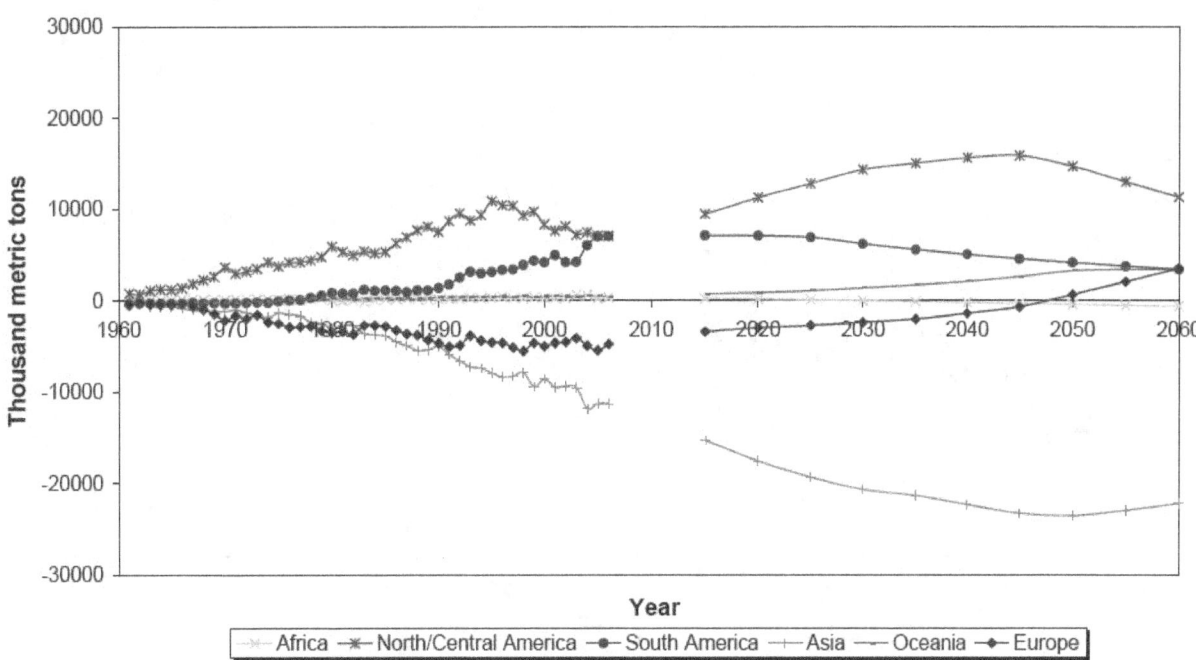

Wood pulp net trade, scenario A1B-Low Fuelwood

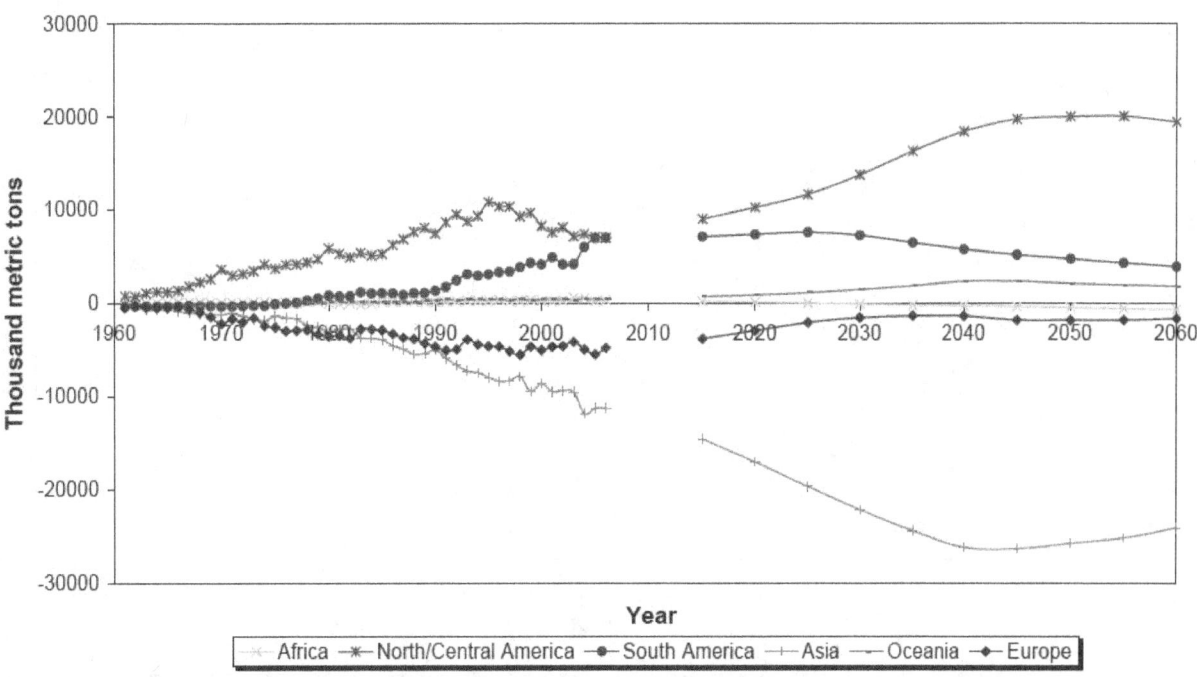

Figure 16 (continued)—Wood pulp net trade by world region, observed and projected with the Global Forest Products Model.

Waste paper recovery rate, scenario A1B

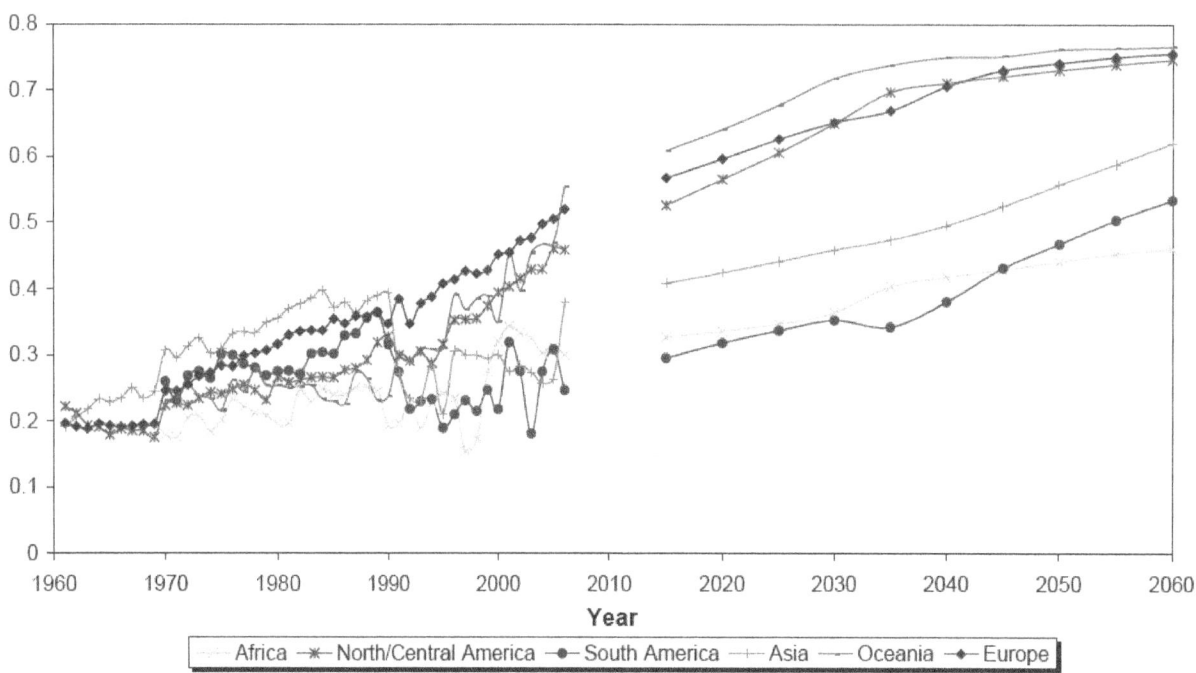

Waste paper recovery rate, scenario A2

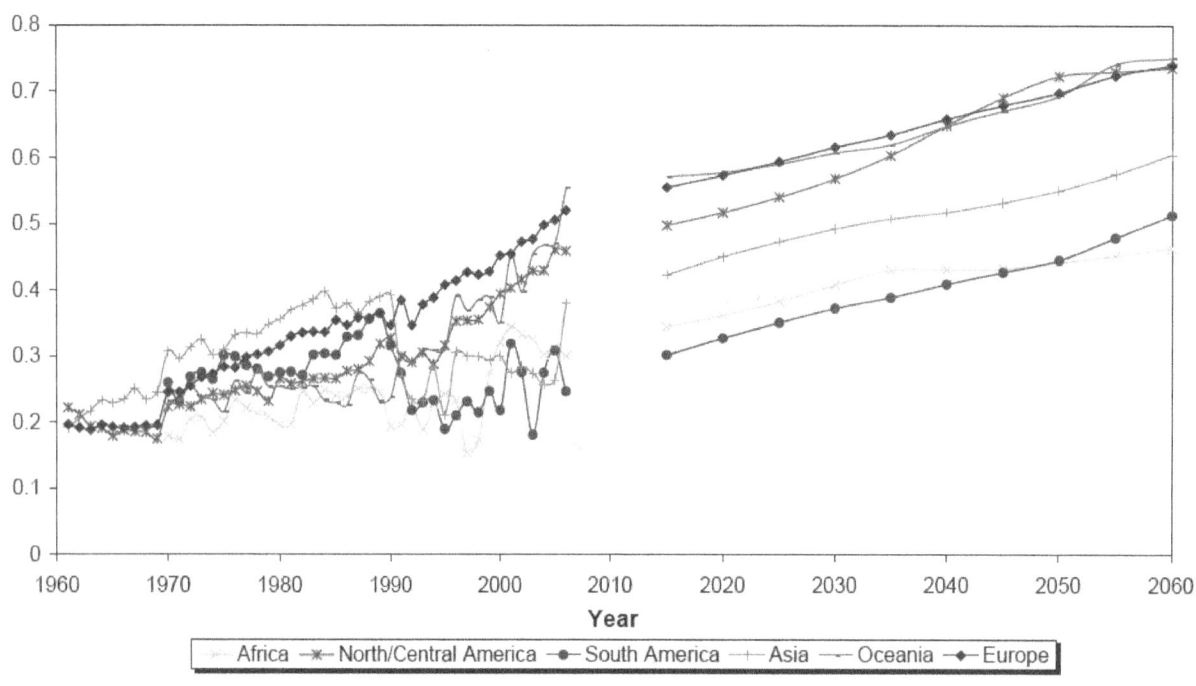

Figure 17—Waste paper recovery rate by world region, observed and projected with the Global Forest Products Model. (continued on next page)

Waste paper recovery rate, scenario B2

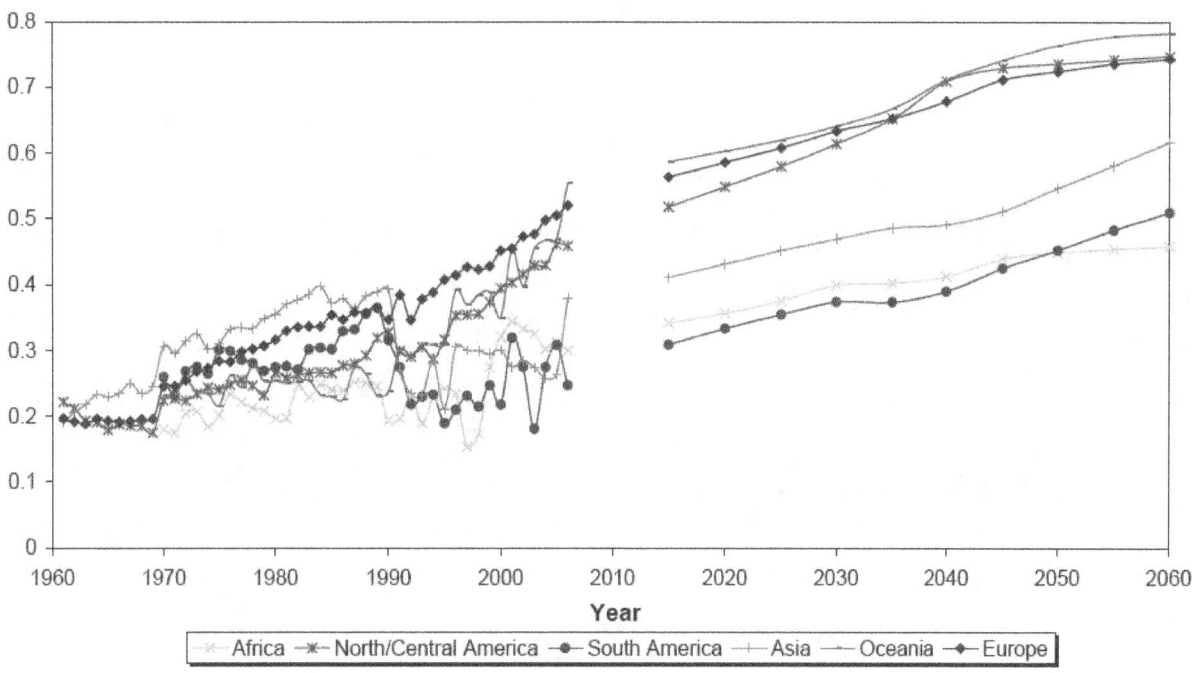

Waste paper recovery rate, scenario A1B-Low Fuelwood

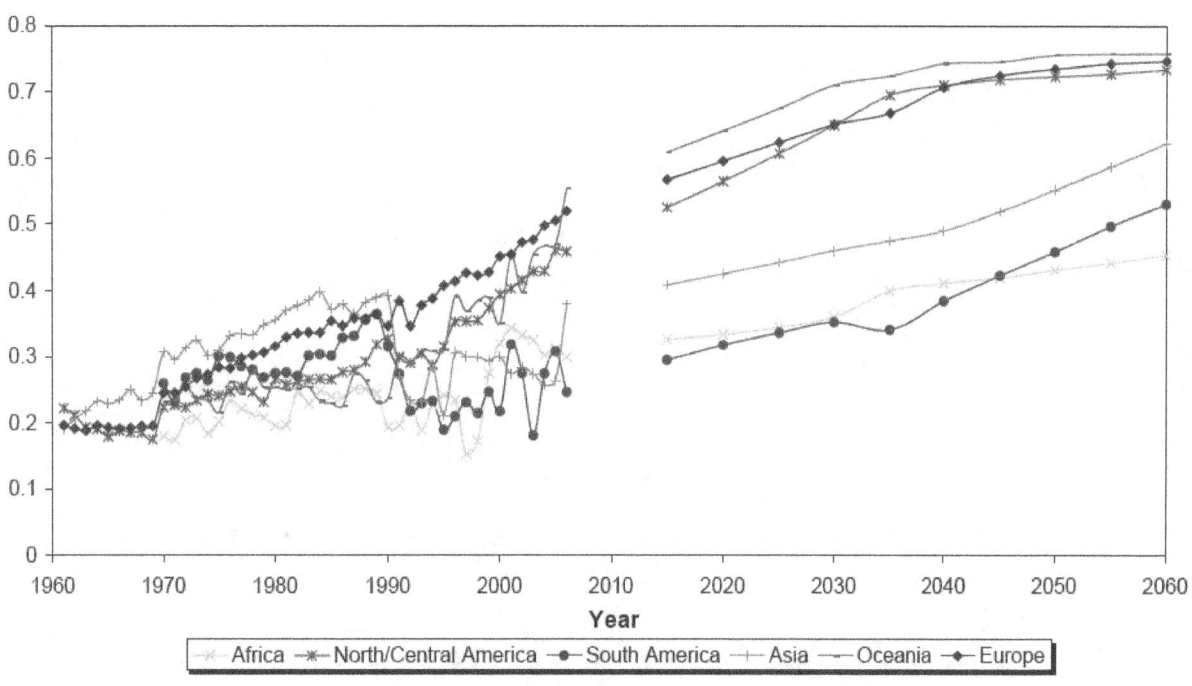

Figure 17 (continued)—Waste paper recovery rate by world region, observed and projected with the Global Forest Products Model.

Waste paper consumption, scenario A1B

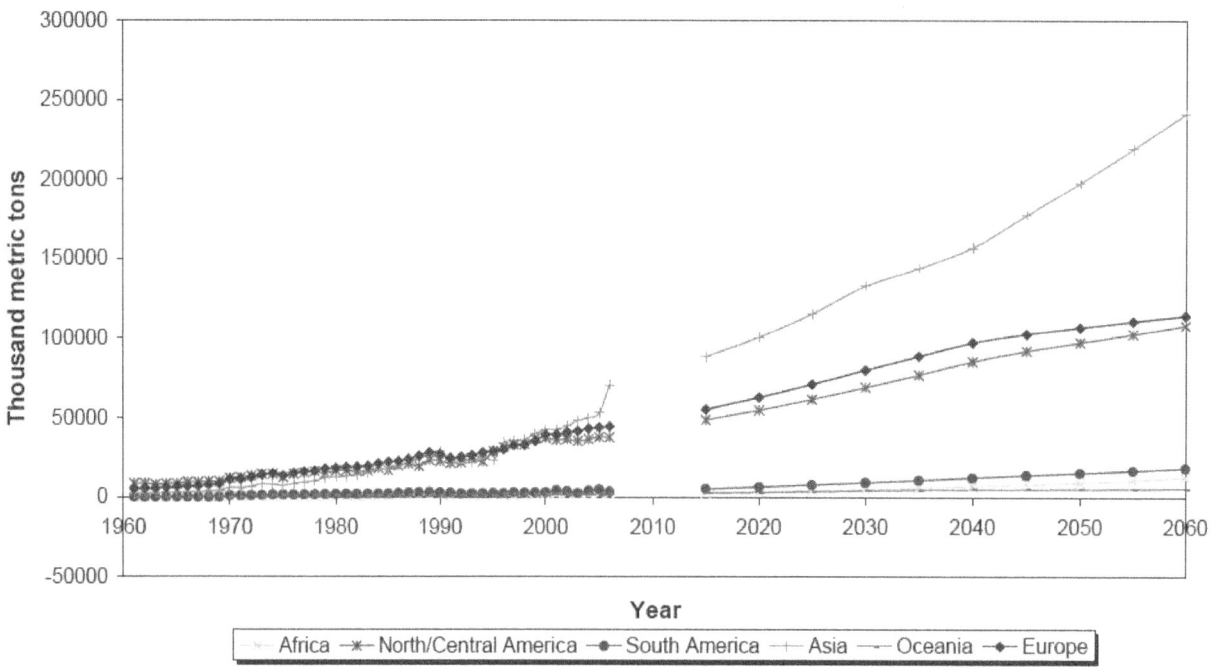

Waste paper consumption, scenario A2

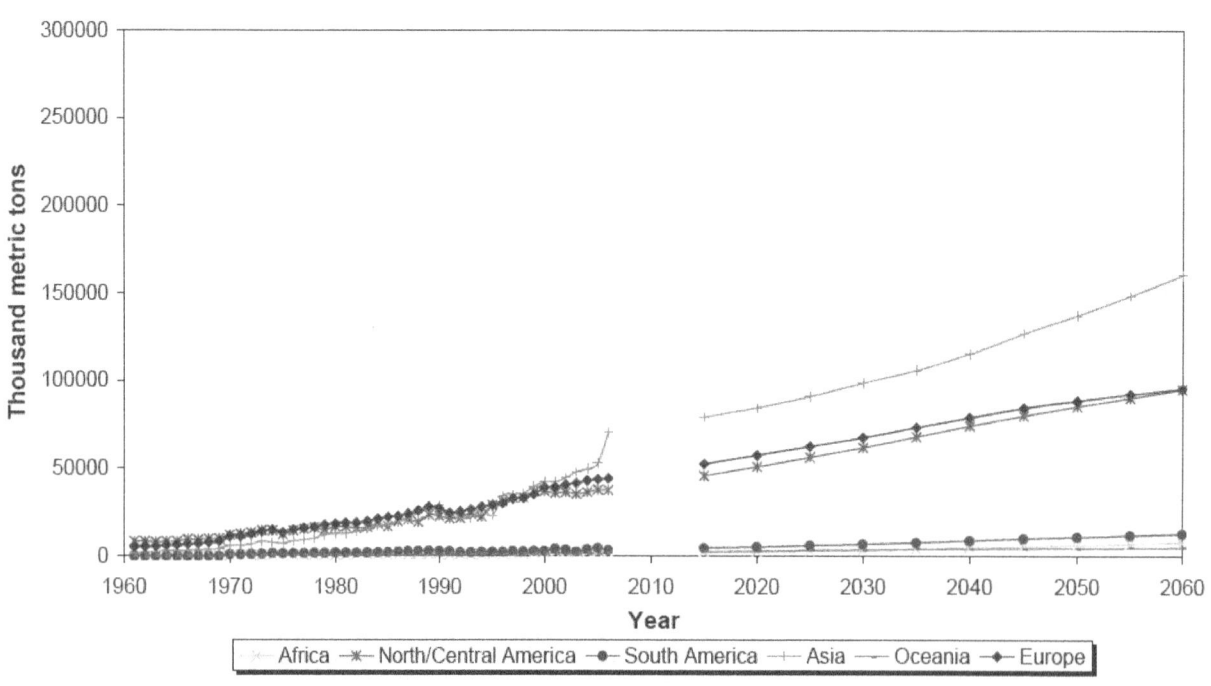

Figure 18—Waste paper consumption by world region, observed and projected with the Global Forest Products Model. (continued on next page)

Waste paper consumption, scenario B2

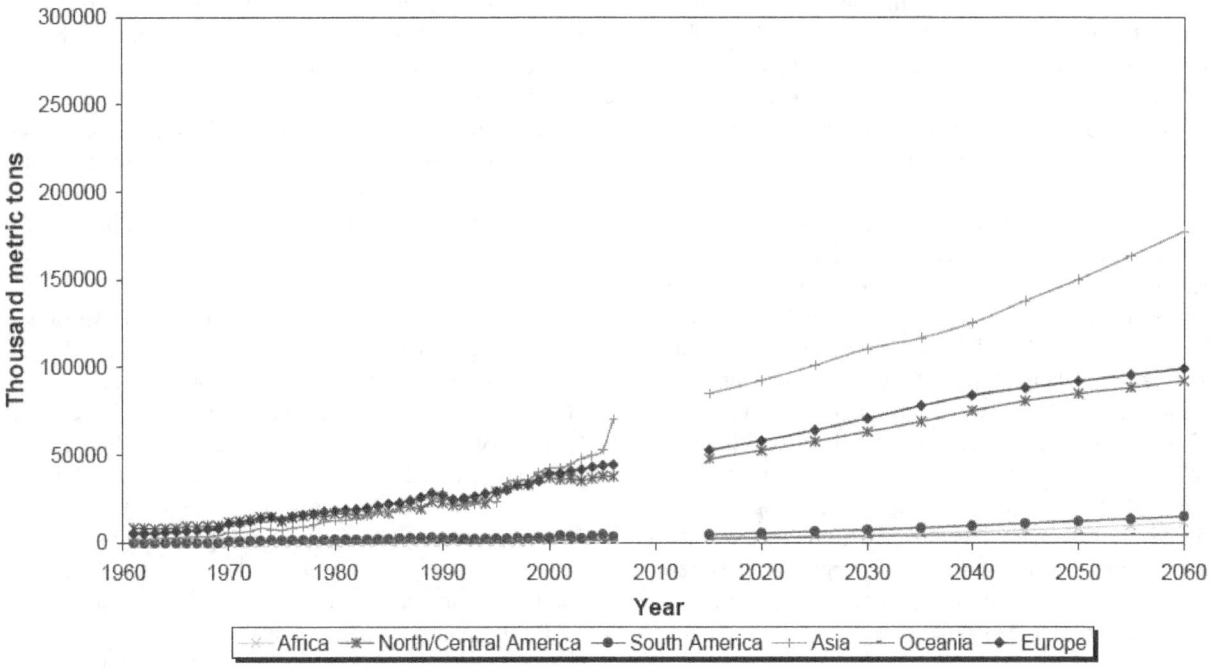

Waste paper consumption, scenario A1B-Low Fuelwood

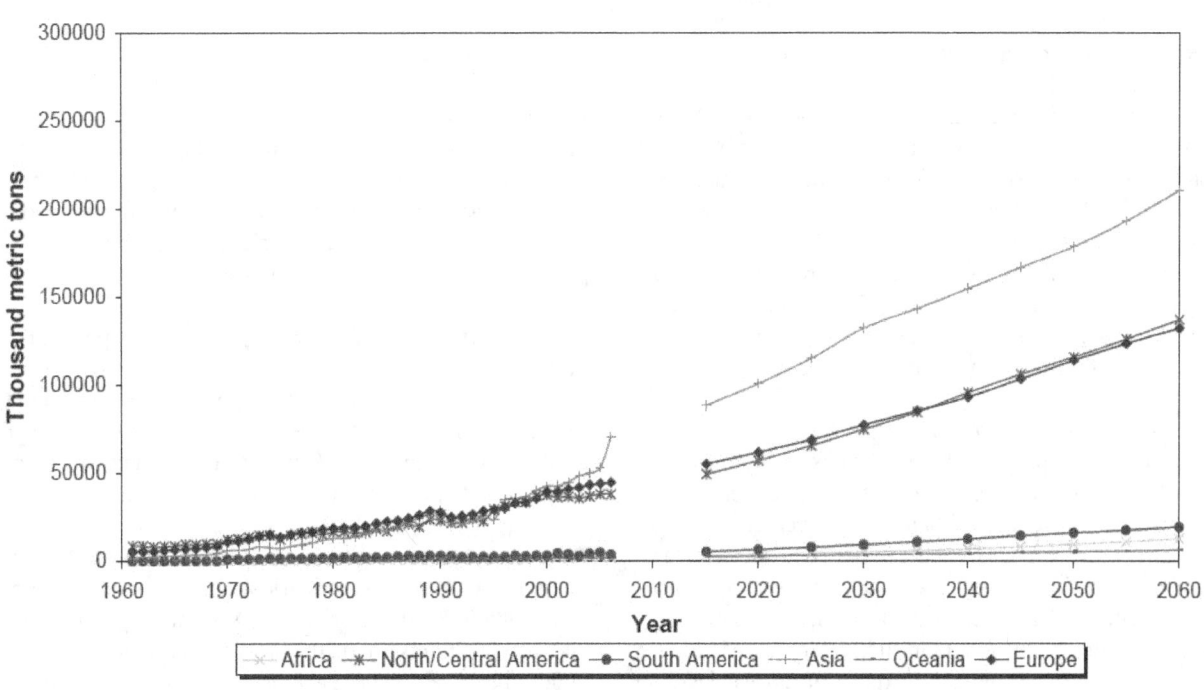

Figure 18 (continued)—Waste paper consumption by world region, observed and projected with the Global Forest Products Model.

Other fiber net trade

While the trade of nonwood fiber pulp was quite small and is expected to remain so (table 37), the world trade of waste paper was 50 percent of the world trade of total papermaking fibers in 2006. Figure 19 shows the historical data of the net trade of waste paper from 1961 to 2006 and the projections to 2060 for each world region. Table 38 shows the same data for selected years and countries within each region.

Observed evolution of waste paper net trade

From 1992 to 2006, developing countries were net importers of waste paper while developed countries were net exporters. The annual net imports of developing countries increased by 23 million mt. Much of this growth of annual net imports was in Asia (18 million mt, with 19 million mt in China, partly compensated by a growth of the Japanese net trade of 4 million mt). Symmetrically, net exports increased in North/Central America by 9 million mt, and by 10 million mt in the United States. The annual net exports of Europe also increased by 9 million mt, including a 4 million mt increase in the United Kingdom. There was little change in the net trade of Africa, while the net exports of Oceania increased by 1 million mt, mostly in Australia.

Projected evolution of waste paper net trade

Scenario A1B—Under scenario A1B, the net imports of developing countries decrease by 17 million mt. The main regional change is in Asia, where net imports decrease by 22 million mt, due principally to China's change from net importer to net exporter, a 41 million mt increase in net trade, and despite a 14 million mt increase of India's net imports. North/Central America changes from net exporter in 2006 to net importer in 2060, with a reduction in annual net trade of 14 million mt, due mostly to a reduction of Canadian annual net imports by 15 million mt. Europe is still a net exporter in 2060, but with 3 million mt less of annual net exports compared to 2006, a change due mostly to Finland going from net exporter to net importer with a reduction of 7 million mt in annual net trade. In Africa, net imports increased by 2 million mt, while there is little change in Oceania.

Scenario A2—Under scenario A2, the annual net imports of waste paper in developing countries decreases by 16 million mt. This is related mostly to a 20 million mt decrease of net imports in Asia, due to a 26 million mt improvement of the net trade of China, which goes from net importer to net exporter, and despite a 6 million mt increase of annual net imports in India. In North/Central America, net trade decreases by 11 million mt, mostly due to a 13 million mt increase in the net imports of Canada. The annual net exports of Europe decrease by 4 million mt, due mostly to a deterioration of Finland's net trade. The annual net imports increases by 2 million mt in South America and 1 million mt in Africa.

Scenario B2—Under scenario B2, the net imports of developing countries decreases by 21 million mt. Asia goes from net importer to net exporter, with a 26 million mt improvement of net trade (+ 36 million mt in China, changing it to a net exporter, against a 9 million mt increase in the net imports of India). Symmetrically, North/Central America goes from net exporter in 2006 to net importer in 2060, mostly due to a 15 million mt increase in the annual imports of Canada. Europe remains a net exporter, but with a reduction of 6 million mt, mostly due to an increase in Finland's imports.

Scenario A1B-Low Fuelwood—Scenario A1B-Low Fuelwood gives the largest increase in the waste paper annual net trade of developing countries among the four scenarios, 56 million mt. Most of the increase is in Asia, where net trade increases by 61 million mt with a 77 million mt improvement in China, which goes from being a large importer to a large exporter, partly compensated by a 12 million mt increase in the net imports of India. The net trade of North/Central America decreases by 39 million mt, and the region becomes a large net importer, mostly due to a 33 million mt increase in Canadian imports. Europe also changes from net exporter in 2006 to net importer in 2060, with a nearly 16 million mt increase in the net imports of Finland. The net imports of Africa increase by 2 million mt, and the net exports of Oceania decrease by 1 million mt, mostly in Australia.

Paper and Paperboard

Prices of paper and paperboard

Figure 20 shows the past and projected values of the world prices of newsprint, printing and writing paper, and other paper and paperboard, expressed by the unit value of world exports in 1997 U.S. dollars. Tables 39, 40, and 41 show the prices in selected years and countries.

Observed evolution of prices of paper and paperboard

Past data show a strong negative trend of the world price of all three commodities, but with large fluctuations around this trend. From 1992 to 2006, the real world price decreased by $124/mt for newsprint, $276/mt for printing and writing paper, and by $183/mt for other paper and paperboard.

Projected evolution of prices of paper and paperboard

Scenario A1B—Under scenario A1B, after a slight decrease from 2006 to 2030, the price of newsprint and of printing and writing paper ends up in 2060 at about the same level as in 2006. The price of other paper and paperboard declines to end at about $96/mt lower than in 2006.

Scenario A2—Under scenario A2, the prices of all three grades of paper decline steadily from 2006 to 2060. The real price of newsprint ends approximately $130/mt lower in 2060 than in 2006, the price of printing and writing paper was $220 lower, and that of other paper and paperboard was $230 lower.

Scenario B2—The price trends for scenario B2 are similar to those of A2, with slightly smaller decreases: -$100/mt for newsprint, -$190/mt for printing and writing paper, and -$200/mt for other paper and paperboard.

Scenario A1B-Low Fuelwood—Under scenario A1B-Low Fuelwood, the price changes are similar to those in scenario B2, except for less decrease of the price of other paper and paperboard (-150$/ton).

Paper and paperboard consumption
Figure 21 shows the historical data and the projections of the annual consumption of total paper and paperboard (newsprint, printing and writing paper, and other paper and paperboard), by world region. More detailed data for each subcommodity group, and for selected years and countries are in tables 42, 43, and 44.

Observed evolution of paper and paperboard consumption
From 1992 to 2006, the world annual consumption of total paper and paperboard increased by 132 million mt, with 81 million mt in developing countries. The main regional growth was in Asia, where annual consumption increased by 73 million mt, with 49 million mt in China and 3 million mt each in India and the Republic of Korea. In Europe, annual consumption increased by 33 million mt, with 5 million mt in Germany and 4 million mt each in Spain and Italy. The annual consumption of North/Central America grew by 19 million mt, with 12 million mt in the United States and 5 million mt in Mexico. In South America, annual consumption increased by 3 million mt, mostly in Brazil, Argentina, and Chile. It increased as much in Africa and by 2 million mt in Oceania.

Projected evolution of paper and paperboard consumption
Scenario A1B—Under scenario A1B, annual world consumption of total paper and paperboard increases by 374 million mt, with 278 million mt in developing countries. Asia is the region of most growth (+244 million mt, with 145 million mt in China, 21 million mt in India, 12 million mt in Indonesia, and 10 million mt in Japan). The second largest growth of annual consumption is in Europe (+55 million mt, with 8 million mt in the Russian Federation, 7 million mt in the United Kingdom, and 5 million each in France and Germany). In North/Central America, the annual consumption increases by 35 million mt, with 17 million mt in the United States, 9 million mt in Mexico, and 5 million mt in Canada. South

America increases its annual consumption by 20 million mt, with more than half in Brazil. Annual consumption increases by 17 million mt in Africa, with 4 million mt each in Egypt and Nigeria, and by 3 million mt in Oceania, most of it in Australia.

Scenario A2—Under scenario A2, the growth of annual consumption of paper and paperboard is about half what it is under scenario A1B: 131 million mt in developing countries and 61 million mt in developed countries. Asia still has the largest growth: 117 million mt growth in aggregate, with 75 million mt growth in China, 8 million mt in India, and 7 million mt in Japan. In Europe, annual consumption grows by 31 million mt, with 6 million mt in the United Kingdom and 4 million mt each in France and Germany. The North/Central American annual consumption increases by 24 million mt, with 14 million mt in the United States and 5 million mt in Canada. Annual consumption grows by 10 million mt in South America (with 5 million mt in Brazil), 8 million mt in Africa, and 3 million mt in Oceania.

Scenario B2—Under scenario B2, the world annual consumption of paper and paperboard grows faster for developing countries (+179 million mt) but slower for developed countries (+48 million mt) than under scenario A2. In Asia, the annual consumption increases by 150 million mt, with 93 million mt in China and 14 million mt in India. In Europe, annual consumption increases by 34 million mt, including 4 million each in the Russian Federation and the United Kingdom. The increase of annual consumption in both Africa (+15 million mt, with 4 million mt in South Africa) and in South America (+4 million mt, with 7 million mt in Brazil) exceeds the increase in North America (+12 million mt, with 5 million mt in Mexico and 3 million mt in Canada).

Scenario A1B-Low Fuelwood—Scenario A1B-Low Fuelwood gives the largest increase in the world annual consumption of paper and paperboard: 404 million mt, with 291 million in developing countries. Relative to scenario A1B, this is due to the lower price of paper and paperboard (fig. 20) in concert with a lower price of wood pulp induced by a lower price of wood stemming from the low use of wood for energy. As in the other scenarios, the largest growth is in Asia, where annual consumption increased by 256 million mt, with 151 million mt in China, 21 million mt in India, 13 million mt in Indonesia, and 12 million mt in Japan. Europe is still the region of second largest growth, with an increase of 63 million mt of annual consumption, principally in the Russian Federation and the United Kingdom (+8 million mt each), Germany (+7 million mt), and France (+6 million mt). In North/Central America, annual consumption increased by 42 million mt, with 22 million mt in the United States, 10 million mt in Mexico, and 6 million mt in Canada. The annual consumption of South America increased by 21 million mt,

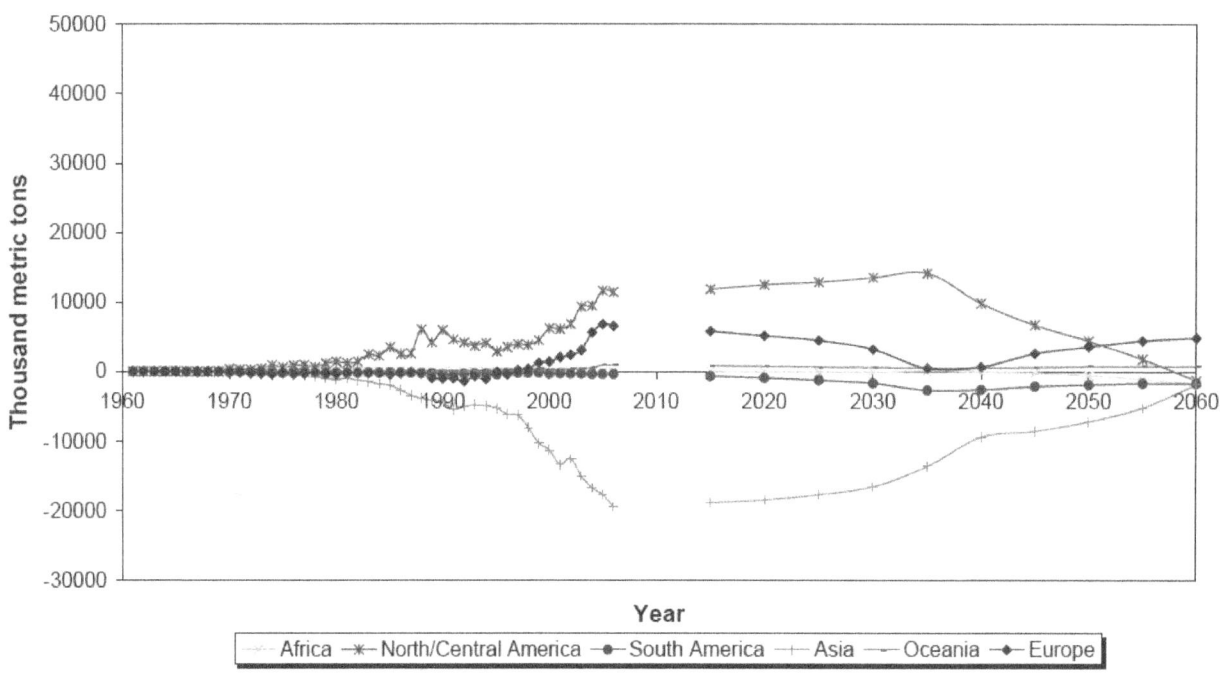

Waste paper net trade, scenario A1B

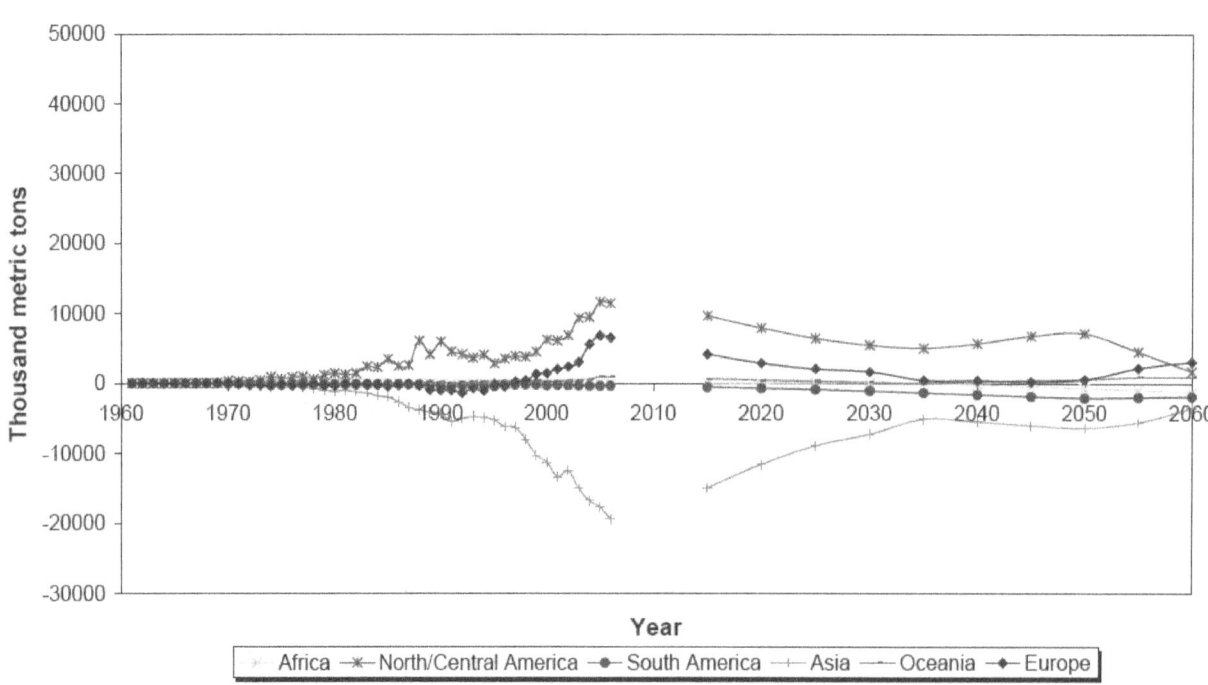

Waste paper net trade, scenario A2

Figure 19—Waste paper net trade by world region, observed and projected with the Global Forest Products Model. (continued on next page)

Waste paper net trade, scenario B2

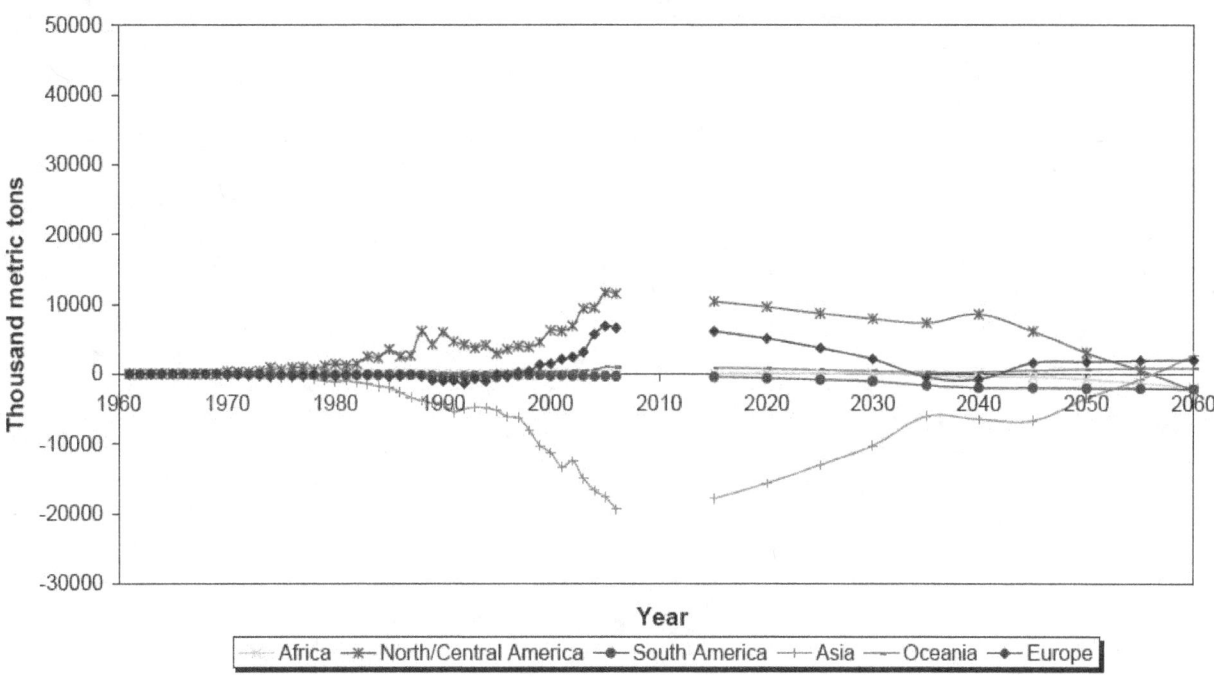

Waste paper net trade, scenario A1B-Low Fuelwood

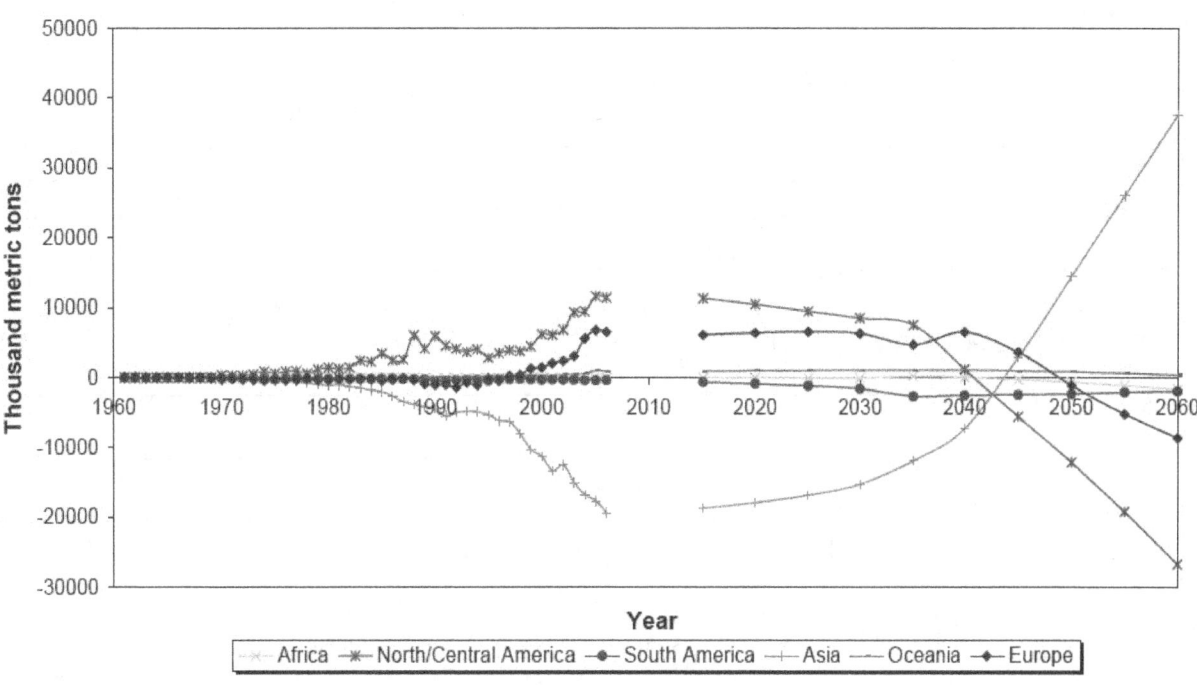

Figure 19 (continued)—Waste paper net trade by world region, observed and projected with the Global Forest Products Model.

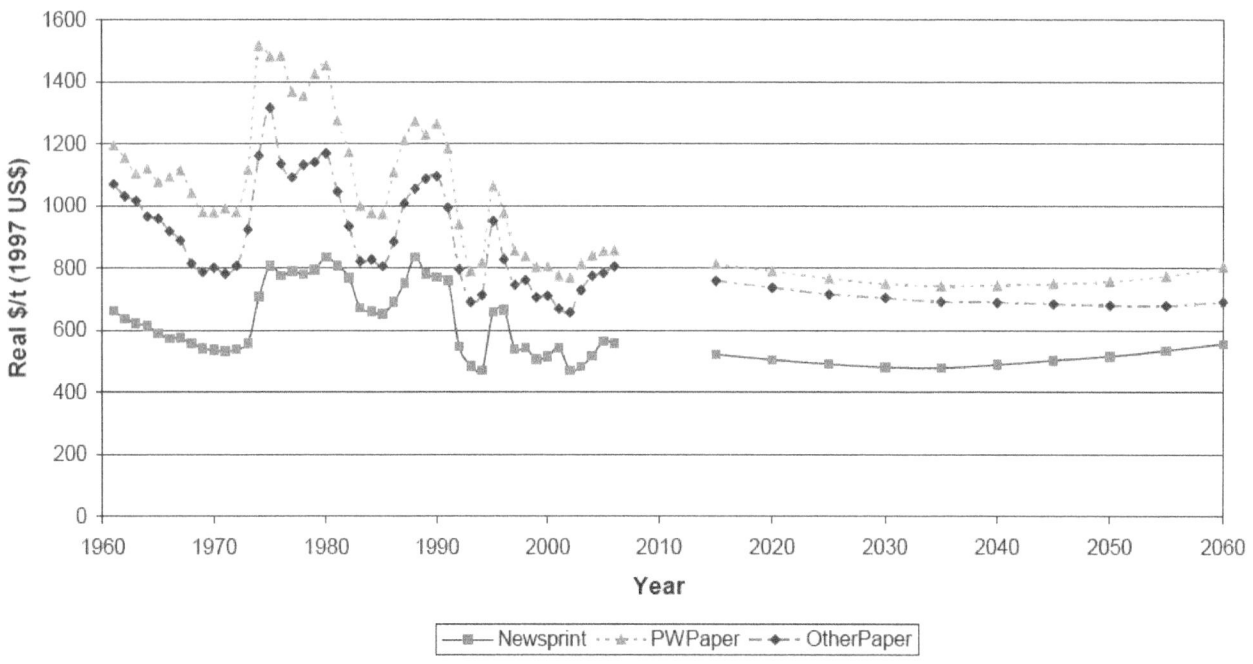

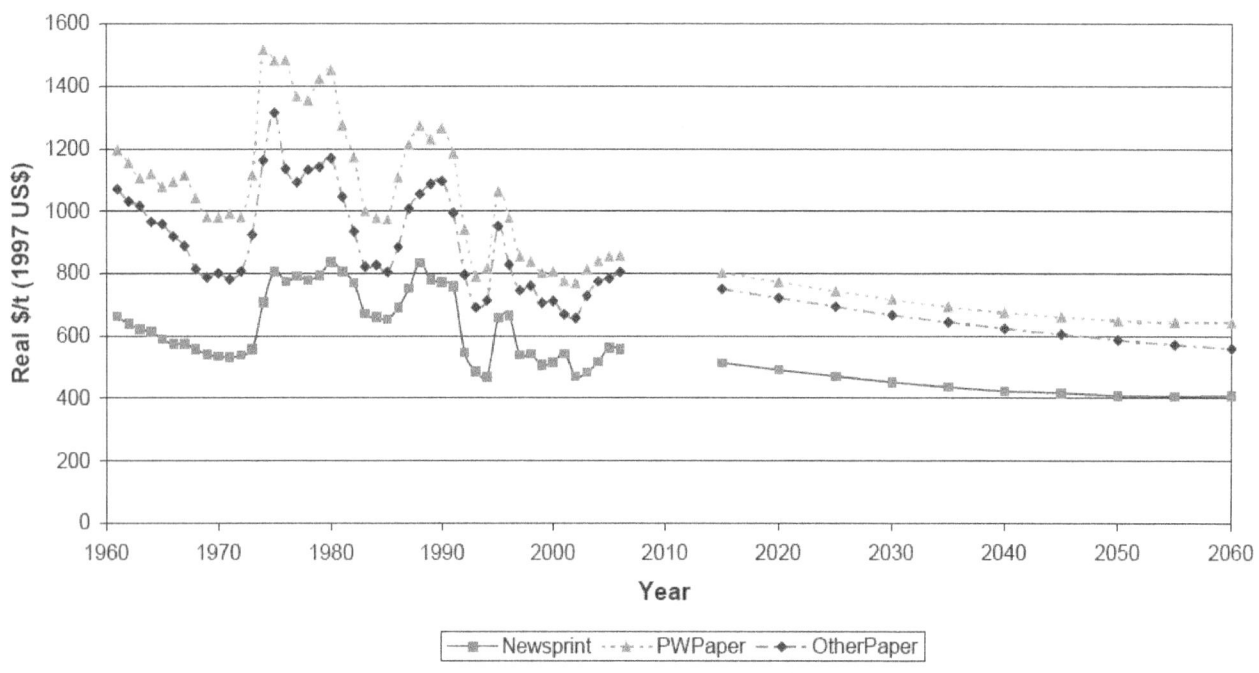

Figure 20—World prices of paper and paperboard by world region, observed and projected with the Global Forest Products Model. (continued on next page)

Paper and paperboard prices, scenario B2

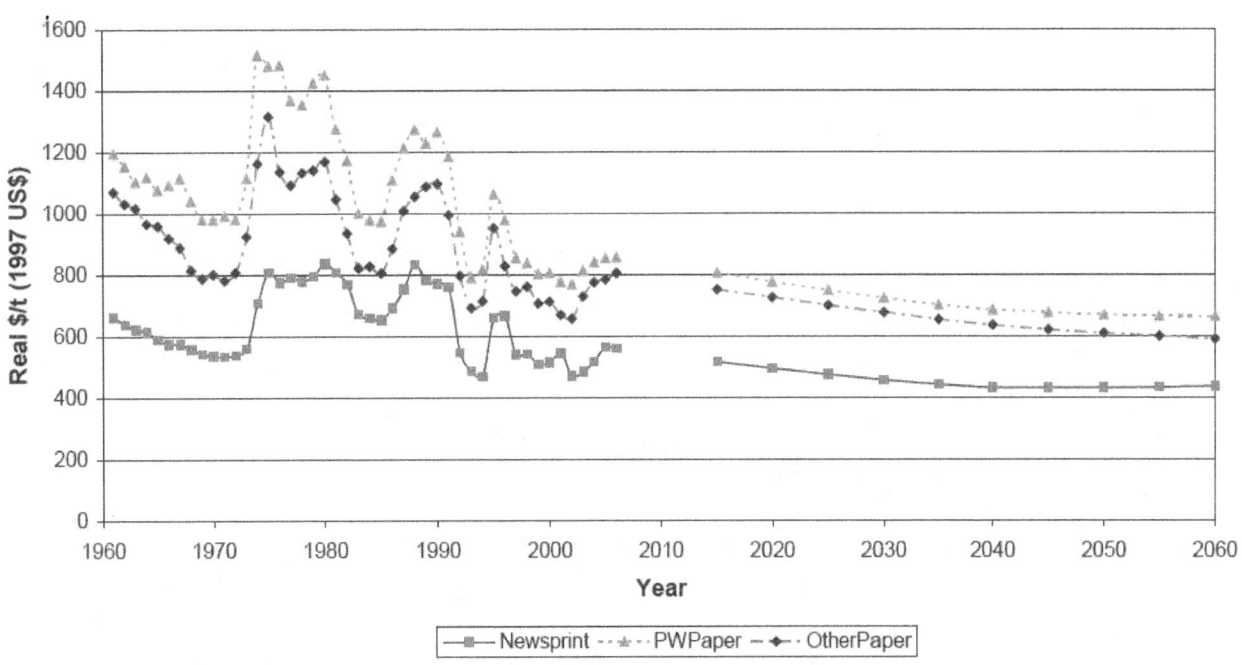

Paper and paperboard prices, scenario A1B-Low Fuelwood

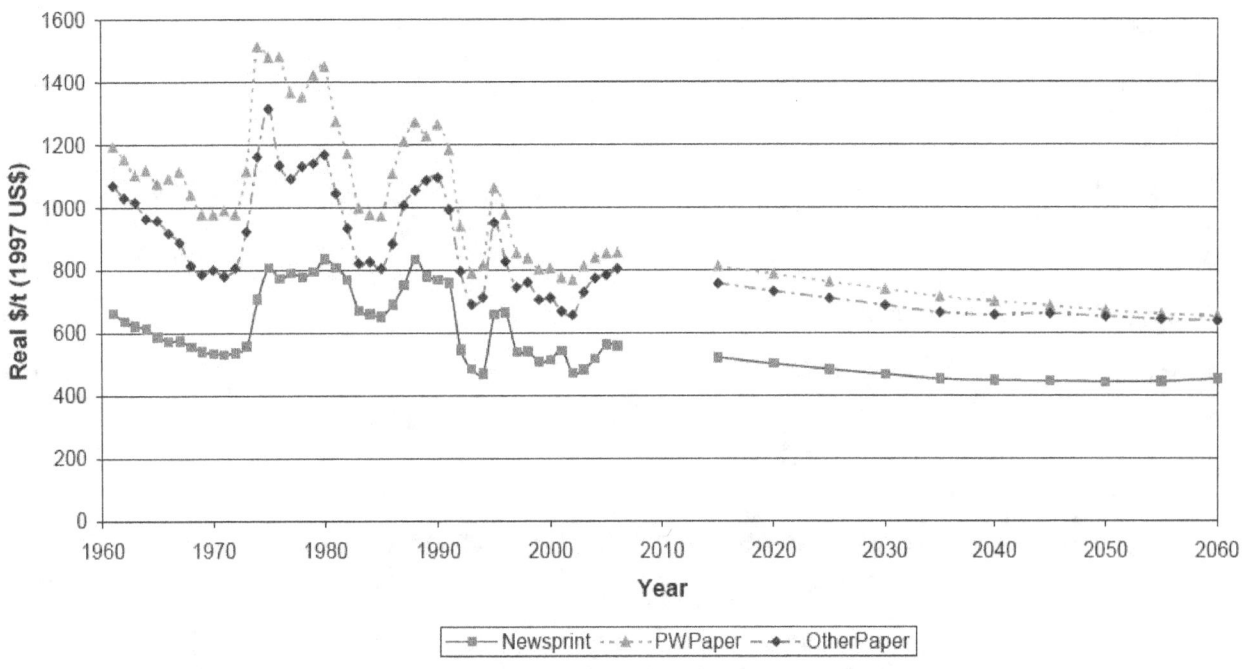

Figure 20 (continued)—World prices of paper and paperboard by world region, observed and projected with the Global Forest Products Model.

Total paper and paperboard consumption, scenario A1B

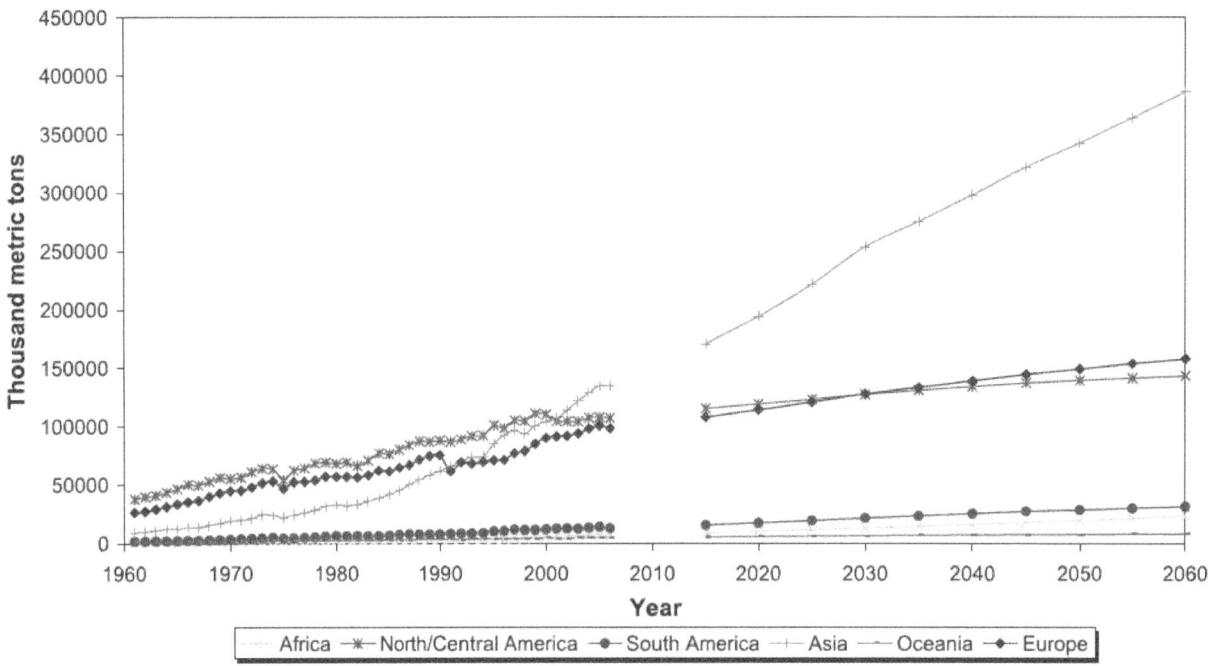

Total paper and paperboard consumption, scenario A2

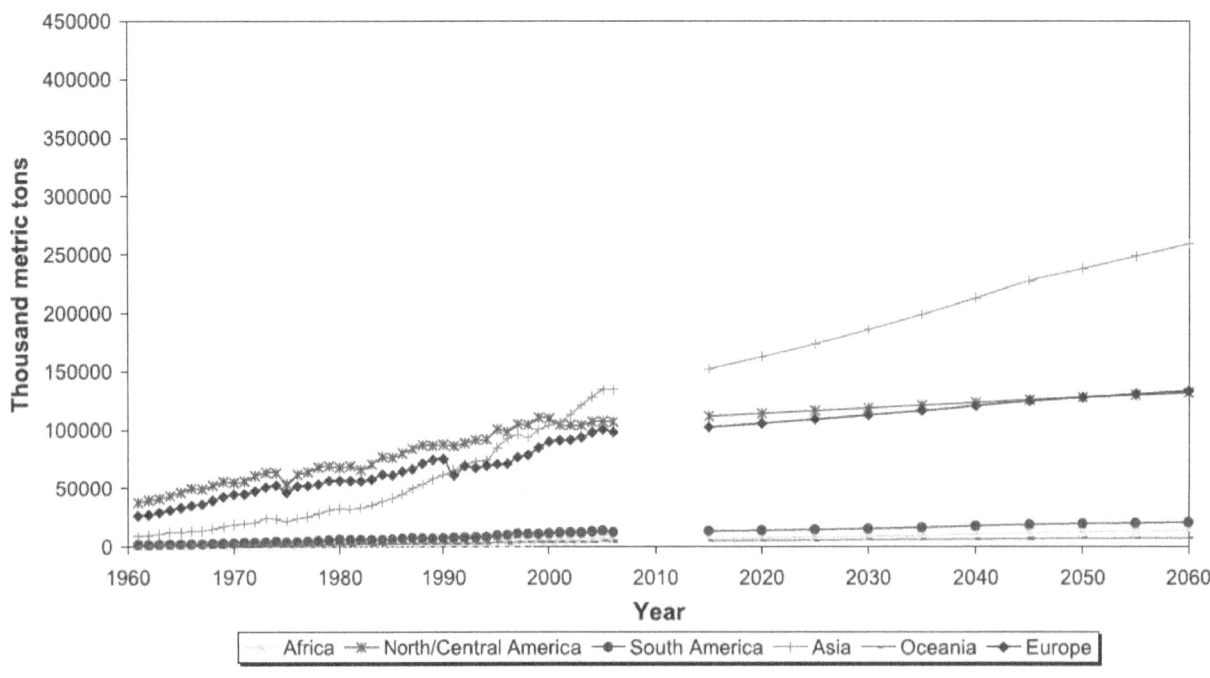

Figure 21—Paper and paperboard consumption by world region, observed and projected with the Global Forest Products Model. (continued on next page)

Total paper and paperboard consumption, scenario B2

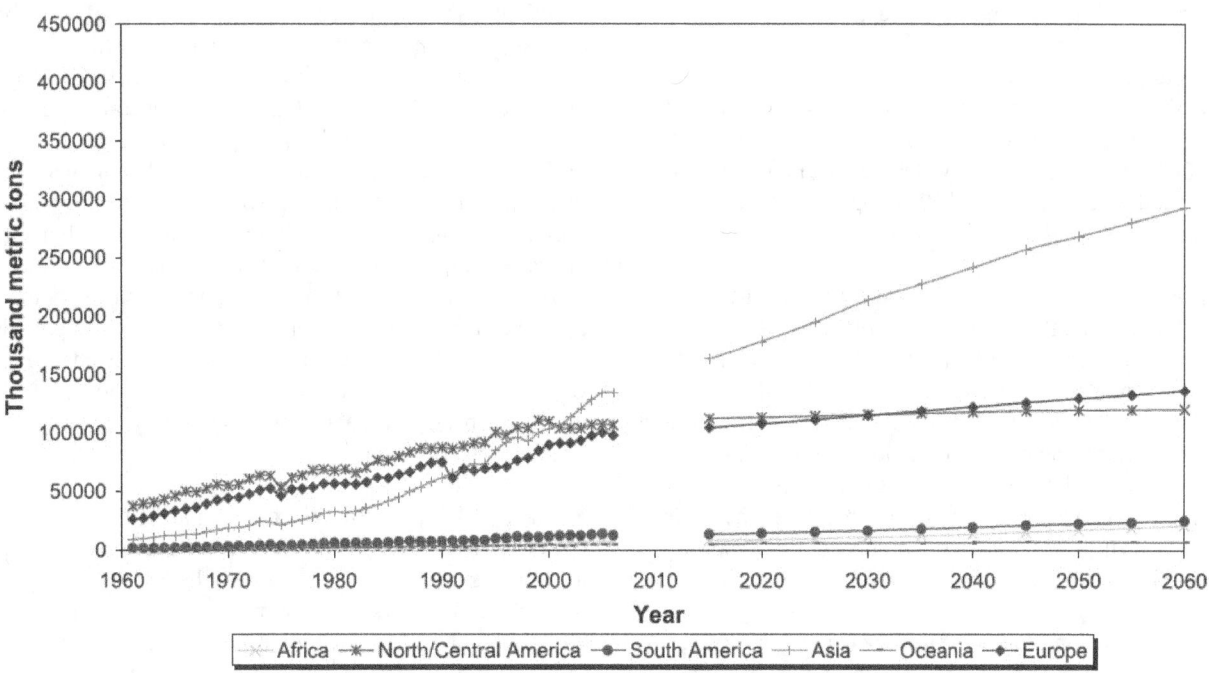

Total paper and paperboard consumption, scenario A1B-Low Fuelwood

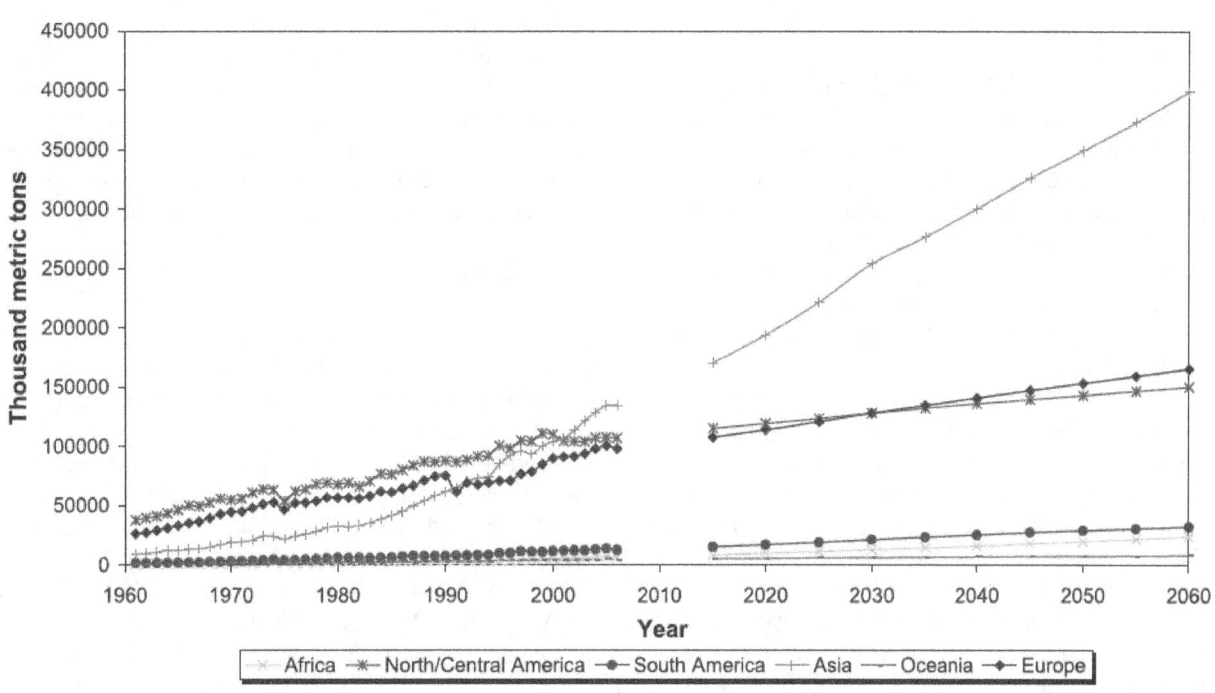

Figure 21 (continued)—Paper and paperboard consumption by world region, observed and projected with the Global Forest Products Model.

with more than half in Brazil. The annual consumption of paper and paperboard grew in Africa by 18 million mt, and in Oceania by 4 million mt, mostly in Australia.

Paper and paperboard net trade

Figure 22 shows the annual net trade (exports minus imports) of total paper and paperboard of world regions, from 1961 to 2060. Tables 45, 46, and 47 show detailed data for newsprint, printing and writing paper, and other paper and paperboard, for selected years and countries.

Observed evolution of paper and paperboard net trade

From 1992 to 2006, the annual net exports of developed countries increased by 5 million mt. The main regional change of annual net trade was in Europe (+9 million mt, with 5 million mt in Finland and 4 million mt each in Germany and Sweden). The annual net exports of North/Central America decreased by 6 million mt during the same period, mostly due to a 3 million mt increase of annual net imports in the United States and a 2 million mt increase in Mexico. Net imports also increased in Africa and Asia by approximately 1 million mt.

Projected evolution of paper and paperboard net trade

Scenario A1B—Under scenario A1B, the annual net imports of paper and paperboard in developing countries increase steadily and then decrease to end up 25 million mt higher in 2060 than in 2006 (13 million mt higher in China and 3 million mt higher in India). The net exports of Europe and North America change symmetrically. In North/Central America, annual net exports increase by 16 million mt, largely due to an increase of 14 million mt of the annual net exports of Canada, while the net imports of the United States decrease by 3 million mt. In Europe, annual net exports increase by 8 million mt, with a decrease of net imports of 6 million mt in the United Kingdom, an increase of net exports of 3 million mt each in France and Germany, and a 7 million mt decrease in the net exports of Sweden. The net imports of Africa increase by 3 million mt, while Oceania changes from being a net importer to net exporter with an overall change in net trade of about 1 million mt.

Scenario A2—Under scenario A2, the annual net imports of developing countries increase by about half of the projection under scenario A1B. The annual imports of Asia decrease by 11 million mt, with a 9 million mt decrease of net imports in China and a 3 million mt decrease of net exports in Indonesia. The annual net exports of North/Central America increase by 8 million mt, with a 6 million mt increase of net exports of Canada, and a decrease of 2 million mt of net imports of Mexico. Europe increases its annual net exports by 4 million mt, with a 6 million mt decrease of net imports in the United Kingdom, and a 3 million mt increase of the net exports from Germany, but with an 8 million mt decrease in the net exports of Sweden.

Scenario B2—Under scenario B2, developing countries increase their annual net imports of paper and paperboard slightly less than under scenario A1B. The annual net imports decrease by 19 million mt in Asia, with a 14 million mt decrease of net imports in China and a 3 million mt decrease of net exports in Indonesia. The North/American annual net trade improves by 15 million mt, with a 13 million mt increase in Canadian annual net exports and a 2 million mt decrease in annual net imports of the United States. The net trade of Europe also improves by 6 million mt, with a 4 million mt increase in the annual net exports of Germany, a 3 million mt increase in the net exports of France, and a 6 million mt decrease in the net imports of the United Kingdom, but with an 8 million mt decrease in the net exports of Sweden. The annual net imports of Africa increase by 2 million mt, and the annual net exports of Oceania increase by 1 million mt, mostly from Australia.

Scenario A1B-Low Fuelwood—Scenario A1B-Low Fuelwood leads to an 84 million mt increase of the annual net imports in developing countries, the largest among the four scenarios. In Asia, annual net imports increase by 76 million mt, with 64 million mt in China and 3 million mt in India, while the net exports of Indonesia decrease by 3 million mt. Symmetrically, the annual net exports of North/Central America increase by 50 million mt, with 37 million mt in Canada and 15 million mt in the United States. In Europe, net exports increase by 31 million mt, with an 18 million mt increase in the net exports of Finland, an 8 million mt increase in the net exports of Germany, and a 6 million mt decrease in the net imports of the United Kingdom, and partly compensated by a decrease in the annual exports of Sweden of 7 million mt. The annual net imports of Africa increase by 3 million mt, while the net exports of Oceania increase by about 1 million mt.

Value Added

Figure 23 shows the data on the annual value added to wood and fiber input in forest industries, defined as the value of production minus the value of wood and fiber consumption, in 1992 and 2006, and projected values for 2006 to 2060, for the world regions. The value added is in real terms at the 1997 value of the U.S. dollar. Table 48 shows the corresponding data for selected years and countries within each region.

Observed evolution of value added to wood and fiber input

From 1992 to 2006, the world annual value added increased by $148 billion, with $80 billion occurred in developing countries. The largest regional increase was in Asia (+$70 billion, with $51 billion in China, $4 billion in the Republic of Korea, and $3 billion in Indonesia). In Europe, the annual value added increased by $42 billion over the same period, with $9 billion in Germany, $5 billion in Finland and $4 billion each in Sweden and Spain. Meanwhile, the North/Central American annual value added grew by $24 billion, of which $12 billion came from the United States and $9 billion from Canada. The annual value added increased by $9 billion in South America, of which $5 billion occurred in Brazil. In Oceania it grew by approximately $2 billion and by $1 billion in Africa.

Projected evolution of value added to wood and fiber input
Scenario A1B—Under scenario A1B, the world value added increases by $86 billion, mostly in developing countries. The main growth is in Asia (+$64 billion, including +$45 billion in China and +$7 billion in India, but with a $4 billion decrease in Japan). In South America, annual value added increases by $6 billion, two-thirds of which is in Brazil. The value added in Africa and Europe also increases by about $6 billion each, spread over several countries, and despite a $6 billion decrease in Germany. In North/Central America, value added increases by $3 billion with a $7 billion decrease in the United States offset by an almost equal increase in Canada. In Oceania, it increased by approximately $1 billion, mostly in Australia.

Scenario A2—Under scenario A2, the world annual value added decreases by $3 billion, with a decrease of $29 billion in developed countries. The main regional change is a $24 billion decrease of value added in North/Central America, with a $33 billion decrease in the United States offset in part by a $7 billion increase in Canada. Meanwhile, the value added increases by $10 billion in Asia, with a $15 billion increase in China, but a $6 billion decrease in Japan. In South America, value added increases by $5 billion from 2006 to 2060, mostly in Brazil. It increases by $4 billion in Africa and $1 billion in Europe, where a $7 billion decrease in Germany is partly offset by an increase of $3 billion in both Sweden and the United Kingdom.

Scenario B2—Under scenario B2, the world annual value added increases by $16 billion, with a decrease of $25 billion in developed countries. The main regional decrease is in North/Central America, with a $27 billion decrease in the United States partly offset by an $8 billion increase in Canada. The annual value added also decreases in Europe, by $1 billion, with a $7 billion decrease in Germany partly offset by rises in several other countries. The annual value added increases in Asia (+$22 billion, with an equal increase in China and despite a $7 billion decrease in Japan). In Africa, annual value added increases by $6 billion.

Scenario A1B-Low Fuelwood—Scenario A1B-Low Fuelwood leads to the largest increase in annual value added: $120 billion, with $75 billion in developing countries. Value added increases in all regions. As under the other scenarios,

the main change is in Asia (+$53 billion, with $33 billion in China and $7 billion in India, but with a $4 billion decrease in Japan). In North/Central America, annual value added increases by $28 billion, with increases of $14 billion in Canada and $11 billion in the United States. The annual value added in Europe increases by $20 billion, with a $5 billion increase in Finland and a $4 billion increase in the United Kingdom, but with decreases of $2 billion and $3 billion in Germany and Sweden, respectively. The value added increases by $7 billion in Africa, and by $1 billion in Oceania, despite an equivalent contraction in New Zealand.

Summary and Conclusion

The main finding concerns the important impact of the high demand for biofuels implied in some of the Intergovernmental Panel on Climate Change (IPCC) scenarios. In particular, scenario A1B, which implies a 5.5-fold increase in the world consumption of fuelwood by 2060, leads to a rapid growth of the real price of fuelwood, which converges with the price of industrial roundwood by about 2030. At that point, industrial roundwood, used in the past to manufacture sawnwood, panels, and pulp, starts to be used for energy production. The price of all wood then continues to rise steadily up to 2060, and the price of manufactured product increases in concert. This results in more roundwood diverted into fuelwood for the rapidly growing economies of Asia, and in response, more roundwood from South America and Europe.

According to the projections of scenario A1B, the large increase in fuelwood demand leads to a total annual roundwood consumption of 11.2 billion m^3 in 2060. This is well above the sustainable production suggested by previous studies (Smeets and Faaij 2007). In fact, the A1B scenario implies less world growing stock in 2060 than in 2006. And even under scenarios A2 and B2, the growing stock of Asia is lower in 2060, suggesting unsustainable levels of harvest. It is likely that existing forest practice laws and sustained-yield policies would not allow this to happen. Scenario A1B in particular is liable to run into those constraints. On the other hand, the economic and demographic assumptions of scenario A1B coupled with a low fuelwood demand, lead to a global harvest of 3.6 billion m^3 only, and to growing stock higher than its current level in 2060, in all regions.

A study for Europe (EEA 2007) up to the year 2030 used the EFI-GTM model (Kallio and others 2004) to estimate the change in the mix of potential sources of biomass for bioenergy (industrial and harvest residues, imports, competition with other uses) at different prices, taking into consideration available biomass resources and competing demands for wood. Like our study, it predicted that at high

Total paper and paperboard net trade, scenario A1B

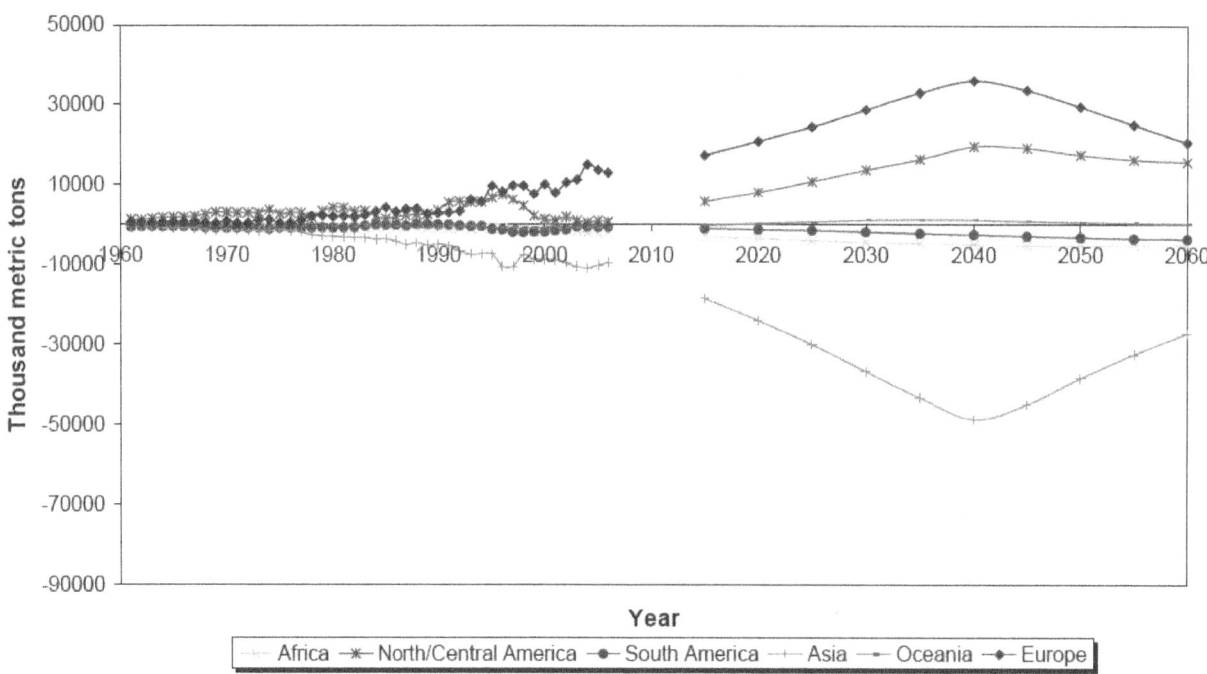

Total paper and paperboard net trade, scenario A2

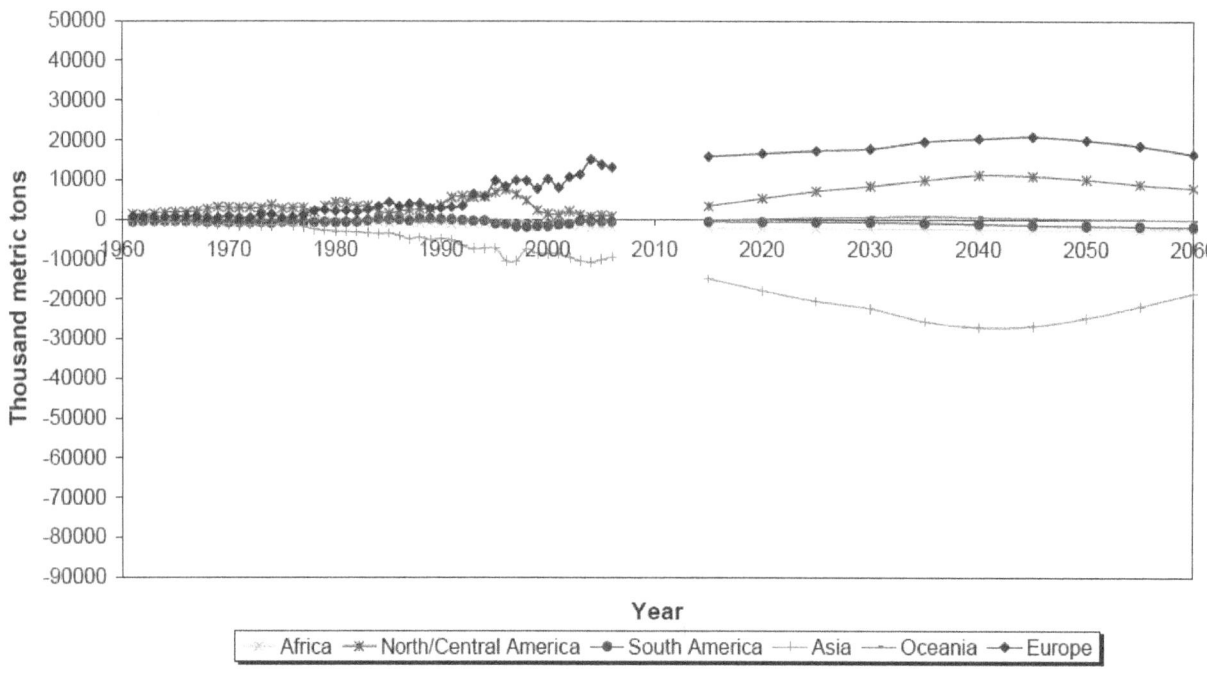

Figure 22—Paper and paperboard net trade by world region, observed and projected with the Global Forest Products Model. (continued on next page)

Total paper and paperboard net trade, scenario B2

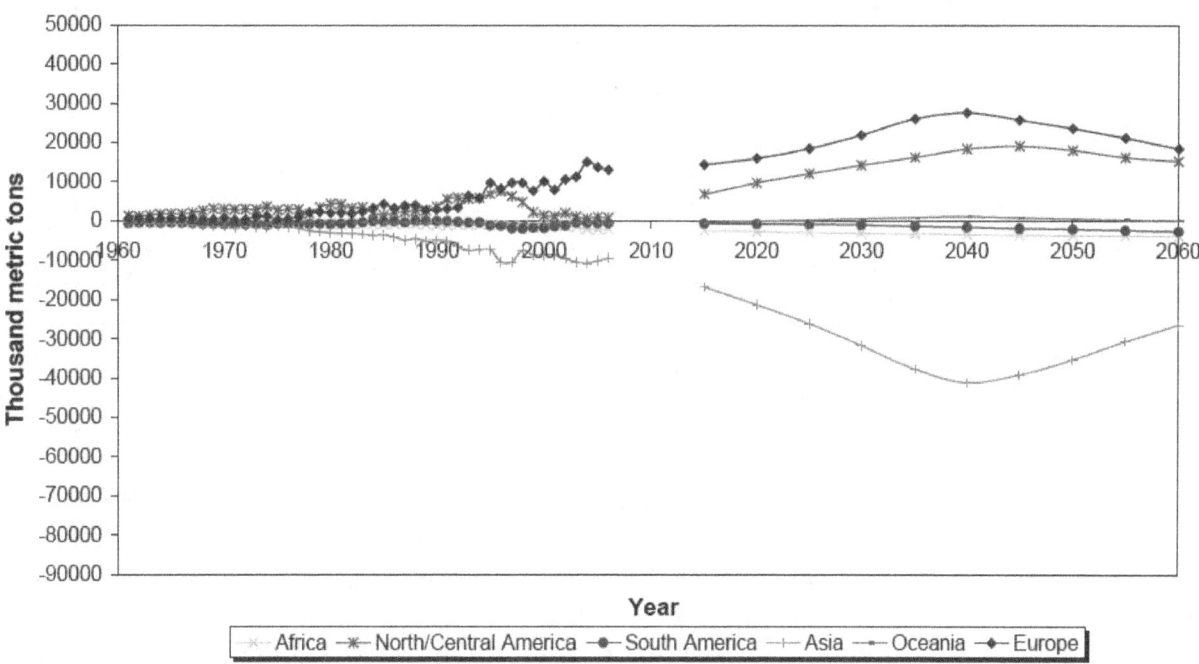

Total paper and paperboard net trade, scenario A1B-Low Fuelwood

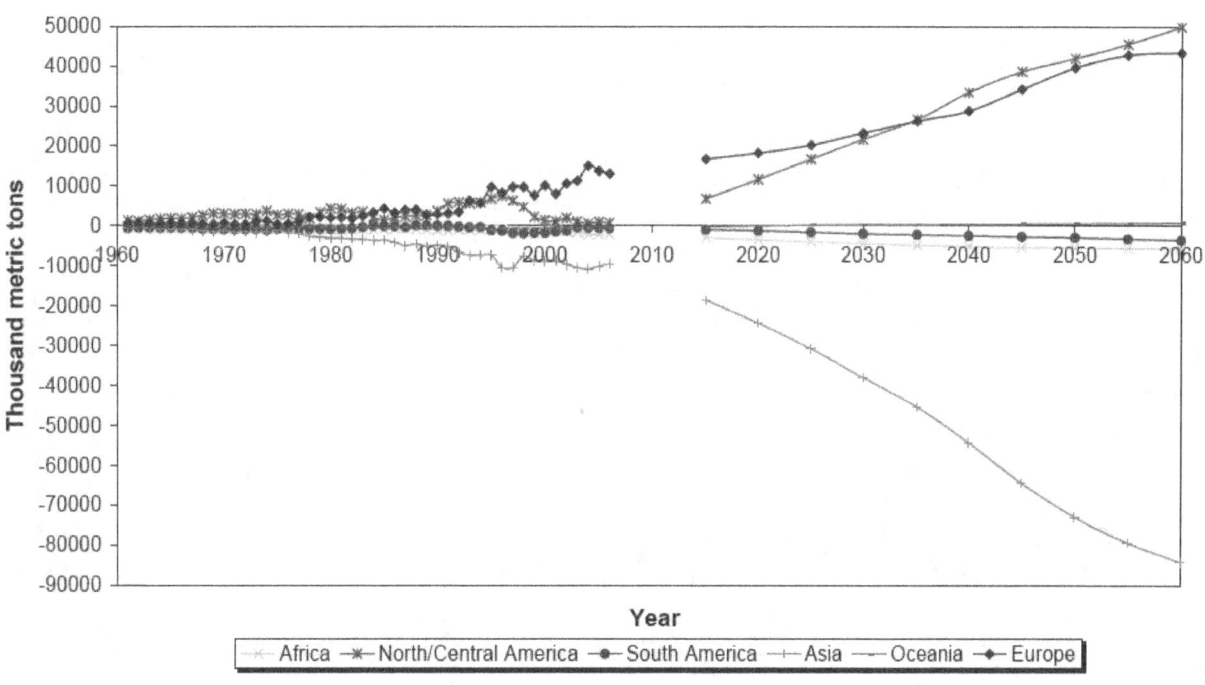

Figure 22 (continued)—Paper and paperboard net trade by world region, observed and projected with the Global Forest Products Model.

Value added, scenario A1B

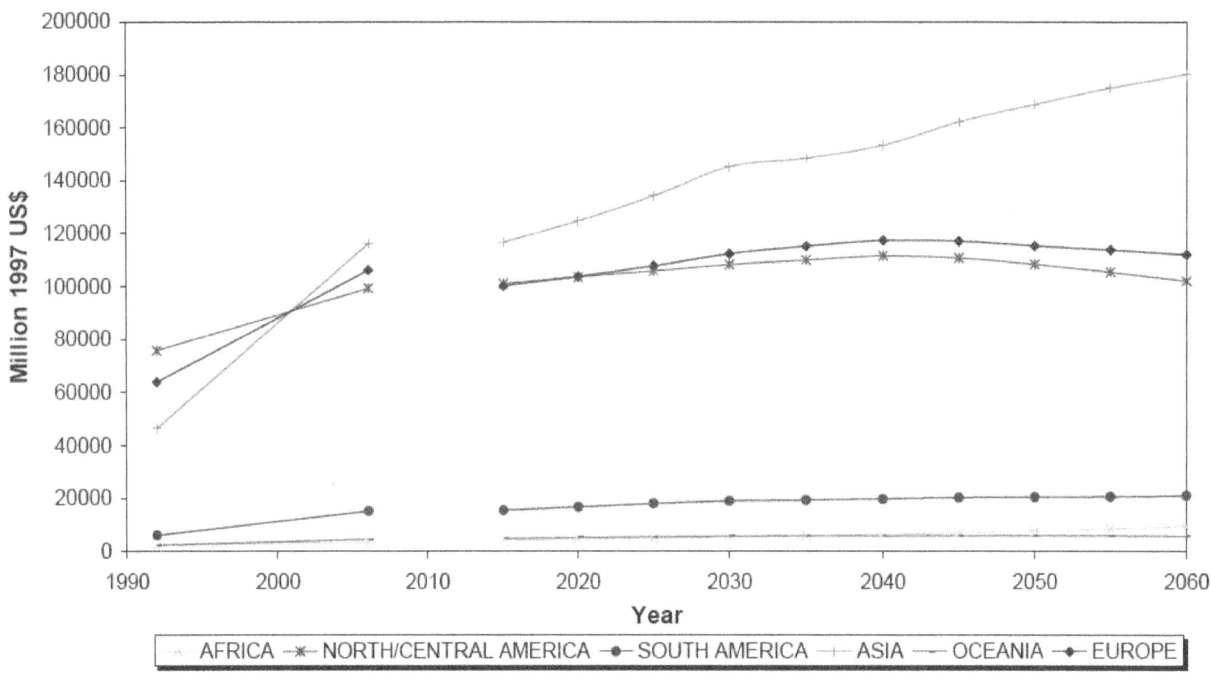

Value added, scenario A2

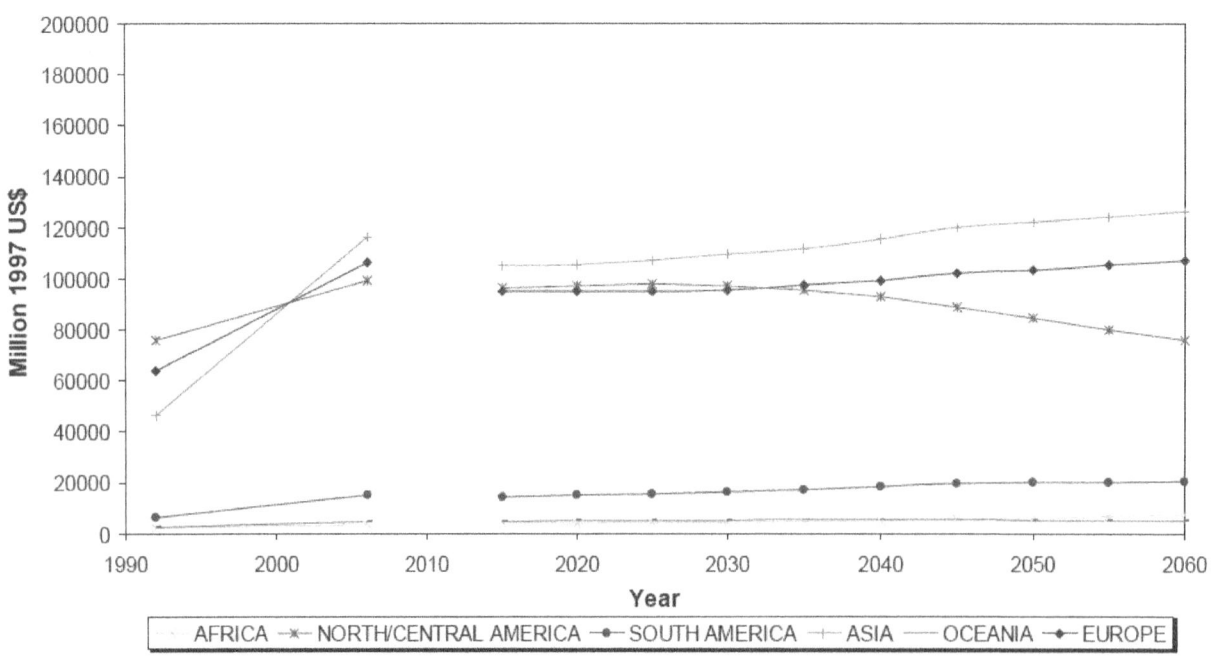

Figure 23 —Value added to wood and fiber in forest industries by world region, observed and projected with the Global Forest Products Model. (continued on next page)

Value added, scenario B2

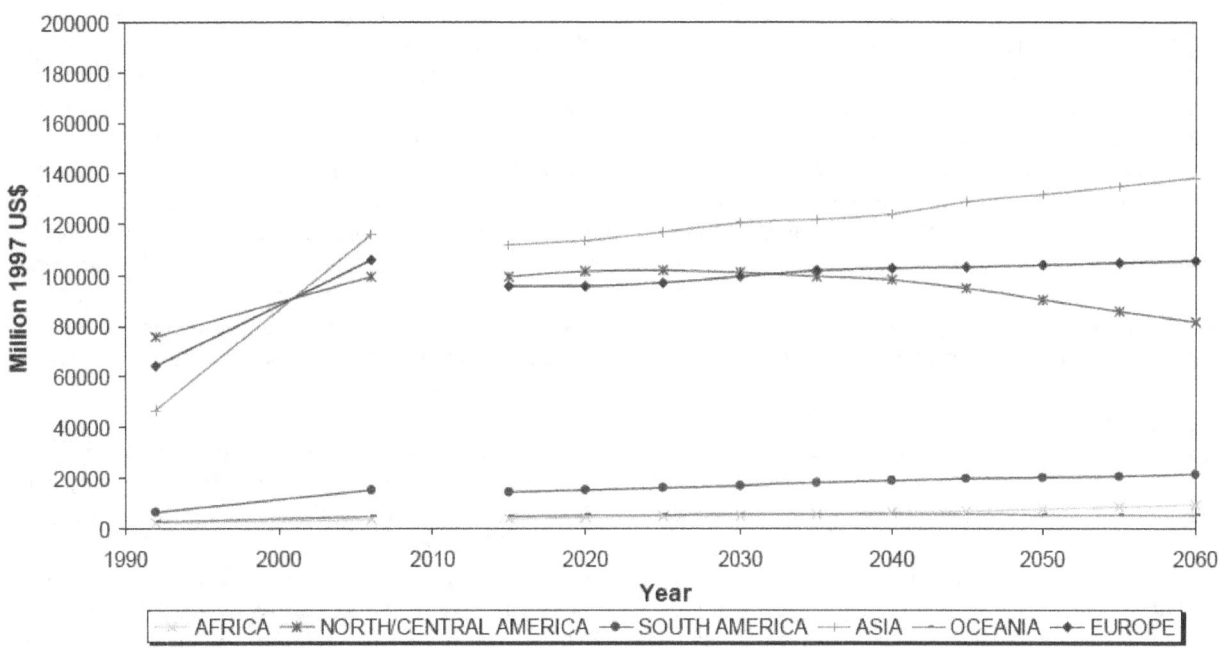

Value added, scenario A1B-Low Fuelwood

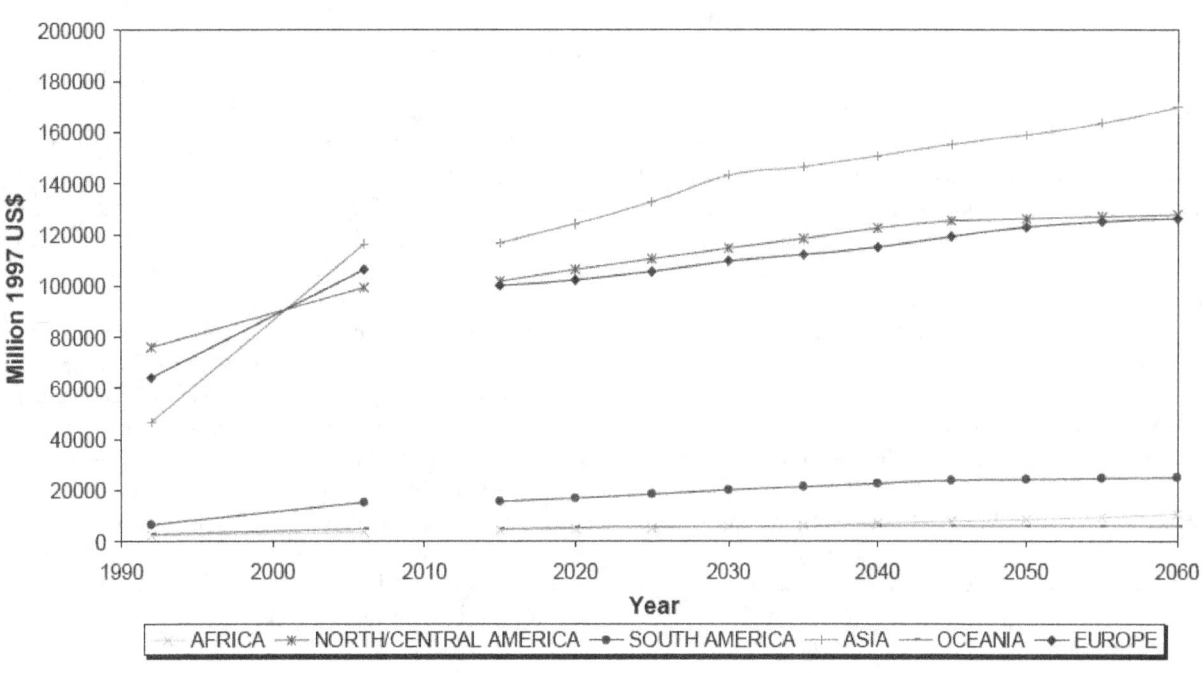

Figure 23 (continued)—Value added to wood and fiber in forest industries by world region, observed and projected with the Global Forest Products Model.

bioenergy prices, wood would be reallocated from other uses, particularly chemical pulp, to bioenergy. As Europe's wood imports also would rise to meet bioenergy demand, this would increase the possibility of illegal logging and unsustainable forest management in some supplying countries. To help avert this, governments in importing and exporting countries could strengthen measures that discourage the production and trade in illegally logged wood. The Lacey Act Amendment of 2008 in the United States and the Forest Law Enforcement, Governance and Trade program of the European Union are examples of such policies.

Another feature of the projections of the present study is the modest growth in the consumption of manufactured wood products under most scenarios, leading to moderate changes in the real prices of wood-based panels and pulp and paper. The price of sawnwood is more affected in scenario A1B because of the large share of the wood price, influenced by the high fuelwood demand, in the cost of sawnwood production.

However, the consumption of all wood products grows rapidly in Asia, due mostly to the fast economic growth of China and India in all the scenarios used here. As a result, Asia would be a large importer of industrial roundwood, largely supplied by South America (Brazil) and Europe (the Russian Federation). Asia would also be the largest importer of paper and paperboard, primarily from Europe but also from North America. Despite these imports, Asia would see the largest regional growth of value added to wood and fiber in forest industries.

The projections presented here have three sources of uncertainty. One is the theoretical Global Forest Products Model (GFPM) structure and its parameters, such as the demand elasticities, input-output coefficients, and forest growth equation parameters. Another is the data describing the past and current state of the world. The third stems from the exogenous predictions: population and GDP growth rates, biofuel demand growth from the IPCC scenarios, and other exogenous changes.

The GFPM was calibrated in such a way that its base-year solution, here for 2006, reproduced the observed data. Earlier tests of prediction errors from 1980 to 2000 showed that the model replicates the observed trends, if not the year-to-year detail. As expected, projections of consumption and production are more accurate than those of trade, and regional projections are more accurate than those for individual countries (Buongiorno and others 2003, Turner 2004).

The base-year data used in the GFPM (FAO 2009, World Bank 2008) are inaccurate, but are the only internationally comparable data. The goal programming approach of

the calibration procedure corrects some errors in the forestry production data of the FAOSTAT (Buongiorno and others 2001). Strong assumptions have been made in the projections. In particular, technical change is reflected mostly by the wood-saving changes in manufacturing and the increasing use of waste paper in paper and paperboard manufacture. The possibility of better recovery of wood in the forest has not been considered explicitly. It is also possible that future carbon pricing policies may have effects on forests and forest industries that are not taken into account in the IPCC scenarios or the model. In addition, future developments of general energy prices may limit the rise in the price of wood energy that occurs under scenario A1B and the substitution of wood for other energy sources, a topic that merits further investigation.

In considering other future studies, the issue of climate change and its impact on the forest sector comes naturally to mind [see Kirilenko and Sedjo (2007) for a review]. As used in this study, the GFPM includes the impact of climate change on future forest growth explicitly only for the United States through the shifts of timber supply. For other countries, climate change is incorporated only to the extent that it is reflected by past growth data. Several studies have used the projections of atmospheric and biological climate change in economic forest sector models, for countries (McCarl and others 2000), regions (Solberg and others 2003), or the world (Perez-Garcia and others 2002, Sohngen and Sedjo 2005). Some studies assume higher growth of forests due to elevated CO_2 concentrations, higher temperatures, and longer growing seasons (Nabuurs and others 2002), factors that in turn lead to increased timber inventories and supply, particularly in South America and Oceania, and hence lower timber prices (Perez-Garcia and others 2002, Sohngen and Mendelsohn 1998, Sohngen and Sedjo 2005, Solberg and others 2003). This growth may be limited by the propagation of pests, diseases, and invasive species (Sohngen and Sedjo 2005).

Still, the main source of uncertainty for the time horizon of this study rests in the future world situation stylized by the IPCC scenarios. Scenario A1B is very different from A2 and B2 in terms of future population, economic growth, and biofuel demand. Given current knowledge, no definite probability may be assigned to each scenario. Yet each scenario represents a plausible outcome. The results presented in this report—with due caution and wisdom—should prove useful in assessing the implications of future world forestry and its implications for the United States.

Acknowledgments

The research leading to this report was supported in part by the U.S. Department of Agriculture, Forest Service, Southern Research Station, in Asheville, NC. We are most grateful to Dali Zhang and James Turner for their earlier contribution to the development of the Global Forest Products Model, and to Peter Ince, Andrew Kramp, and David Wear for their collaboration, especially concerning the United States data. We also acknowledge with thanks the helpful review comments of David Darr, Sun Joseph Chang, Shashi Kant, Susan Phelps, and Linda Langner.

Literature Cited

Alcamo, J.D.; van Vuuren, D.; Ringer, C.; [and others] 2005. Changes in nature's balance sheet: model-based estimates of future worldwide ecosystem services. Ecology and Society 10(2): 1-19

Buongiorno, J. 2009. International trends in forest products consumption: is there convergence? International Forestry Review 11(4): 490-500.

Buongiorno, J.; Liu, C.S.; Turner, J.A. 2001. Estimating international wood and fiber utilization accounts in the presence of measurement errors. Journal of Forest Economics 7(2): 101-124.

Buongiorno, J., Zhu, S.; Zhang, D.;[and others] 2003. The Global Forest Products Model: structure, estimation, and applications. Academic Press/Elsevier. San Diego. 301 p.

Buongiorno, J.; Zhu, S. 2011a. Using the Global Forest Products Model (GFPM version 2011). Staff Paper Series # 71, Department of Forest and Wildlife Ecology, University of Wisconsin Madison. http://fwe.wisc.edu/facstaff/buongiorno/. [Date accessed: November 1, 2011].

Buongiorno, J.; Zhu, S. 2011b. Calibrating and updating the Global Forest Products Model (GFPM version 2010). Staff Paper Series #70, Department of Forest and Wildlife Ecology, University of Wisconsin Madison. http://fwe.wisc.edu/facstaff/buongiorno/. [Date accessed: November 1, 2011].

FAO (Food and Agriculture Organization of the United Nations). 2009. FAOSTAT Forestry data 1961-2006. http://faostat fao.org/site/626/default.aspx#ancor [Date accessed: June 19, 2009].

FAO 2006. Global forest resources assessment 2005. FAO Forestry Paper 147, Food and Agriculture Organization of the United Nations, Rome. 320 p.

Ince, P.J.; Kramp, A.D.; Skog, K.E.; [and others] 2011. U.S. Forest Product Model: A technical document supporting the Forest Service 2010 RPA Assessment. Res. Pap. FPL-RP-662. Madison, WI: U.S. Department of Agriculture Forest Service, Forest Products Laboratory. 61 p.

Kallio, A.M.I.; Moiseyev, A.; Solberg, B. 2004. The global forest sector model EFI-GTM. The model structure. European Forest Institute, Joensuu, EFI Internal Report 15.

Kando, I.; Buongiorno, J. 2009. Efficiency in wood and fiber utilization in OECD countries. Journal of Forest Research 14(6): 321-327.

Katsigris, E.; Bull, G.Q.; White, A.; [and others] 2005. The China forest products trade: overview of Asia-Pacific supplying countries, impacts and implications. International Forestry Review 6(3-4): 237-253.

Kirilenko, A.P.; Sedjo, R.A. 2007. Climate change impacts on forestry. Proceedings of the National Academy of Sciences 104(50): 19697-19702.

McCarl, B.; Adams, D.M.; Alig, R.J.; [and others] 2000. Effects of global climate change on the U.S. forest sector: response functions derived from a dynamic resource and market simulator. Climate Research 15:195-205.

Nabuurs, G.J.; Prussinen, A.; Karjalainen, T.; [and others] 2002. Stem volume increment changes in European forests due to climate change—a simulation study with the EFISCEN model. Global Change Biology 8:304-316.

Nakicenovic, N.; Alcamo, J.; Davis, G.; [and others] 2001. Special Report on Emissions Scenarios. Intergovernmental Panel on Climate Change http://www.grida no/climate/ipcc/emission/index.htm. [Date accessed: November 1, 2011].

Perez-Garcia, J.; Joyce, L.A.; McGuire, A.D.; Xiao, X. 2002. Impacts of climate change on the global forest sector. Climatic Change 54: 439-461.

Sala-i-Martin, X. 2006. The world distribution of income: Falling poverty and ...convergence, period. Quarterly Journal of Economics. CXXI (2): 351-397.

Samuelson, P.A. 1952. Spatial price equilibrium and linear programming. American Economic Review 42: 283-303.

Simangunsong, B.; Buongiorno, J. 2001. International demand equations for forest products: a comparison of methods. Scandinavian Journal of Forest Research 16: 155-172.

Smeets, E.M.W.; Faaij, A.P.C. 2007. Bioenergy potentials from forestry in 2050: an assessment of the drivers that determine the potentials. Climatic Change 81: 353-390.

Sohngen, B.; Mendelsohn, R. 1998. Valuing the impact of large-scale ecological change in a market: the effect of climate change on U.S. timber. American Economic Review 88(4): 689-710.

Sohngen, B.; Sedjo, R. 2005. Impacts of climate change on forest product markets: implications for North American producers. The Forestry Chronicle 81(5): 689-674.

Solberg, B.; Moiseyev, A.; Kallio, A.M.I. 2003. Economic impacts of accelerating forest growth in Europe. Forest Policy and Economics 5(2): 157-171.

Turner, J.A. 2004. Trade liberalization and forest resources: a global modeling approach. Ph.D. Dissertation, University of Wisconsin, Madison. 303 p.

Turner, J.A.; Buongiorno, J.; Zhu, S. 2006. An economic model of international wood supply, forest stock and forest area change. Scandinavian Journal of Forest Research 21: 73-86.

USDA Forest Service. 2012. Future scenarios: a technical document supporting the Forest Service 2010 RPA Assessment. Gen. Tech. Rep. RMRS-GTR-272. Fort Collins, CO: U.S. Department of Agriculture, Forest Service, Rocky Mountain Research Station. 34 p.

World Bank. 2008. World Development Indicators. http://data.worldbank.org/data-catalog/world-development-indicators. [Date accessed: November 1, 2011].

Index of Tables

Index of Tables (continued)

Index of Tables (continued)

Table 1—Countries and world regions represented in the Global Forest Products Model

AFRICA	Uganda	Brunei Darussalam	New Zealand
Algeria	Congo, Dem. Rep. Zambia	Cambodia	Papua New Guinea
Angola	Zimbabwe	China	Samoa
Benin	**NORTH/CENTRAL AMERICA**	Cyprus	Solomon Islands
Botswana	Bahamas	Georgia	Tonga
Burkina Faso	Barbados	Hong Kong	Vanuatu
Burundi	Belize	India	**EUROPE**
Cameroon	Canada	Indonesia	Albania
Cape Verde	Cayman Islands	Iran, Islamic Rep. of	Austria
Central African Rep	Costa Rica	Iraq	Belgium
Chad	Cuba	Israel	Belarus
Congo, Rep	Dominica	Japan	Bosnia and Herzegovina
Côte d'Ivoire	Dominican Rep	Jordan	Bulgaria
Djibouti	El Salvador	Kazakhstan	Croatia
Egypt	Guatemala	Korea, Dem. Peop Rep	Czech Republic
Equatorial Guinea	Haiti	Korea, Rep	Denmark
Ethiopia	Honduras	Kuwait	Estonia
Gabon	Jamaica	Kyrgyzstan	Finland
Gambia	Martinique	Lao People's Dem. Rep.	France
Ghana	Mexico	Lebanon	Germany
Guinea	Netherlands Antilles	Macau	Greece
Guinea-Bissau	Nicaragua	Malaysia	Hungary
Kenya	Panama	Mongolia	Iceland
Lesotho	Saint Vincent/Grenadines	Myanmar	Ireland
Liberia	Trinidad and Tobago	Nepal	Italy
Libyan Arab Jam.	United States of America	Oman	Latvia
Madagascar	**SOUTH AMERICA**	Pakistan	Lithuania
Malawi	Argentina	Philippines	Macedonia, The fmr Yug. Rep. of
Mali	Bolivia, Plurinational State of	Qatar	Malta
Mauritania	Brazil	Saudi Arabia	Moldova, Rep
Mauritius	Chile	Singapore	Netherlands
Morocco	Colombia	Sri Lanka	Norway
Mozambique	Ecuador	Syrian Arab Rep.	Poland
Niger	French Guiana	Tajikistan	Portugal
Nigeria	Guyana	Thailand	Romania
Réunion	Paraguay	Turkey	Russian Federation
Rwanda	Peru	Turkmenistan	Slovakia
São Tomé and Príncipe	Suriname	United Arab Emirates	Slovenia
Senegal	Uruguay	Uzbekistan	Spain
Sierra Leone	Venezuela, Boliv Rep.	Vietnam	Sweden
Somalia	**ASIA**	Yemen	Switzerland
South Africa	Afghanistan	**OCEANIA**	Ukraine
Sudan	Armenia	Australia	United Kingdom
Swaziland	Azerbaijan, Rep.	Cook Islands	Serbia and Montenegro
Tanzania, United Rep.	Bahrain	Fiji Islands	
Togo	Bangladesh	French Polynesia	
Tunisia	Bhutan	New Caledonia	

Table 2—Elasticity of demand for end products in the Global Forest Products Model with respect to Gross Domestic Product (GDP), price, and yearly rate of shift

	GDP	Price	Year
Fuelwood-developing countries	**0.05**[1]	**-0.10**	[2]
Fuelwood-developed countries	**0.22**[1]	**-0.10**	[2]
Sawnwood	**0.22**	**-0.10**	**-0.003**
Standard error	0.03	0.02	0.001
Plywood & veneer	**0.41**	**-0.29**	**-0.009**
Standard error	0.04	0.02	0.002
Particleboard	**0.54**	**-0.29**	**-0.006**
Standard error	0.07	0.02	0.002
F berboard	**0.35**	**-0.46**	**-0.002**
Standard error	0.06	0.02	0.002
Newsprint	**0.58**	**-0.25**	**-0.008**
Standard error	0.04	0.02	0.001
Printing & Writing	**0.45**	**-0.37**	**0.003**
Standard error	0.03	0.02	0.001
Other paper & Paperboard	**0.43**	**-0.23**	**-0.004**
Standard error	0.03	0.02	0.001

[1] Used only in Scenario A1B-Low Fuelwood
[2] Annual rates of shift set to conform with Intergovernmental Climate Control Panel biofuel projections (see text)

Table 4—Intergovernmental Panel on Climate Change global scenario characteristics

	Scenario		
	A1B	A2	B2
Population growth	low	high	medium
GDP[1] growth	very high	medium	medium
Energy use	very high	high	medium
Land- use changes	low	medium/high	medium
Resource availability	medium	low	medium
Pace of technological change	rapid	slow	medium

[1] Gross Domestic Product

Table 3—Rates of shift in wood supply and of forest area change in the United States assumed in the Global Forest Products Model scenarios

	2006-2007	2007-2010	2010-2015	2015-2030	2030-2045	2045-2060
Annual rate of wood supply shift						
Scenarios A1B and A1B-Low Fuelwood	0.0000	0.0000	0.0175	0.0047	0.0135	-0.0094
Scenario A2	0.0000	0.0000	0.0038	0.0070	0.0065	0.0030
Scenario B2	0.0000	0.0000	0.0184	0.0050	0.0033	0.0038
Annual rate of forest area change						
Scenarios A1B and A1B-Low Fuelwood	-0.0044	-0.0045	-0.0015	-0.0009	0.0006	-0.0046
Scenario A2	-0.0053	-0.0053	-0.0012	-0.0045	0.0028	0.0044
Scenario B2	-0.0037	-0.0037	-0.0013	-0.0012	0.0014	-0.0043

Table 5—Projected percent growth rate of Gross Domestic Product for world regions and selected countries in the Global Forest Products Model[1]

	Scenario A1B		Scenario A2		Scenario B2	
	2006-2030	2030-2060	2006-2030	2030-2060	2006-2030	2030-2060
AFRICA	**7.1**	**5.4**	**3.4**	**4.1**	**5.0**	**5.9**
Egypt	7.2	5.1	3.8	4.4	4.6	5.2
Nigeria	8.9	6.1	5.0	4.7	7.0	7.0
South Africa	4.1	3.1	0.6	1.7	3.2	3.6
NORTH/CENTRAL AMERICA	**2.6**	**2.3**	**1.9**	**1.8**	**1.7**	**1.4**
Canada	2.2	1.9	1.7	1.3	1.6	0.8
Mexico	5.2	3.2	1.8	2.1	2.5	3.1
United States	2.3	2.1	1.9	1.8	1.6	1.1
SOUTH AMERICA	**5.3**	**3.3**	**2.0**	**2.5**	**2.7**	**3.4**
Argentina	4.7	2.8	1.4	1.9	2.0	2.7
Brazil	5.2	3.2	1.8	2.2	2.4	3.0
Chile	4.9	2.9	2.1	2.5	3.0	3.6
ASIA	**5.5**	**3.8**	**2.5**	**2.4**	**3.7**	**2.8**
China	7.4	3.8	3.9	3.2	5.6	2.8
India	8.8	5.1	4.2	3.2	6.8	4.0
Indonesia	8.2	4.5	3.9	2.8	5.7	2.9
Japan	1.4	1.2	0.9	0.6	0.6	0.1
Korea, Republic of	4.9	1.7	0.8	-0.1	2.9	0.3
Malaysia	6.5	2.7	2.7	1.4	4.5	1.5
OCEANIA	**2.9**	**2.1**	**2.2**	**1.6**	**2.2**	**0.9**
Australia	2.6	1.9	2.1	1.6	2.0	0.8
New Zealand	2.6	2.0	2.3	1.8	2.4	1.1
EUROPE	**2.3**	**2.0**	**1.2**	**1.1**	**1.3**	**1.3**
EU-27	1.9	1.7	1.2	1.0	1.1	0.9
Austria	1.4	1.2	0.9	0.5	0.9	0.4
Finland	1.3	1.1	0.9	0.5	0.9	0.5
France	1.9	1.6	1.4	1.0	1.1	0.6
Germany	1.5	1.3	1.0	0.7	0.8	0.3
Italy	1.3	1.2	0.8	0.5	0.6	0.2
Spain	1.7	1.6	1.3	0.9	1.1	0.6
Sweden	1.3	1.1	0.8	0.5	1.1	0.6
United Kingdom	2.0	1.7	1.5	1.1	1.3	0.8
Russian Federation	5.7	3.2	1.1	2.9	2.9	3.0
DEVELOPED, ALL	**2.3**	**2.0**	**1.5**	**1.4**	**1.4**	**1.2**
DEVELOPING, ALL	**6.7**	**4.2**	**3.1**	**3.0**	**4.6**	**3.7**
WORLD	**3.9**	**3.2**	**1.9**	**2.0**	**2.4**	**2.4**

[1]Projections based on population projections of the International Panel on Climate Change and on the projections of gross domestic product per capita in Table 6.

Table 6—Observed and projected Gross Domestic Product per capita for world regions and selected countries in the Global Forest Products Model ($U.S. of 1990)[1]

		Scenario A1B		Scenario A2		Scenario B2	
	2006	2030	2060	2030	2060	2030	2060
AFRICA	**1027**	**3449**	**13545**	**1417**	**3307**	**1987**	**7755**
Egypt	1240	4756	17495	1929	4256	2724	9996
Nigeria	475	2326	11626	966	2927	1400	7430
South Africa	4451	12318	30137	5226	7615	6492	14278
NORTH/CENTRAL AMERICA	**19677**	**29684**	**50391**	**23592**	**30083**	**22940**	**27454**
Canada	27162	39205	61551	34505	43524	34798	43857
Mexico	4558	12537	30442	5044	6844	6533	14059
United States	28679	41021	62485	35884	46269	32933	34262
SOUTH AMERICA	**4378**	**11953**	**29322**	**5023**	**7408**	**6564**	**15364**
Argentina	6778	16849	36044	6982	8638	8845	16925
Brazil	4528	12477	30358	4997	6790	6501	14019
Chile	5865	15128	33892	7084	10777	9584	24292
ASIA	**2352**	**7016**	**20939**	**3141**	**4908**	**4515**	**9226**
China	1016	5431	19510	2051	4170	3295	7499
India	616	3741	15767	1255	2579	2365	6646
Indonesia	1030	5490	19630	1865	3267	3132	6568
Japan	29518	41711	63769	36580	44166	36747	44684
Korea, Republic of	11909	33965	55616	13072	11392	21685	23975
Malaysia	5773	19809	40868	7547	8541	12349	16696
OCEANIA	**18860**	**28943**	**49811**	**23107**	**29233**	**25107**	**32288**
Australia	24629	36449	59039	31751	41582	32768	43297
New Zealand	18744	29742	52562	26272	38419	26805	38764
EUROPE	**15225**	**26595**	**51409**	**20035**	**27489**	**21823**	**35509**
EU-27	20291	31703	55194	26676	35845	27343	39164
Austria	27521	39591	61896	35505	44611	35179	44214
Finland	36042	48398	69424	43606	50531	44063	52379
France	28108	40217	62453	35577	44425	35823	44859
Germany	28416	40545	62744	36207	45066	36161	45196
Italy	25384	37278	59803	33241	42779	32829	41868
Spain	18861	29880	52702	27012	39209	26428	37256
Sweden	36520	48875	69814	44029	50815	44519	52731
United Kingdom	22360	33918	56660	30001	40373	29647	39004
Russian Federation	3786	15034	43203	4961	10464	8434	23430
DEVELOPED, ALL	**18808**	**30362**	**53982**	**24132**	**32046**	**24595**	**33838**
DEVELOPING, ALL	**1607**	**5939**	**18836**	**2357**	**4239**	**3510**	**8675**
WORLD	**5158**	**10275**	**24889**	**6013**	**8289**	**7143**	**12576**

[1] Data for 2006 are from World Bank (2008), and projections are based on projections of the Intergovernmental Panel for Climate Change with the method described in Appendix B.

Table 7—Observed and projected forest area (thousand ha) for world regions and selected countries in the Global Forest Products Model[1]

	Observed		Scenario A1B		Scenario A2		Scenario B2		Scenario A1B-Low Fuelwood	
	1992	2006	2030	2060	2030	2060	2030	2060	2030	2060
AFRICA	678886	621478	557314	601973	542215	494239	543351	528537	557314	601973
Egypt	47	69	90	166	87	130	87	142	90	166
Nigeria	16323	10724	5237	2506	5144	2108	5159	2266	5237	2506
South Africa	9203	9203	10189	13995	9474	10610	9468	11429	10189	13995
NORTH/CENTRAL AMERICA	709453	705105	687181	686483	683035	665927	683561	679249	687181	686483
Canada	310134	310134	310134	310134	310134	310134	310134	310134	310134	310134
Mexico	68306	63982	64557	78295	59686	57918	59861	63649	64557	78295
United States of America	299374	303393	289317	274456	291161	278722	291414	284490	289317	274456
SOUTH AMERICA	883014	827570	746999	799827	697526	610124	699499	667058	746999	799827
Argentina	34958	32889	33345	36816	30646	29423	30680	32105	33345	36816
Brazil	514550	474832	416039	423027	384549	312091	385710	343158	416039	423027
Chile	15376	16186	19709	28814	18413	23991	18564	26654	19709	28814
ASIA	571242	572212	538150	650391	517377	509967	524906	556983	538150	650391
China	160926	201631	210764	297789	202732	226462	205279	244506	210764	297789
India	64646	67701	71072	95958	68918	74077	69843	81819	71072	95958
Indonesia	112557	86726	58360	45368	55816	33198	56623	36225	58360	45368
Japan	24935	24868	24868	24868	24868	24868	24868	24868	24868	24868
Korea, Republic of	6357	6259	6533	6533	6339	6356	6575	7251	6533	6533
Malaysia	22217	20744	20252	21049	18572	16789	19302	19732	20252	21049
OCEANIA	211391	205720	203331	207719	201607	198256	202212	201284	203331	207719
Australia	167247	163515	163678	163678	163678	163678	163678	163678	163678	163678
New Zealand	7819	8326	8769	8769	8814	8889	8825	8963	8769	8769
EUROPE	990882	1002045	969796	1050580	872526	827293	914467	996283	969796	1050580
EU-25	136105	145990	156797	171371	154033	165226	155754	175161	156797	171371
Austria	3788	3866	3871	3871	3865	3865	3870	3870	3871	3871
Finland	22250	22500	22500	22500	22500	22500	22500	22500	22500	22500
France	14697	15601	15807	15807	15762	15762	15872	15872	15807	15807
Germany	10807	11076	11076	11076	11076	11076	11076	11076	11076	11076
Italy	8586	10089	12151	12272	12380	13361	12518	14130	12151	12272
Russian Federation	809014	808790	763025	816943	672553	612273	710711	761223	763025	816943
Spain	14024	18220	20301	20658	20413	21479	20449	22236	20301	20658
Sweden	27388	27528	27528	27528	27528	27528	27528	27528	27528	27528
United Kingdom	2646	2857	3037	3037	3075	3094	3097	3161	3037	3037
DEVELOPED, ALL	1825647	1837684	1793207	1867801	1695758	1639910	1738676	1819737	1793207	1867801
DEVELOPING, ALL	2219221	2096446	1909564	2129172	1818528	1665897	1829318	1809658	1909564	2129172
WORLD	4044868	3934130	3702771	3996973	3514286	3305807	3567994	3629395	3702771	3996973

[1]Observations derived from FAO (2001), projections obtained with the Global Forest Products Model.

Table 8—Observed and projected forest stock (million m³) for world regions and selected countries in the Global Forest Products Model[1]

	Observed		Scenario A1B		Scenario A2		Scenario B2		Scenario A1B-Low Fuelwood	
	1992	2006	2030	2060	2030	2060	2030	2060	2030	2060
AFRICA	67818	64970	60721	60342	60870	58456	60565	61007	62473	73653
Egypt	6	9	0	0	0	0	0	0	0	0
Nigeria	1962	1467	291	10	443	39	406	32	426	90
South Africa	635	653	262	33	294	97	271	88	316	216
NORTH/CENTRAL AMERICA	72449	75574	76266	60810	77514	76049	76991	75354	77690	84877
Canada	32983	33214	32591	27882	32801	32722	32769	32195	32688	33673
Mexico	3144	3144	2285	633	2226	1061	2256	1071	2503	2061
United States of America	32543	35856	38814	30663	39852	40283	39364	40041	39739	46420
SOUTH AMERICA	128286	121704	129673	139228	122626	122041	122605	130605	131206	165942
Argentina	2091	1825	2048	1721	1922	1863	1922	2010	2097	2619
Brazil	87732	81321	88267	94029	83009	81767	82966	87556	89363	113693
Chile	1587	1945	2384	1374	2384	2728	2367	2708	2508	3959
ASIA	50474	47015	39509	28534	40872	35930	40674	36376	42477	47956
China	10831	13295	9725	3403	10275	6123	10171	5793	10853	10974
India	4421	4698	2102	254	2646	893	2521	780	2717	1887
Indonesia	12123	4893	2327	271	2598	652	2462	584	2684	1231
Japan	3247	4249	6456	8058	6514	9587	6507	9358	6472	9847
Korea, Republic of	274	529	1186	1194	1199	1950	1227	2045	1224	2176
Malaysia	5011	5311	6375	6982	5916	6659	6127	7627	6412	8586
OCEANIA	12616	12559	12620	10959	12681	12396	12697	12398	12747	13302
Australia	10203	10203	10666	9861	10718	10944	10723	10935	10738	11409
New Zealand	1181	1181	970	449	997	741	998	720	989	820
EUROPE	104210	109662	116775	109632	107755	109748	112210	127601	118497	146481
EU-25	17439	21023	25861	17164	26290	29174	26474	29867	26791	36576
Austria	974	1192	1413	1002	1447	1672	1449	1579	1455	1871
Finland	1939	2158	2464	1431	2559	2886	2546	2641	2523	3218
France	2113	2559	2897	841	3181	2430	3137	2329	3157	3441
Germany	2899	2899	3828	2219	3982	4280	3949	4178	3957	5291
Italy	1095	1475	2127	1801	2231	2700	2239	2720	2220	2780
Russian Federation	80086	80479	80236	81495	71374	67897	75243	83139	80728	92458
Spain	627	913	1247	844	1295	1541	1291	1482	1286	1662
Sweden	2838	3155	3284	1835	3403	3219	3380	3214	3361	3865
United Kingdom	274	355	405	185	428	395	429	377	414	460
DEVELOPED, ALL	186017	196091	207720	188215	200048	205422	203996	222540	210634	250657
DEVELOPING, ALL	249836	235393	227844	221289	222270	209197	221746	220802	234457	281553
WORLD	435853	431484	435563	409504	422318	414619	425741	443342	445091	532210

[1]Observations derived from FAO (2006), projections obtained with the Global Forest Products Model.

Table 9—Observed and projected fuelwood prices (1997$/m³) for selected countries in the Global Forest Products

	Observed		Scenario A1B		Scenario A2		Scenario B2		Scenario A1B-Low Fuelwood	
	1992	2006	2030	2060	2030	2060	2030	2060	2030	2060
AFRICA										
Egypt	56	46	101	266	71	128	78	135	69	73
Nigeria	44	46	101	266	71	128	78	135	69	73
South Africa	53	46	101	266	71	128	78	135	69	73
NORTH/CENTRAL AMERICA										
Canada	44	46	99	256	70	118	77	125	59	63
Mexico	53	46	95	265	70	127	71	134	59	63
United States of America	53	56	88	338	77	194	77	189	48	60
SOUTH AMERICA										
Argentina	44	46	91	266	71	128	76	127	59	63
Brazil	44	46	91	256	61	118	68	125	59	63
Chile	44	46	91	256	61	118	68	125	59	63
ASIA										
China	44	61	107	282	75	136	83	144	68	73
India	44	56	100	265	70	127	77	134	68	72
Indonesia	44	46	101	266	71	128	78	135	69	73
Japan	53	56	100	265	70	127	77	134	59	63
Korea, Republic of	44	46	91	266	61	118	68	135	59	63
Malaysia	44	67	91	256	73	118	75	125	59	63
OCEANIA										
Australia	53	46	91	256	71	128	75	125	59	63
New Zealand	44	0	91	262	71	121	76	127	59	66
EUROPE										
EU-25										
Austria	53	56	91	256	68	118	68	125	59	63
Finland	53	56	91	256	61	118	68	125	59	63
France	44	46	91	265	64	127	68	125	59	63
Germany	53	56	91	265	70	127	77	129	59	63
Italy	53	56	100	265	70	127	77	134	59	63
Russian Federation	44	46	91	256	61	118	68	125	59	63
Spain	53	46	100	265	70	127	77	134	59	63
Sweden	44	56	91	256	70	127	71	125	59	63
United Kingdom	44	46	100	265	70	127	77	134	59	63
DEVELOPED, ALL										
DEVELOPING, ALL										
WORLD	52	39	91	256	61	118	68	125	59	63

[1]Observations derived from FAO (2009), projections obtained with the Global Forest Products Model.

Table 10—Observed and projected industrial roundwood prices (1997$/m³) for selected countries in the Global Forest Products Model[1]

	Observed		Scenario A1B		Scenario A2		Scenario B2		Scenario A1B-Low Fuelwood	
	1992	2006	2030	2060	2030	2060	2030	2060	2030	2060
AFRICA										
Egypt	96	91	107	281	92	138	94	146	97	82
Nigeria	86	80	150	642	123	342	128	376	131	232
South Africa	86	80	117	318	102	166	107	164	101	91
NORTH/CENTRAL AMERICA										
Canada	101	94	92	255	81	117	82	124	84	62
Mexico	111	102	112	291	96	144	98	154	101	86
United States of America	86	80	87	336	76	193	76	188	67	59
SOUTH AMERICA										
Argentina	86	80	91	264	74	127	75	126	78	64
Brazil	86	80	88	254	74	115	75	123	78	63
Chile	86	80	88	256	73	118	75	125	78	63
ASIA										
China	96	91	103	265	90	134	92	141	93	80
India	98	94	103	272	87	133	89	140	92	78
Indonesia	86	80	108	310	91	164	96	174	98	101
Japan	101	94	99	265	82	127	83	134	90	72
Korea, Republic of	102	95	102	261	86	115	88	132	91	76
Malaysia	86	80	91	255	74	117	75	124	78	64
OCEANIA										
Australia	86	80	90	256	74	127	75	124	77	62
New Zealand	86	80	86	240	73	111	74	117	75	69
EUROPE										
EU-25										
Austria	101	95	91	256	80	118	81	125	84	64
Finland	102	95	93	256	80	118	83	125	86	63
France	86	80	88	264	73	126	75	125	77	64
Germany	86	80	90	263	72	125	74	127	76	62
Italy	100	93	100	264	85	128	86	134	89	76
Russian Federation	86	80	87	251	76	113	77	121	78	65
Spain	101	94	98	263	85	125	85	133	89	76
Sweden	102	95	102	255	88	126	90	125	92	63
United Kingdom	104	80	100	273	85	135	85	141	88	80
DEVELOPED, ALL										
DEVELOPING, ALL										
WORLD	117	72	88	256	73	118	75	125	78	63

[1]Observations derived from FAO (2009), projections obtained with the Global Forest Products Model.

Table 11—Observed and projected sawnwood prices (1997$/m³) for selected countries in the Global Forest Products Model[1]

	Observed		Scenario A1B		Scenario A2		Scenario B2		Scenario A1B-Low Fuelwood	
	1992	2006	2030	2060	2030	2060	2030	2060	2030	2060
AFRICA										
Egypt	266	281	220	346	188	189	192	198	198	126
Nigeria	228	241	257	407	222	235	227	245	233	168
South Africa	253	268	273	400	229	220	247	236	236	158
NORTH/CENTRAL AMERICA										
Canada	228	241	222	392	207	244	207	251	210	183
Mexico	228	281	260	436	241	271	241	288	244	211
United States of America	253	268	244	482	229	320	229	320	217	181
SOUTH AMERICA										
Argentina	276	241	234	408	209	255	211	254	215	184
Brazil	228	241	232	397	209	245	212	253	216	185
Chile	228	241	231	397	207	245	210	253	214	184
ASIA										
China	261	276	251	394	236	254	236	262	240	199
India	329	348	290	414	269	260	272	268	276	199
Indonesia	228	241	240	392	222	253	227	261	230	198
Japan	258	273	246	386	229	248	230	255	237	194
Korea, Republic of	266	281	254	388	238	239	240	256	243	200
Malaysia	228	241	229	378	211	240	213	247	216	184
OCEANIA										
Australia	266	281	258	396	230	255	232	252	236	183
New Zealand	228	241	228	384	210	243	212	249	215	192
EUROPE										
EU-25										
Austria	228	241	222	384	210	243	211	249	214	187
Finland	228	241	222	395	206	245	209	251	214	183
France	256	271	241	394	224	250	226	248	229	185
Germany	256	241	228	387	211	248	213	250	215	184
Italy	256	271	251	395	231	256	231	271	235	206
Russian Federation	228	241	229	396	204	246	207	252	212	183
Spain	256	271	246	387	231	248	231	256	235	199
Sweden	228	241	222	392	199	250	202	249	206	178
United Kingdom	256	271	251	392	231	254	231	260	235	201
DEVELOPED, ALL										
DEVELOPING, ALL										
WORLD	**238**	**228**	**222**	**392**	**203**	**250**	**203**	**249**	**206**	**178**

[1]Observations derived from FAO (2009), projections obtained with the Global Forest Products Model.

Table 12—Observed and projected fuelwood consumption (thousand m³) for world regions and selected countries in the Global Forest Products Model[1]

	Observed		Scenario A1B		Scenario A2		Scenario B2		Scenario A1B-Low Fuelwood	
	1992	2006	2030	2060	2030	2060	2030	2060	2030	2060
AFRICA	**385835**	**593599**	**701913**	**1136946**	**468373**	**474802**	**461414**	**461605**	**603427**	**659620**
Egypt	14635	17059	37967	105943	27998	53116	22403	32768	17400	18652
Nigeria	52854	61628	87065	137594	55595	49764	59776	59725	64160	69740
South Africa	12609	12000	25152	64528	16258	24005	22801	52391	14057	17148
NORTH/CENTRAL AMERICA	**172042**	**131625**	**359046**	**1694285**	**303738**	**1320517**	**281122**	**1132446**	**139808**	**150294**
Canada	6227	2869	14293	114737	13010	92903	11082	66010	2953	3316
Mexico	34918	38516	78882	194067	60174	106273	54677	85437	39308	40899
United States of America	90452	44949	205517	1276662	186870	1070749	176209	939550	50700	56765
SOUTH AMERICA	**166209**	**192331**	**318148**	**673299**	**239628**	**344650**	**208271**	**257774**	**197120**	**205488**
Argentina	2872	4372	16911	85196	12503	44118	11243	35335	4679	4844
Brazil	123251	138783	201735	322909	157362	182356	135590	133380	140890	146642
Chile	9000	13488	19905	32809	13495	13517	11618	9866	13542	14045
ASIA	**790243**	**790676**	**1486215**	**4662336**	**866970**	**1727169**	**1152119**	**2504305**	**846462**	**902026**
China	196145	203510	429999	1053636	253936	320514	351141	676775	220920	231820
India	283869	306331	526808	1027229	289151	264957	392849	538087	327066	350364
Indonesia	115666	70718	128186	260601	75088	77586	102530	159581	76630	81368
Japan	184	106	4017	351145	3670	285244	3023	187861	118	127
Korea, Republic of	2611	2469	14793	137346	7259	27456	10285	60951	2515	2562
Malaysia	3845	3025	12318	65785	6485	16091	9061	34157	3320	3434
OCEANIA	**9875**	**10915**	**29488**	**104306**	**24309**	**79725**	**21998**	**55230**	**13664**	**14942**
Australia	4021	5042	17613	75600	16357	65079	12883	38704	6020	6782
New Zealand	50	1	3396	11338	3158	9879	2723	7148	1414	1590
EUROPE	**114722**	**153397**	**364106**	**1593968**	**265344**	**953840**	**271521**	**856294**	**163305**	**191523**
EU-25	42367	82300	208174	1132441	174397	808950	159009	631966	75841	84611
Austria	3271	4977	8576	20425	7493	15301	7043	13262	4407	4741
Finland	2895	5455	8877	16264	8019	12797	7086	9906	5613	5981
France	9692	32682	58799	193232	53339	154308	44467	104523	23880	26263
Germany	3836	8758	33417	224435	29402	171556	25325	125412	7493	8115
Italy	5145	6703	24834	131345	21899	98438	19105	73791	6823	7337
Russian Federation	63879	45800	98321	248860	56558	70830	71749	123689	60063	73551
Spain	2433	1461	10129	83955	8789	60564	7905	48648	1992	2194
Sweden	3788	6088	12103	27430	10659	20933	10076	18557	6420	6849
United Kingdom	225	176	3007	166158	2723	131933	2372	98630	132	146
DEVELOPED, ALL	**228775**	**219234**	**639883**	**3687497**	**508318**	**2578852**	**504363**	**2230209**	**239768**	**278916**
DEVELOPING, ALL	**1410152**	**1653310**	**2619033**	**6177644**	**1660044**	**2321849**	**1892082**	**3037445**	**1724019**	**1844979**
WORLD	**1638927**	**1872543**	**3258916**	**9865141**	**2168362**	**4900701**	**2396445**	**5267654**	**1963787**	**2123894**

[1]Observations derived from FAO (2009), projections obtained with the Global Forest Products Model.

Table 13—Observed and projected fuelwood net trade (thousand m^3) for world regions and selected countries in the Global Forest Products Model[1]

	Observed		Scenario A1B		Scenario A2		Scenario B2		Scenario A1B-Low Fuelwood	
	1992	2006	2030	2060	2030	2060	2030	2060	2030	2060
AFRICA	-8	2	-22124	137885	18087	137508	75914	192186	-142116	-271513
Egypt	-5	0	-37956	-105909	-27998	-53115	-22400	-32762	-17400	-18652
Nigeria	0	1	-47538	-133642	-15303	-42829	-18211	-53750	-27048	-61607
South Africa	-9	0	-11080	-59797	-5904	-17591	-12046	-46253	-3357	-10006
NORTH/CENTRAL AMERICA	2	94	7923	221624	-14381	-43588	6621	77377	10031	3446
Canada	161	128	0	372114	-7310	35457	-4612	92684	1620	1818
Mexico	-8	5	0	-124768	-7273	-55480	0	-31113	8495	0
United States of America	-152	-35	-196	-46	-1657	-29099	-601	-526	562	10038
SOUTH AMERICA	16	0	278957	2175234	102585	576349	184171	854061	147901	296522
Argentina	0	0	633	-5659	-2531	-10496	0	0	3872	9635
Brazil	0	0	229398	1895183	86755	449178	147027	653857	109704	212791
Chile	16	0	28674	133588	14592	108135	20621	131503	14611	39089
ASIA	-44	-326	-416088	-3413247	-106748	-837568	-311396	-1595339	-115959	-283345
China	0	-5	-79319	-693683	-14853	-35681	-82998	-391468	0	0
India	1	-79	-222719	-928776	-39464	-103789	-123863	-391067	-80424	-181764
Indonesia	0	1	-24538	-225503	0	-38946	-21913	-123372	-1610	-45722
Japan	-22	-1	-2962	-191596	-3399	-232073	-2714	-126106	98	246
Korea, Republic of	0	0	2739	-57670	3463	21551	2381	-48	7950	18844
Malaysia	7	-12	17037	91514	0	36963	0	32393	434	7963
OCEANIA	-1	-1	15626	77444	-2446	2180	3039	24861	5351	11512
Australia	-1	0	3465	58219	-4681	-9192	0	16273	3228	7349
New Zealand	0	0	4411	0	-1018	0	0	0	263	0
EUROPE	-137	757	136466	801820	3663	165880	42411	447615	95553	244138
EU-25	-272	-740	56980	-227761	-27638	-114468	6832	77903	54830	138217
Austria	-277	-272	2058	7246	0	15018	550	20747	1887	4271
Finland	-17	-165	3990	10740	18	57287	2179	50334	1963	5381
France	108	516	19433	-103092	0	-33436	13146	8277	24163	31084
Germany	-41	-468	16026	-56781	-14594	-43737	-6484	0	4277	15270
Italy	-313	-1097	-4610	-72777	-8428	-63031	-3733	-35742	3940	7609
Russian Federation	21	200	34774	760488	14008	136870	14102	203548	15792	26805
Spain	-133	146	-906	-37542	-2935	-30151	-1271	-15157	2690	4526
Sweden	12	-188	1216	1	-763	0	0	1230	1407	3063
United Kingdom	0	141	-1872	-164489	-1958	-130422	-1500	-97090	465	582
DEVELOPED, ALL	-166	844	128237	819806	-22541	-149956	19975	320671	98122	254136
DEVELOPING, ALL	-6	-318	-127477	-819047	23301	150716	-19215	-319912	-97362	-253376
WORLD	-172	526	760	760	760	760	760	760	760	760

[1]Observations derived from FAO (2009), projections obtained with the Global Forest Products Model.

Table 14—Observed and projected industrial roundwood consumption (except energy wood) (thousand m³) for world regions and selected countries in the Global Forest Products Model[1]

	Observed		Scenario A1B		Scenario A2		Scenario B2		Scenario A1B-Low Fuelwood	
	1992	2006	2030	2060	2030	2060	2030	2060	2030	2060
AFRICA	**52971**	**65082**	**65908**	**48101**	**61897**	**51787**	**63988**	**53110**	**68458**	**62163**
Egypt	223	321	4516	3734	3624	3112	3811	3458	4596	4190
Nigeria	8258	8770	8695	5768	7610	5002	8287	6333	9044	7389
South Africa	14455	17923	11660	5471	11058	5689	11218	7172	11863	7698
NORTH/CENTRAL AMERICA	**554822**	**602667**	**567997**	**357308**	**510785**	**212955**	**539576**	**280653**	**590147**	**444764**
Canada	165929	186345	182408	108805	160897	136851	162125	123611	166861	109436
Mexico	7113	6296	7887	4008	11255	10824	8244	3385	8751	10338
United States of America	378169	405418	372506	238842	334051	60224	364466	148127	409262	318677
SOUTH AMERICA	**111002**	**158217**	**155835**	**90991**	**146305**	**96523**	**147417**	**96844**	**165241**	**110503**
Argentina	7024	9466	9671	6544	8787	5158	8668	5734	10268	7500
Brazil	78909	100681	109613	59571	103595	65317	104555	63686	118343	75002
Chile	13166	33106	21295	11835	20492	12404	20424	12629	21370	12970
ASIA	**306059**	**321210**	**381658**	**424614**	**303524**	**339337**	**324668**	**358790**	**375046**	**462807**
China	100229	148261	185017	211081	146102	172242	155702	181930	184094	240757
India	25630	27232	35145	36003	26833	24644	31214	30156	35330	37988
Indonesia	42621	27534	23708	17656	19944	13183	21129	14090	24220	20384
Japan	65900	38660	45947	50914	36809	45937	37431	42315	41218	48810
Korea, Republic of	9431	10314	15278	21009	11006	12941	12124	15193	14033	18668
Malaysia	27208	18407	12681	12741	10692	9853	11560	10298	12852	13277
OCEANIA	**21278**	**38081**	**35903**	**31691**	**34305**	**24205**	**34434**	**27022**	**35784**	**26860**
Australia	10248	21919	21704	12210	20899	12301	20840	11445	21718	14460
New Zealand	10241	15589	13413	18809	12742	11327	12866	14959	13276	11681
EUROPE	**432219**	**492240**	**495197**	**383611**	**460390**	**449167**	**467174**	**398800**	**500742**	**418194**
EU-25										
Austria	14371	22815	16194	12209	13950	14496	14240	11533	14985	13868
Finland	40966	59466	53870	29897	46373	36717	47918	30082	50213	36277
France	30887	27498	32376	27325	31019	27566	30431	26584	31977	31447
Germany	27893	51873	52821	48531	48163	47498	48444	49298	52820	60691
Italy	9174	8622	10344	15832	8745	14537	7866	11573	9184	13556
Russian Federation	153539	94219	70875	49949	65304	49210	64462	44901	71376	54761
Spain	13811	17726	19829	18522	17595	18697	17541	16902	18627	20093
Sweden	54408	62361	83121	46514	97115	104880	97900	73129	99139	44195
United Kingdom	6263	7884	12847	20441	11024	19426	11052	18250	11262	18834
DEVELOPED, ALL	**1077553**	**1179684**	**1146285**	**822594**	**1039369**	**725147**	**1079127**	**750697**	**1168436**	**934272**
DEVELOPING, ALL	**400799**	**497813**	**556213**	**513722**	**477837**	**448826**	**498129**	**464521**	**566982**	**591018**
WORLD	**1478352**	**1677497**	**1702499**	**1336316**	**1517206**	**1173974**	**1577256**	**1215219**	**1735418**	**1525290**

[1]Observations derived from FAO (2009), projections obtained with the Global Forest Products Model.

Table 15—Observed and projected industrial roundwood net trade (thousand m³) for world regions and selected countries in the Global Forest Products Model[1]

	Observed		Scenario A1B		Scenario A2		Scenario B2		Scenario A1B-Low Fuelwood	
	1992	2006	2030	2060	2030	2060	2030	2060	2030	2060
AFRICA	**4026**	**3150**	**-19455**	**-14923**	**-12425**	**-15026**	**-14524**	**-19948**	**-15976**	**-25995**
Egypt	-98	-116	-4511	-3729	-3622	-3109	-3809	-3456	-4593	-4186
Nigeria	5	41	-4531	-4621	-2725	-3350	-3522	-4624	-3877	-4951
South Africa	818	140	0	-1417	0	0	-329	-1808	0	-1213
NORTH/CENTRAL AMERICA	**22463**	**5519**	**5531**	**7449**	**-5940**	**-10747**	**-912**	**-2420**	**17673**	**98929**
Canada	-2421	-1148	0	663	0	5	0	21	0	7004
Mexico	-68	-165	-2860	0	-7185	-7758	-4005	-97	-3881	-7213
United States of America	24933	6717	9768	9730	2368	-655	4329	296	22944	102647
SOUTH AMERICA	**7248**	**2495**	**48819**	**12995**	**16551**	**89436**	**19706**	**39333**	**21203**	**65505**
Argentina	553	33	0	0	424	0	437	0	522	1
Brazil	355	87	28027	574	1793	77884	4099	37488	2817	38796
Chile	6191	111	21539	22	15349	12028	16280	14	19117	28527
ASIA	**-38810**	**-51465**	**-156336**	**-233579**	**-87621**	**-154626**	**-107394**	**-182844**	**-134577**	**-247235**
China	-7788	-33023	-98323	-131247	-66275	-98822	-75100	-108979	-97598	-166694
India	-723	-4040	-24694	-32580	-15883	-19005	-20543	-24993	-23339	-31832
Indonesia	490	565	-1586	-9294	0	-3765	-1124	-5108	-1688	-10574
Japan	-38786	-10550	0	0	0	0	0	0	0	0
Korea, Republic of	-8308	-6367	-5431	0	-2835	0	-3537	0	-5106	-5567
Malaysia	17830	4771	0	122	12705	3	11282	13	16534	11432
OCEANIA	**13907**	**9650**	**-329**	**282**	**4733**	**-181**	**4624**	**-169**	**5424**	**-274**
Australia	6406	1063	0	460	0	0	179	17	487	1
New Zealand	4774	5568	0	0	2924	0	2639	0	2917	0
EUROPE	**-937**	**31018**	**119986**	**225991**	**82916**	**89358**	**96715**	**164262**	**104467**	**107285**
EU-25	-11623	-23166	28948	202351	20268	-7924	23855	75847	24589	43374
Austria	-4516	-8384	0	28809	0	4	0	17	0	0
Finland	-5361	-13946	0	77974	0	1267	0	15964	0	6136
France	1697	1094	4864	0	3432	0	4612	11	4883	0
Germany	5165	3888	0	0	17720	0	16905	0	17463	5787
Italy	-5649	-4471	-4878	-1660	-3921	-5453	-2896	-1813	-4151	-8603
Russian Federation	10461	50384	83810	2304	49339	93578	58827	80633	64673	59666
Spain	-2187	-3617	0	0	0	0	0	0	0	-296
Sweden	-4688	-3660	0	93223	-26052	0	-25379	31675	-24331	7810
United Kingdom	-72	229	0	-1174	0	-1347	0	0	0	-7871
DEVELOPED, ALL	**-5493**	**32158**	**125813**	**207740**	**86517**	**76272**	**101414**	**145740**	**128271**	**211298**
DEVELOPING, ALL	**13390**	**-31790**	**-127598**	**-209525**	**-88302**	**-78057**	**-103199**	**-147525**	**-130056**	**-213083**
WORLD	**7897**	**368**	**-1785**	**-1785**	**-1785**	**-1785**	**-1785**	**-1785**	**-1785**	**-1785**

[1]Observations derived from FAO (2009), projections obtained with the Global Forest Products Model.

Table 16—Observed and projected sawnwood consumption (thousand m³) for world regions and selected countries in the Global Forest Products Model[1]

	Observed		Scenario A1B		Scenario A2		Scenario B2		Scenario A1B-Low Fuelwood	
	1992	2006	2030	2060	2030	2060	2030	2060	2030	2060
AFRICA	**10452**	**12638**	**16671**	**19805**	**14050**	**16057**	**15204**	**19252**	**16823**	**21589**
Egypt	1633	1465	2055	2463	1756	2101	1825	2291	2075	2724
Nigeria	2675	1979	2827	3596	2373	2876	2615	3655	2853	3931
South Africa	2254	2515	3046	3240	2584	2611	2930	3365	3090	3557
NORTH/CENTRAL AMERICA	**118741**	**159609**	**168456**	**162902**	**164431**	**161674**	**162201**	**153425**	**170224**	**179840**
Canada	12543	21271	22093	21212	21662	20991	21563	20109	22215	22968
Mexico	2675	6779	7825	8223	6622	6785	6876	7469	7874	8866
United States of America	101286	128405	135263	129913	133317	130816	130796	122403	136840	144176
SOUTH AMERICA	**25256**	**32503**	**37260**	**39109**	**31869**	**33064**	**33022**	**36153**	**37527**	**42319**
Argentina	1663	1833	1811	1850	1547	1547	1595	1682	1827	2010
Brazil	18137	20764	24524	25669	20822	21319	21511	23167	24702	27790
Chile	2181	5377	6152	6344	5376	5632	5634	6300	6198	6871
ASIA	**106710**	**101150**	**122794**	**134483**	**105880**	**112497**	**113497**	**121030**	**123361**	**144479**
China	21336	32438	36548	40195	30765	33867	33487	35930	36719	43122
India	17472	14943	20848	25158	16744	18621	19057	22308	20949	27079
Indonesia	7683	2610	3623	4143	2949	3161	3233	3470	3640	4447
Japan	36566	21042	21443	19963	20973	19493	20692	18578	21521	21440
Korea, Republic of	4338	5155	6163	5947	5026	4504	5603	5122	6190	6367
Malaysia	3994	3525	4085	4175	3399	3326	3720	3645	4109	4499
OCEANIA	**6209**	**7641**	**8550**	**8366**	**8397**	**8325**	**8422**	**7979**	**8618**	**9034**
Australia	4187	5010	5472	5358	5408	5353	5376	5057	5521	5795
New Zealand	1648	2324	2649	2576	2630	2625	2651	2534	2664	2769
EUROPE	**134916**	**120144**	**126706**	**122519**	**118162**	**113979**	**120461**	**116084**	**127437**	**131877**
EU-25	74241	102783	105068	100253	99982	95107	100790	95173	105658	107795
Austria	3821	5499	5272	4863	5165	4752	5162	4710	5291	5242
Finland	2797	5077	5397	4915	5314	4877	5302	4849	5418	5327
France	11429	12426	12638	11987	12411	11821	12195	11364	12699	12963
Germany	17540	20851	19348	18010	18988	17622	18832	17050	19463	19460
Italy	8215	9441	9114	8490	8934	8253	8831	7949	9173	9081
Russian Federation	47368	6242	9287	9756	7432	7944	8140	8755	9361	10567
Spain	4378	7062	7126	6799	6996	6671	6923	6455	7159	7282
Sweden	4028	5467	6029	5502	5944	5406	6028	5525	6073	5974
United Kingdom	9208	10455	11117	10702	10919	10531	10764	10153	11189	11472
DEVELOPED, ALL	**293914**	**302904**	**319198**	**307594**	**306785**	**298183**	**306761**	**290853**	**321832**	**335609**
DEVELOPING, ALL	**108370**	**130781**	**161240**	**179590**	**136004**	**147413**	**146045**	**163070**	**162158**	**193529**
WORLD	**402283**	**433685**	**480437**	**487184**	**442789**	**445595**	**452807**	**453922**	**483990**	**529138**

[1]Observations derived from FAO (2009), projections obtained with the Global Forest Products Model.

Table 17—Observed and projected sawnwood net trade (thousand m³) for world region and selected countries in the Global Forest Products Model[1]

	Observed		Scenario A1B		Scenario A2		Scenario B2		Scenario A1B-Low Fuelwood	
	1992	2006	2030	2060	2030	2060	2030	2060	2030	2060
AFRICA	**-2354**	**-3424**	**-2265**	**-850**	**-599**	**6072**	**-1547**	**1021**	**-1908**	**2274**
Egypt	-1633	-1463	-440	-95	-440	-95	-440	-95	-440	-95
Nigeria	40	21	6	1	6	10	6	4	6	10
South Africa	-436	-424	-1357	-1189	-416	-59	-1198	-419	-1357	-379
NORTH/CENTRAL AMERICA	**11004**	**-2770**	**-2082**	**-12182**	**-15239**	**-99824**	**-1556**	**-34477**	**-3953**	**-3068**
Canada	27595	37438	16513	3545	12899	12842	13173	2828	14042	3015
Mexico	21	-4129	-6050	-7879	-1996	-594	-4333	-7119	-5677	-4201
United States of America	-16136	-35501	-12029	-7501	-25743	-111915	-9945	-29840	-11817	-1572
SOUTH AMERICA	**1449**	**6983**	**2194**	**1162**	**2463**	**3565**	**2398**	**2196**	**2198**	**1527**
Argentina	-191	270	69	15	69	15	69	15	69	15
Brazil	491	3033	945	203	945	566	945	203	945	203
Chile	839	3341	875	188	930	904	918	197	875	188
ASIA	**-9492**	**-21081**	**-11690**	**-6528**	**-14093**	**-5173**	**-21409**	**-8558**	**-15173**	**-7678**
China	-1580	-6662	-2518	-829	-3597	-772	-10628	-2513	-5213	-1237
India	-12	-154	-26	-6	-26	-6	-26	-6	-26	-6
Indonesia	755	1623	506	109	506	109	506	99	506	109
Japan	-9289	-8488	-2756	-590	-4086	-875	-4098	-880	-3047	-654
Korea, Republic of	-825	-789	-232	-49	-232	-48	-232	-50	-232	-50
Malaysia	5375	1604	550	764	550	764	550	238	550	118
OCEANIA	**-303**	**1631**	**390**	**556**	**392**	**433**	**392**	**304**	**389**	**229**
Australia	-1146	-226	-133	-103	-133	-29	-133	-29	-133	-29
New Zealand	896	1910	523	514	523	310	523	187	523	112
EUROPE	**-797**	**25547**	**17523**	**21914**	**31147**	**99000**	**25793**	**43587**	**22518**	**10787**
EU-25	-7605	5057	11695	20199	19123	86695	18401	41947	16955	9749
Austria	3199	5008	2029	2302	1635	2277	1635	351	1635	351
Finland	4533	7150	2217	476	2121	5904	2121	455	2121	455
France	-941	-2434	-732	-157	-732	-98	-732	-98	-732	-157
Germany	-4044	3569	720	1785	720	959	720	155	720	155
Italy	-6392	-7693	-6808	-2699	-7514	-2820	-7699	-4962	-7568	-5895
Russian Federation	6002	15884	4411	947	9728	9374	6085	1306	4424	950
Spain	-1910	-3256	-2283	-479	-3452	-730	-3410	-732	-3139	-855
Sweden	8100	12833	27581	24090	38050	84361	38050	53535	36674	26615
United Kingdom	-7113	-7548	-6233	-1513	-7547	-2541	-7221	-2086	-7430	-5130
DEVELOPED, ALL	**173**	**18388**	**16648**	**15000**	**12864**	**-1543**	**22657**	**14009**	**19083**	**9904**
DEVELOPING, ALL	**-667**	**-11502**	**-12577**	**-10928**	**-8793**	**5616**	**-18586**	**-9937**	**-15013**	**-5832**
WORLD	**-494**	**6886**	**4071**	**4072**	**4071**	**4072**	**4071**	**4072**	**4071**	**4072**

[1]Observations derived from FAO (2009), projections obtained with the Global Forest Products Model.

Table 18—Observed and projected veneer and plywood prices (1997$/m³) for selected countries in the Global Forest Products Model[1]

	Observed		Scenario A1B		Scenario A2		Scenario B2		Scenario A1B-Low Fuelwood	
	1992	2006	2030	2060	2030	2060	2030	2060	2030	2060
AFRICA										
Egypt	545	571	488	621	441	452	447	462	456	386
Nigeria	524	422	408	565	353	381	360	393	371	310
South Africa	461	483	452	665	425	488	428	498	429	416
NORTH/CENTRAL AMERICA										
Canada	403	422	395	594	370	430	372	438	373	364
Mexico	444	465	431	631	393	458	398	468	405	390
United States of America	436	457	428	688	405	462	404	472	391	365
SOUTH AMERICA										
Argentina	465	487	424	569	376	406	381	406	389	331
Brazil	403	422	395	594	358	430	363	438	370	363
Chile	403	422	404	594	370	430	374	439	381	366
ASIA										
China	469	422	418	618	394	451	398	460	403	385
India	403	422	419	604	394	448	398	457	403	388
Indonesia	403	422	428	616	400	448	407	457	412	383
Japan	448	470	440	606	413	446	416	454	417	405
Korea, Republic of	465	487	456	588	429	429	432	448	433	397
Malaysia	403	422	411	610	381	433	385	443	389	364
OCEANIA										
Australia	440	461	431	595	387	444	389	440	397	368
New Zealand	403	422	410	601	389	436	391	443	394	378
EUROPE										
EU-25										
Austria	403	422	391	641	366	429	369	438	373	343
Finland	403	422	394	594	370	430	372	438	373	363
France	448	470	438	605	409	442	412	440	417	370
Germany	448	470	440	652	413	462	416	462	417	372
Italy	448	470	440	609	413	462	416	463	417	405
Russian Federation	403	422	410	595	381	432	385	441	391	368
Spain	448	470	436	667	408	449	408	461	417	373
Sweden	448	470	440	594	413	441	416	440	417	376
United Kingdom	448	470	440	648	413	475	416	485	417	405
DEVELOPED, ALL										
DEVELOPING, ALL										
WORLD	491	442	395	594	370	430	372	438	373	363

[1]Observations derived from FAO (2009), projections obtained with the Global Forest Products Model.

Table 19—Observed and projected particleboard prices (1997$/m³) for selected countries in the Global Forest Products Model[1]

	Observed		Scenario A1B		Scenario A2		Scenario B2		Scenario A1B-Low Fuelwood	
	1992	2006	2030	2060	2030	2060	2030	2060	2030	2060
AFRICA										
Egypt	235	319	300	415	270	271	274	280	280	215
Nigeria	235	304	353	446	317	289	322	299	329	228
South Africa	235	284	330	469	286	284	304	301	294	229
NORTH/CENTRAL AMERICA										
Canada	235	236	235	402	219	253	220	261	222	192
Mexico	268	270	269	439	253	281	253	294	256	222
United States of America	246	248	249	486	232	323	232	322	219	192
SOUTH AMERICA										
Argentina	276	236	249	404	223	265	226	264	231	201
Brazil	235	236	263	415	239	276	243	284	247	221
Chile	235	236	240	388	217	251	220	259	223	195
ASIA										
China	283	284	275	408	258	269	261	276	264	214
India	235	319	300	407	278	268	283	276	287	214
Indonesia	235	257	260	401	241	262	246	270	250	208
Japan	259	260	258	400	241	262	242	269	247	208
Korea, Republic of	264	265	265	402	248	253	248	271	251	218
Malaysia	235	236	239	393	221	255	223	262	226	197
OCEANIA										
Australia	256	257	258	391	227	262	229	259	234	198
New Zealand	235	236	242	397	224	257	226	263	229	207
EUROPE										
EU-25										
Austria	235	236	235	392	222	254	223	261	226	200
Finland	235	236	235	393	219	255	222	262	227	199
France	235	236	244	423	224	269	226	267	230	199
Germany	264	236	242	400	224	262	226	264	229	198
Italy	264	265	262	407	247	268	248	276	251	213
Russian Federation	235	294	279	391	255	253	259	260	263	198
Spain	266	267	260	400	247	262	246	269	251	213
Sweden	264	236	259	386	235	256	238	255	243	193
United Kingdom	264	265	265	421	248	272	248	279	251	216
DEVELOPED, ALL										
DEVELOPING, ALL										
WORLD	278	260	235	402	219	310	220	309	222	192

[1]Observations derived from FAO (2009), projections obtained with the Global Forest Products Model.

Table 20—Observed and projected fiberboard prices (1997$/m³) for selected countries in the Global Forest Products Model[1]

	Observed		Scenario A1B		Scenario A2		Scenario B2		Scenario A1B-Low Fuelwood	
	1992	2006	2030	2060	2030	2060	2030	2060	2030	2060
AFRICA										
Egypt	376	455	397	501	364	357	369	366	376	301
Nigeria	391	474	426	600	404	436	406	447	413	370
South Africa	301	421	379	538	358	389	360	398	366	328
NORTH/CENTRAL AMERICA										
Canada	301	364	328	476	308	337	310	346	315	282
Mexico	313	379	342	490	322	351	324	360	329	296
United States of America	301	383	343	555	325	355	327	404	316	280
SOUTH AMERICA										
Argentina	301	364	335	484	308	345	310	346	315	282
Brazil	301	364	334	476	308	337	310	346	315	283
Chile	301	364	333	476	309	338	312	346	317	283
ASIA										
China	360	364	352	475	336	336	338	344	342	282
India	301	493	406	490	384	352	388	360	392	298
Indonesia	301	364	343	490	324	352	329	359	333	298
Japan	322	390	346	483	331	345	331	353	337	292
Korea, Republic of	338	409	360	485	343	337	346	354	350	298
Malaysia	376	364	333	476	314	337	316	346	320	284
OCEANIA										
Australia	329	364	335	476	308	347	310	345	315	282
New Zealand	301	364	328	478	311	340	313	346	315	291
EUROPE										
EU-25										
Austria	301	364	326	524	308	342	310	352	315	280
Finland	301	409	349	474	332	336	335	344	340	282
France	301	364	332	484	311	346	314	346	318	285
Germany	338	364	330	483	313	346	315	348	318	283
Italy	338	409	358	491	343	352	344	359	348	297
Russian Federation	301	455	381	475	358	338	361	345	366	283
Spain	301	409	333	494	319	349	319	356	324	298
Sweden	338	409	363	474	340	344	343	343	348	281
United Kingdom	338	409	367	512	345	356	345	364	351	295
DEVELOPED, ALL										
DEVELOPING, ALL										
WORLD	366	328	328	476	308	337	310	346	315	282

[1]Observations derived from FAO (2009), projections obtained with the Global Forest Products Model.

Table 21—Observed and projected veneer and plywood consumption (thousand m³) for world regions and selected countries in the Global Forest Products Model[1]

	Observed		Scenario A1B		Scenario A2		Scenario B2		Scenario A1B-Low Fuelwood	
	1992	2006	2030	2060	2030	2060	2030	2060	2030	2060
AFRICA	**930**	**737**	**1168**	**1521**	**849**	**1024**	**980**	**1440**	**1188**	**1765**
Egypt	157	145	249	328	187	239	200	281	254	377
Nigeria	75	55	102	146	75	97	89	151	105	172
South Africa	84	96	102	102	74	67	95	108	104	117
NORTH/CENTRAL AMERICA	**19864**	**22723**	**23263**	**19962**	**22372**	**20400**	**21759**	**18336**	**23834**	**24047**
Canada	2020	1987	1879	1589	1821	1565	1803	1443	1910	1841
Mexico	337	944	1168	1165	866	817	925	982	1188	1346
United States of America	17305	19552	19898	16882	19443	17772	18767	15609	20412	20484
SOUTH AMERICA	**1825**	**643**	**1657**	**1657**	**1254**	**1230**	**1339**	**1456**	**1689**	**1923**
Argentina	101	107	117	115	88	83	93	97	120	134
Brazil	1088	184	877	866	652	614	692	718	894	1003
Chile	55	125	237	230	186	185	203	227	242	266
ASIA	**21274**	**37242**	**54105**	**56306**	**40726**	**41060**	**46528**	**46041**	**54761**	**64665**
China	5469	20987	34078	36410	24866	26754	29067	29859	34460	41993
India	239	2108	3672	4612	2450	2638	3116	3693	3713	5270
Indonesia	386	817	1520	1774	1041	1084	1234	1288	1537	2046
Japan	9917	8348	7399	5924	7138	5708	6951	5216	7513	6685
Korea, Republic of	1871	1798	2463	2140	1695	1276	2073	1621	2501	2404
Malaysia	849	550	823	774	588	515	695	609	836	904
OCEANIA	**356**	**745**	**723**	**629**	**705**	**631**	**709**	**583**	**736**	**725**
Australia	217	370	372	325	367	325	363	293	381	375
New Zealand	65	352	323	279	319	291	323	272	326	321
EUROPE	**8702**	**8707**	**9075**	**7964**	**7906**	**6908**	**8202**	**7232**	**9205**	**9214**
EU-25	6864	7063	6995	5921	6460	5457	6505	5462	7097	6855
Austria	140	7	41	31	40	31	40	30	42	38
Finland	136	272	217	166	211	164	211	162	220	193
France	768	651	610	510	594	499	574	463	619	590
Germany	1726	1228	1109	880	1074	861	1058	811	1127	1042
Italy	1165	671	716	573	692	543	676	512	727	648
Russian Federation	1141	1083	1435	1443	947	987	1122	1182	1455	1666
Spain	179	501	472	383	460	383	451	359	478	457
Sweden	164	237	215	171	209	166	215	173	219	196
United Kingdom	1420	1360	1345	1123	1304	1098	1268	1025	1366	1293
DEVELOPED, ALL	**38406**	**39686**	**39542**	**33593**	**37406**	**32996**	**36902**	**30642**	**40349**	**39642**
DEVELOPING, ALL	**14546**	**31111**	**50450**	**54446**	**36405**	**38257**	**42615**	**44445**	**51063**	**62698**
WORLD	**52952**	**70797**	**89992**	**88039**	**73811**	**71253**	**79517**	**75087**	**91413**	**102340**

[1]Observations derived from FAO (2009), projections obtained with the Global Forest Products Model.

Table 22—Observed and projected particleboard consumption (thousand m³) by world region and country in the Global Forest Products Model[1]

	Observed		Scenario A1B		Scenario A2		Scenario B2		Scenario A1B-Low Fuelwood	
	1992	2006	2030	2060	2030	2060	2030	2060	2030	2060
AFRICA	613	1146	1965	3167	1290	1856	1613	3006	2012	3880
Egypt	41	15	31	52	21	34	23	43	31	63
Nigeria	40	42	106	213	68	122	87	220	108	259
South Africa	277	582	790	970	528	572	718	1068	817	1201
NORTH/CENTRAL AMERICA	17374	36049	40900	38493	39396	39533	37750	34031	42325	51072
Canada	1667	3625	3420	3242	3266	3223	3231	2892	3476	4061
Mexico	440	176	410	486	272	308	298	390	416	597
United States of America	15160	32112	36807	34414	35677	35767	34019	30439	38164	45986
SOUTH AMERICA	1370	4331	6738	8254	4607	5499	5007	6796	6870	10004
Argentina	188	421	632	706	430	459	463	563	646	872
Brazil	634	2372	3826	4567	2564	2892	2776	3549	3896	5518
Chile	210	497	707	807	509	608	571	800	722	993
ASIA	5384	18245	31739	41755	22510	29784	26161	33559	32109	50695
China	1383	9222	17024	22823	11185	15211	13744	17578	17215	27678
India	58	101	227	383	133	184	182	287	230	462
Indonesia	228	207	471	694	285	363	357	456	476	845
Japan	1288	1691	1730	1520	1642	1457	1587	1294	1752	1852
Korea, Republic of	727	1731	2691	2579	1635	1326	2138	1812	2731	3101
Malaysia	119	0	28	30	18	18	22	22	28	37
OCEANIA	741	1178	1435	1426	1394	1425	1384	1256	1473	1745
Australia	646	1034	1241	1236	1216	1242	1198	1082	1277	1514
New Zealand	92	137	157	154	155	164	158	150	160	188
EUROPE	30988	46375	58468	59764	46153	46526	50344	53187	59292	72281
EU-25	23743	36838	44287	42319	37645	35555	39490	38099	44899	50915
Austria	877	930	940	809	896	777	895	759	950	994
Finland	273	270	281	237	271	234	270	231	284	291
France	2641	3110	3611	3242	3481	3206	3330	2912	3673	4079
Germany	8279	9196	9456	8299	9050	7996	8872	7373	9609	10278
Italy	2652	3781	3936	3466	3738	3287	3631	3020	3985	4211
Russian Federation	4507	5209	8154	10202	4703	6204	5882	7862	8287	12447
Spain	1912	3548	3864	3618	3694	3507	3601	3233	3901	4374
Sweden	598	463	774	676	748	654	774	689	788	831
United Kingdom	2829	3555	4058	3837	3879	3767	3746	3441	4119	4697
DEVELOPED, ALL	50205	86471	104407	103807	89684	90480	92686	92529	106760	130169
DEVELOPING, ALL	6265	20853	36838	49052	25665	34141	29573	39305	37321	59508
WORLD	56470	107324	141245	152858	115349	124622	122259	131834	144081	189677

[1]Observations derived from FAO (2009), projections obtained with the Global Forest Products Model.

Table 23—Observed and projected fiberboard consumption (thousand m³) for world regions and selected countries in the Global Forest Products Model[1]

	Observed		Scenario A1B		Scenario A2		Scenario B2		Scenario A1B-Low Fuelwood	
	1992	2006	2030	2060	2030	2060	2030	2060	2030	2060
AFRICA	177	907	1357	1817	1051	1435	1186	1843	1380	2298
Egypt	5	232	381	548	301	451	319	516	390	692
Nigeria	16	40	87	131	66	98	77	142	89	165
South Africa	49	320	374	414	288	312	354	466	380	523
NORTH/CENTRAL AMERICA	7188	12909	14807	13993	14338	15746	14018	13865	15307	19211
Canada	545	1349	1358	1303	1338	1397	1326	1295	1382	1673
Mexico	42	916	1159	1280	901	1022	954	1189	1178	1627
United States of America	6498	10408	11919	10990	11799	12964	11417	10948	12366	15370
SOUTH AMERICA	645	3577	4194	4637	3340	3882	3532	4465	4297	5921
Argentina	84	234	399	422	317	346	332	394	411	546
Brazil	416	1921	2451	2710	1927	2192	2027	2488	2516	3468
Chile	98	624	658	710	541	639	581	759	673	908
ASIA	4063	33880	52872	62871	41398	52909	46528	57711	53600	80370
China	1752	23962	37934	45859	29183	38323	33314	41888	38453	58647
India	47	276	469	684	336	459	411	608	477	859
Indonesia	8	33	230	290	168	206	194	237	233	367
Japan	1055	936	1533	1398	1493	1471	1462	1356	1551	1778
Korea, Republic of	415	2068	2935	2872	2146	2028	2545	2458	2974	3613
Malaysia	20	1401	2221	2344	1681	1787	1936	2053	2262	3001
OCEANIA	268	747	847	827	842	895	842	832	868	1056
Australia	100	533	571	558	572	603	566	551	587	715
New Zealand	157	199	250	242	250	272	253	256	254	308
EUROPE	5686	18080	20735	21020	18180	19710	19122	21212	21071	26956
EU-25	3453	14743	16259	15918	14879	15580	15299	16231	16517	20431
Austria	67	575	480	408	472	450	471	439	487	553
Finland	101	248	253	231	250	248	248	245	256	295
France	257	937	903	837	893	892	867	838	921	1078
Germany	729	3789	3625	3271	3559	3451	3510	3270	3691	4226
Italy	261	1537	1648	1520	1608	1587	1576	1496	1671	1927
Russian Federation	1518	1672	2319	2754	1641	2152	1895	2498	2360	3495
Spain	335	1401	1180	1087	1158	1161	1139	1096	1195	1387
Sweden	174	299	367	342	363	359	370	372	374	436
United Kingdom	493	1706	1874	1803	1848	1944	1807	1825	1912	2340
DEVELOPED, ALL	14198	32193	37328	36650	34345	37295	35005	36819	38191	48240
DEVELOPING, ALL	3829	37907	57483	68515	44803	57282	50223	63108	58333	87570
WORLD	18027	70100	94811	105165	79148	94577	85228	99927	96524	135811

[1]Observations derived from FAO (2009), projections obtained with the Global Forest Products Model.

Table 24—Observed and projected veneer and plywood net trade (thousand m³) for world regions and selected countries in the Global Forest Products Model[1]

	Observed		Scenario A1B		Scenario A2		Scenario B2		Scenario A1B-Low Fuelwood	
	1992	2006	2030	2060	2030	2060	2030	2060	2030	2060
AFRICA	-82	33	288	1051	606	1308	532	1194	305	1020
Egypt	-122	-120	-35	-7	-35	-7	-35	-7	-35	-7
Nigeria	-3	0	0	0	0	0	0	0	0	0
South Africa	-37	-58	-102	-101	-74	-66	-95	-107	-104	-116
NORTH/CENTRAL AMERICA	-57	-6635	-2648	-1127	-5736	-17115	-4104	-12640	-372	-366
Canada	319	265	3295	2455	2583	902	2920	3253	1883	380
Mexico	-167	-810	-200	-54	-193	-39	-192	-39	-200	-40
United States of America	-106	-5901	-5487	-3260	-7933	-17772	-6623	-15609	-1795	-385
SOUTH AMERICA	450	3646	8173	2803	10254	15144	10028	11569	9840	10106
Argentina	-30	-16	-1	0	-1	1	-1	2	-1	5
Brazil	446	2860	7631	1843	9320	13889	9320	10250	9320	9478
Chile	30	679	260	59	598	129	390	79	262	53
ASIA	3135	7344	-3322	-2014	-3613	-2671	-4048	-2673	-5871	-7690
China	-3342	7112	1302	262	1302	262	1302	262	1302	262
India	10	22	9	2	9	2	9	2	9	2
Indonesia	9769	2995	1163	234	1135	229	1162	234	1164	235
Japan	-3689	-5034	-4042	-815	-4819	-1629	-4646	-1370	-5755	-4743
Korea, Republic of	-923	-1285	-1140	-227	-1006	-311	-1398	-373	-1727	-1148
Malaysia	2451	4883	1348	272	1329	268	1337	269	1348	272
OCEANIA	-45	-183	-50	-42	-42	-18	-45	-18	-51	-40
Australia	-81	-225	-56	-44	-56	-11	-56	-11	-56	-11
New Zealand	44	52	24	19	24	3	24	5	24	-9
EUROPE	-2877	-1282	-863	907	109	4928	-786	4145	-2276	-1453
EU-25	-3050	-2866	-1499	-203	-587	3609	-1464	2800	-2899	-2256
Austria	35	171	206	72	287	1505	218	1090	144	717
Finland	347	1143	1404	1376	2269	3382	1464	2479	711	158
France	-226	-220	-60	-28	-61	-12	-60	-12	-75	-38
Germany	-878	-993	-627	-236	-704	-338	-713	-186	-778	-400
Italy	-255	-337	-309	-66	-494	-304	-486	-212	-516	-602
Russian Federation	219	1531	404	81	441	89	439	89	404	81
Spain	-9	-33	-8	-32	-7	-2	-7	-2	-68	-55
Sweden	-96	-145	-81	-16	-47	-23	-70	-19	-117	-89
United Kingdom	-1413	-1360	-1345	-1123	-1304	-1098	-1268	-1025	-1366	-1293
DEVELOPED, ALL	-6414	-12341	-7517	-1140	-10360	-13860	-9509	-9998	-8368	-6695
DEVELOPING, ALL	6938	15264	9093	2717	11937	15437	11087	11576	9944	8273
WORLD	524	2923	1577	1577	1577	1576	1577	1578	1577	1578

[1]Observations derived from FAO (2009), projections obtained with the Global Forest Products Model.

Table 25—Observed and projected particleboard net trade (thousand m³) for world regions and selected countries in the Global Forest Products Model[1]

	Observed		Scenario A1B		Scenario A2		Scenario B2		Scenario A1B-Low Fuelwood	
	1992	2006	2030	2060	2030	2060	2030	2060	2030	2060
AFRICA	**-2**	**-196**	**-429**	**-1060**	**-350**	**-208**	**-374**	**-429**	**-435**	**-456**
Egypt	0	-9	-1	0	-1	0	-1	0	-1	0
Nigeria	0	-2	-10	-19	-10	-5	-10	-9	-10	-9
South Africa	19	-60	-192	-798	-192	-124	-192	-281	-192	-246
NORTH/CENTRAL AMERICA	**402**	**-943**	**6512**	**3743**	**3679**	**-1217**	**5980**	**917**	**8661**	**10662**
Canada	1890	8909	15960	12844	13897	33957	11238	27504	11821	10843
Mexico	-26	-76	-384	-253	-219	-47	-266	-134	-388	-578
United States of America	-1453	-9737	-8918	-8683	-9902	-35029	-4882	-26314	-2622	659
SOUTH AMERICA	**21**	**198**	**-92**	**-171**	**366**	**1016**	**288**	**807**	**-62**	**-139**
Argentina	-10	164	29	12	29	31	29	23	29	12
Brazil	26	128	4	5	4	11	4	11	4	5
Chile	24	25	47	37	439	1076	370	910	76	79
ASIA	**-667**	**-1439**	**-3968**	**-1648**	**-2304**	**-433**	**-3589**	**-1009**	**-4829**	**-3030**
China	-141	-706	-167	-11	-168	0	-163	1	-167	-11
India	2	-77	-34	-4	-20	-2	-29	-3	-34	-4
Indonesia	122	-82	-66	-12	-17	6	-70	-10	-57	-49
Japan	-125	-446	-326	-36	-370	-40	-395	-44	-698	-88
Korea, Republic of	-451	-954	-1551	-272	-799	-114	-1464	-255	-1885	-1434
Malaysia	31	453	91	132	76	142	77	132	84	43
OCEANIA	**63**	**62**	**-33**	**-26**	**-10**	**10**	**-15**	**6**	**-22**	**-34**
Australia	-4	-32	-17	-18	-7	3	-7	3	-7	0
New Zealand	70	101	21	28	20	27	20	28	21	9
EUROPE	**-1879**	**3595**	**-1240**	**-89**	**-630**	**1582**	**-1542**	**459**	**-2563**	**-6252**
EU-25	-2302	4539	-609	416	-292	1448	-999	730	-1827	-5364
Austria	729	1495	442	909	280	663	280	678	284	132
Finland	81	170	30	38	43	128	30	96	30	15
France	27	1650	221	127	221	337	221	337	221	127
Germany	-828	1644	294	758	294	553	294	758	294	204
Italy	-387	-56	-37	18	-171	47	-638	-28	-307	-39
Russian Federation	15	-492	-66	13	-66	34	-66	22	-66	6
Spain	-232	-232	-50	39	-97	53	-154	27	-50	15
Sweden	-17	78	-45	26	-45	39	-45	39	-45	9
United Kingdom	-1092	-929	-982	-105	-944	-109	-804	-73	-1468	-1311
DEVELOPED, ALL	**-1511**	**1634**	**4071**	**2208**	**2132**	**11**	**3255**	**710**	**4529**	**4017**
DEVELOPING, ALL	**-551**	**-357**	**-3321**	**-1458**	**-1381**	**740**	**-2506**	**41**	**-3779**	**-3267**
WORLD	**-2062**	**1277**	**750**	**750**	**750**	**750**	**750**	**751**	**750**	**750**

[1]Observations derived from FAO (2009), projections obtained with the Global Forest Products Model.

Table 26—Observed and projected fiberboard net trade (thousand m³) for world regions and selected countries in the Global Forest Products Model[1]

	Observed		Scenario A1B		Scenario A2		Scenario B2		Scenario A1B-Low Fuelwood	
	1992	2006	2030	2060	2030	2060	2030	2060	2030	2060
AFRICA	**-83**	**-662**	**-912**	**-962**	**-675**	**-715**	**-790**	**-1000**	**-914**	**-1207**
Egypt	-2	-214	-104	-16	-72	-11	-78	-12	-102	-16
Nigeria	-16	-40	-87	-131	-66	-98	-77	-142	-89	-165
South Africa	8	-162	-374	-413	-288	-311	-354	-466	-380	-522
NORTH/CENTRAL AMERICA	**403**	**-2785**	**142**	**949**	**-3996**	**-12433**	**-998**	**-3146**	**-53**	**106**
Canada	127	598	2244	3000	784	1744	1058	3173	2015	1363
Mexico	-7	-762	-1066	-1279	-727	-1000	-811	-1182	-1028	-1598
United States of America	301	-2475	-817	-523	-3877	-12964	-1056	-4884	-817	655
SOUTH AMERICA	**350**	**1249**	**603**	**15**	**2729**	**1284**	**1934**	**455**	**1184**	**514**
Argentina	12	421	303	47	759	128	562	114	490	290
Brazil	282	373	254	43	1775	1186	1252	381	650	310
Chile	73	512	184	29	282	44	216	45	199	31
ASIA	**-834**	**-32**	**-2911**	**-2796**	**-2491**	**-2592**	**-2627**	**-2901**	**-2988**	**-4091**
China	-270	740	-49	138	-49	44	-49	44	-49	44
India	1	-146	-23	-4	-23	-4	-23	-4	-23	-4
Indonesia	45	394	79	12	75	12	77	12	80	13
Japan	-126	-41	-162	-25	-336	-53	-274	-43	-176	-27
Korea, Republic of	-61	-420	-88	-14	-91	-10	-91	-14	-88	-14
Malaysia	-10	1223	281	387	246	78	256	140	278	43
OCEANIA	**360**	**1002**	**667**	**434**	**382**	**43**	**502**	**104**	**894**	**671**
Australia	-1	309	302	83	181	28	293	92	549	646
New Zealand	372	708	391	378	222	35	233	36	371	58
EUROPE	**-55**	**1121**	**1742**	**1692**	**3382**	**13744**	**1310**	**5819**	**1208**	**3338**
EU-25	-106	1458	1261	1205	2920	11844	1081	4373	930	3220
Austria	26	406	328	79	181	548	201	294	267	1601
Finland	0	-118	-19	-1	-19	-1	-19	-1	-19	-1
France	168	453	185	29	162	25	161	66	195	31
Germany	-141	2144	977	829	524	82	597	199	859	134
Italy	-11	-326	-82	-13	-83	-13	-82	-13	-82	-13
Russian Federation	47	-220	-32	6	-32	-5	-32	6	-32	-5
Spain	65	-103	52	8	52	8	52	8	52	8
Sweden	-11	-145	-43	-5	-43	-7	-44	-5	-43	-5
United Kingdom	-337	-834	-221	-35	-217	-34	-222	-35	-221	-35
DEVELOPED, ALL	**528**	**-287**	**2931**	**3848**	**-220**	**1953**	**868**	**3379**	**2367**	**5082**
DEVELOPING, ALL	**-387**	**180**	**-3600**	**-4517**	**-448**	**-2622**	**-1537**	**-4048**	**-3036**	**-5751**
WORLD	**141**	**-107**	**-669**	**-669**	**-668**	**-669**	**-669**	**-669**	**-669**	**-669**

[1]Observations derived from FAO (2009), projections obtained with the Global Forest Products Model.

Table 27—Observed and projected mechanical pulp prices (1997$/mt) for selected countries in the Global Forest Products Model[1]

	Observed		Scenario A1B		Scenario A2		Scenario B2		Scenario A1B-Low Fuelwood	
	1992	2006	2030	2060	2030	2060	2030	2060	2030	2060
AFRICA										
Egypt	337	442	378	680	331	396	337	412	345	289
Nigeria	330	463	397	719	379	428	394	443	403	326
South Africa	337	390	436	736	375	419	400	448	385	309
NORTH/CENTRAL AMERICA										
Canada	337	390	343	633	318	361	320	376	324	255
Mexico	382	442	403	703	366	417	371	431	378	302
United States of America	364	421	360	792	337	512	336	501	318	250
SOUTH AMERICA										
Argentina	390	390	358	628	313	357	318	355	325	230
Brazil	337	451	376	657	337	386	342	401	349	278
Chile	337	455	379	632	346	361	349	376	355	254
ASIA										
China	364	421	371	671	345	397	348	412	354	288
India	364	1155	368	675	342	398	345	412	349	301
Indonesia	364	421	368	665	342	394	346	409	352	287
Japan	364	421	358	654	332	383	334	398	344	277
Korea, Republic of	364	421	362	656	338	365	342	399	347	288
Malaysia	337	421	363	643	331	370	336	386	343	265
OCEANIA										
Australia	337	421	381	636	335	385	337	379	344	258
New Zealand	337	390	339	646	313	369	316	383	320	272
EUROPE										
EU-25										
Austria	364	421	360	758	332	403	335	422	342	266
Finland	337	390	342	631	314	362	319	376	328	255
France	364	421	366	654	333	383	337	380	343	261
Germany	364	421	354	702	325	402	329	407	333	264
Italy	364	421	362	669	340	396	342	411	346	288
Russian Federation	337	390	349	633	315	362	320	376	326	254
Spain	337	421	377	817	347	442	347	462	357	308
Sweden	337	390	359	631	327	374	332	374	338	254
United Kingdom	**364**	**421**	**378**	**671**	**348**	**397**	**348**	**411**	**356**	**288**
DEVELOPED, ALL										
DEVELOPING, ALL										
WORLD	**406**	**349**	**339**	**646**	**313**	**369**	**316**	**383**	**320**	**272**

[1]Observations derived from FAO (2009), projections obtained with the Global Forest Products Model.

Table 28—Observed and projected chemical pulp prices (1997$/mt) for selected countries in the Global Forest Products Model[1]

	Observed		Scenario A1B		Scenario A2		Scenario B2		Scenario A1B-Low Fuelwood	
	1992	2006	2030	2060	2030	2060	2030	2060	2030	2060
AFRICA										
Egypt	532	598	565	855	521	604	525	617	536	499
Nigeria	543	592	665	881	598	603	606	624	619	495
South Africa	469	512	585	871	521	585	548	612	533	488
NORTH/CENTRAL AMERICA										
Canada	469	512	480	778	449	537	451	549	457	439
Mexico	507	553	539	820	494	577	500	589	508	476
United States of America	469	553	526	920	495	666	495	657	471	436
SOUTH AMERICA										
Argentina	469	512	508	798	456	555	461	554	470	442
Brazil	469	512	500	779	456	537	462	550	471	440
Chile	469	512	501	779	460	537	466	550	472	441
ASIA										
China	507	553	539	818	496	577	500	589	511	476
India	507	553	539	818	496	577	501	589	514	476
Indonesia	507	512	539	809	491	561	502	575	510	465
Japan	507	553	527	796	496	554	500	567	511	459
Korea, Republic of	507	553	539	800	496	553	500	589	511	476
Malaysia	507	553	539	797	496	546	500	564	511	456
OCEANIA										
Australia	507	553	521	778	459	553	463	548	472	441
New Zealand	469	512	502	789	471	542	475	552	480	454
EUROPE										
EU-25										
Austria	507	553	501	778	467	533	472	546	480	437
Finland	469	512	478	778	442	537	449	549	460	438
France	507	553	531	798	489	554	495	551	501	446
Germany	507	553	539	818	496	577	500	586	510	438
Italy	507	553	539	818	496	577	500	589	511	476
Russian Federation	469	512	504	779	465	537	470	550	478	440
Spain	469	512	495	793	458	551	459	564	471	465
Sweden	469	512	499	778	459	547	464	549	472	437
United Kingdom	508	638	539	818	496	577	500	589	511	476
DEVELOPED, ALL										
DEVELOPING, ALL										
WORLD	565	481	499	778	456	537	460	549	471	436

[1]Observations derived from FAO (2009), projections obtained with the Global Forest Products Model.

Table 29—Observed and projected other fiber pulp prices (1997$/mt) for selected countries in the Global Forest Products Model[1]

	Observed		Scenario A1B		Scenario A2		Scenario B2		Scenario A1B-Low Fuelwood	
	1992	2006	2030	2060	2030	2060	2030	2060	2030	2060
AFRICA										
Egypt	1083	1247	1135	1089	989	895	1051	937	1110	967
Nigeria										
South Africa	920	1062	979	919	826	740	883	779	980	806
NORTH/CENTRAL AMERICA										
Canada	994	1147	1058	919	826	740	915	779	1059	806
Mexico	920	1147	979	919	829	740	883	779	980	806
United States of America	920	1062	979	919	826	740	883	779	980	806
SOUTH AMERICA										
Argentina	920	1227	1132	966	856	569	931	703	1133	949
Brazil	920	1147	979	919	826	740	883	779	980	806
Chile										
ASIA										
China	994	1147	1058	998	905	819	962	858	1059	885
India	994	1148	1004	839	826	611	909	713	1004	816
Indonesia	921	1062	979	919	826	740	883	779	980	806
Japan	994	1147	1058	998	905	819	962	858	1059	885
Korea, Republic of			1058	998	905	819	962	858	1059	885
Malaysia	920	1147	1058	998	905	819	962	858	1059	885
OCEANIA										
Australia	920		1058	998	905	819	962	858	1059	885
New Zealand										
EUROPE										
EU-25										
Austria	921		1058	998	905	819	962	858	1059	885
Finland			1058	998	905	819	962	858	1059	885
France	994	1062	979	919	826	740	883	779	980	806
Germany	994		1058	998	905	819	962	858	1059	885
Italy	994	1147	1056	658	905	589	960	532	1059	709
Russian Federation	920		1143	1079	980	887	1041	928	1144	958
Spain	920	1062	979	919	826	740	883	779	980	806
Sweden			1058	998	905	819	962	858	1059	885
United Kingdom			1058	998	905	819	962	858	1059	885
DEVELOPED, ALL										
DEVELOPING, ALL										
WORLD	1096	979	979	919	826	740	883	779	980	806

[1]Observations derived from FAO (2009), projections obtained with the Global Forest Products Model.

Table 30—Observed and projected waste paper prices (1997$/mt) for selected countries in the Global Forest Products Model[1]

	Observed		Scenario A1B		Scenario A2		Scenario B2		Scenario A1B-Low Fuelwood	
	1992	2006	2030	2060	2030	2060	2030	2060	2030	2060
AFRICA										
Egypt	150	162	184	298	190	195	178	229	174	291
Nigeria	150	0	108	298	101	195	106	229	109	309
South Africa	138	124	138	250	105	154	130	186	138	260
NORTH/CENTRAL AMERICA										
Canada	138	149	178	275	150	179	157	211	180	285
Mexico	138	149	178	269	150	179	157	210	180	260
United States of America	115	124	153	250	125	154	132	186	155	260
SOUTH AMERICA										
Argentina	148	159	190	288	161	190	168	223	192	298
Brazil	138	149	209	275	150	179	166	211	210	285
Chile	149	161	192	296	162	193	170	227	194	306
ASIA										
China	138	149	178	250	139	154	154	186	180	260
India	138	140	178	275	150	179	157	211	180	285
Indonesia	126	149	178	256	150	154	157	186	180	263
Japan	138	124	153	250	125	154	132	186	155	260
Korea, Republic of	138	149	159	272	138	179	136	209	155	260
Malaysia	115	149	178	275	150	179	157	211	181	285
OCEANIA										
Australia	115	124	153	250	127	154	132	186	155	260
New Zealand	115	124	175	250	130	154	144	186	162	267
EUROPE										
EU-25										
Austria	138	149	178	275	150	179	157	211	180	285
Finland	138	124	178	275	150	179	157	211	180	285
France	138	124	153	250	125	154	132	186	155	260
Germany	115	124	173	250	134	154	143	187	155	285
Italy	138	124	153	250	132	154	132	186	155	260
Russian Federation	115	124	153	250	125	154	132	186	155	260
Spain	138	149	178	250	150	179	157	186	180	260
Sweden	138	149	178	275	150	179	157	211	180	285
United Kingdom	115	124	153	250	125	154	132	186	155	260
DEVELOPED, ALL										
DEVELOPING, ALL										
WORLD	**138**	**119**	**153**	**250**	**125**	**154**	**132**	**186**	**155**	**260**

[1]Observations derived from FAO (2009), projections obtained with the Global Forest Products Model.

Table 31—Observed and projected mechanical pulp consumption (thousand mt) for world regions and selected countries in the Global Forest Products Model[1]

	Observed		Scenario A1B		Scenario A2		Scenario B2		Scenario A1B-Low Fuelwood	
	1992	2006	2030	2060	2030	2060	2030	2060	2030	2060
AFRICA	352	465	1041	1451	741	919	919	1413	1048	1533
Egypt	8	2	15	85	17	80	12	88	16	62
Nigeria	0	16	48	113	40	73	43	120	48	150
South Africa	285	348	708	750	505	457	648	772	713	801
NORTH/CENTRAL AMERICA	15968	15389	19814	12772	16600	10157	17768	11301	18655	17426
Canada	9968	11262	15109	8092	12146	6082	13272	7397	13662	12392
Mexico	56	50	398	1297	335	1022	321	1020	395	1060
United States of America	5935	4042	4176	2920	4014	2715	4066	2470	4470	3493
SOUTH AMERICA	671	1122	1411	1343	1144	946	1165	1115	1358	1399
Argentina	39	66	216	364	148	236	159	279	217	378
Brazil	412	500	564	526	423	351	450	414	566	564
Chile	179	515	499	168	474	146	448	159	443	161
ASIA	3491	4330	12408	31675	9562	21912	10486	23699	12324	28370
China	512	874	5155	17216	3722	11797	4264	12911	5160	13701
India	185	4	278	1304	195	661	210	884	279	1123
Indonesia	91	455	672	1381	462	769	540	920	673	1428
Japan	2235	1677	2840	4918	2704	4575	2627	4113	2848	5208
Korea, Republic of	165	883	1571	2399	1195	1501	1342	1737	1503	2375
Malaysia	12	11	92	504	62	338	74	372	89	543
OCEANIA	823	975	1289	1109	1095	1030	1121	927	1189	1200
Australia	459	377	759	987	712	952	698	845	706	1092
New Zealand	364	595	524	116	379	75	418	79	477	103
EUROPE	13073	20638	24668	24738	20337	21764	21506	21449	23697	30281
EU-25	10206	17153	21335	22140	17676	19699	18607	19162	20369	27376
Austria	539	855	888	557	681	464	740	489	811	690
Finland	3140	6016	6196	2671	4505	2417	5077	2472	5672	6188
France	957	648	1565	2838	1477	2575	1446	2506	1510	3024
Germany	1554	2967	4952	5720	4290	5429	4492	5142	4835	6733
Italy	451	483	950	1782	900	1635	885	1522	939	1852
Russian Federation	1366	1300	1206	641	820	410	952	482	1211	634
Spain	102	167	609	1458	584	1357	565	1269	593	1538
Sweden	2349	3386	2037	483	1636	198	1790	250	1946	493
United Kingdom	626	424	1313	3160	1235	2916	1182	2674	1288	3314
DEVELOPED, ALL	32345	38976	48875	42691	40862	36727	43309	37247	46662	53545
DEVELOPING, ALL	2032	3943	11755	30397	8617	20001	9656	22656	11609	26664
WORLD	34377	42919	60630	73088	49479	56728	52965	59903	58270	80209

[1]Observations derived from FAO (2009), projections obtained with the Global Forest Products Model.

Table 32—Observed and projected chemical pulp consumption (thousand mt) for world regions and selected countries in the Global Forest Products Model[1]

	Observed		Scenario A1B		Scenario A2		Scenario B2		Scenario A1B-Low Fuelwood	
	1992	2006	2030	2060	2030	2060	2030	2060	2030	2060
AFRICA	**1339**	**1552**	**1981**	**2777**	**1510**	**1778**	**1752**	**2633**	**1995**	**2877**
Egypt	53	59	103	273	157	241	103	270	109	216
Nigeria	9	15	58	304	55	194	58	318	59	372
South Africa	966	1133	1002	879	713	533	917	893	1009	920
NORTH/CENTRAL AMERICA	**55496**	**50655**	**46891**	**30306**	**43794**	**27305**	**44299**	**25465**	**51103**	**36270**
Canada	4172	3106	5138	4242	3942	2872	4431	3588	4935	6171
Mexico	649	1208	1293	1398	1156	1150	1140	1133	1276	1162
United States of America	50641	46267	40313	24470	38581	23142	38603	20567	44747	28735
SOUTH AMERICA	**4605**	**6295**	**7788**	**6073**	**5810**	**4237**	**6189**	**4966**	**7811**	**6447**
Argentina	554	505	1016	1011	724	677	772	792	1022	1054
Brazil	3138	4809	5502	3822	4101	2605	4364	3047	5526	4126
Chile	181	333	302	228	248	176	258	213	292	232
ASIA	**18965**	**30059**	**38388**	**40041**	**30811**	**28323**	**33190**	**30682**	**38358**	**37181**
China	2490	9415	14476	17478	11105	12364	12419	13544	14527	14249
India	783	391	1356	1998	917	1028	1085	1409	1357	1849
Indonesia	1160	2362	2843	2669	2029	1519	2318	1806	2854	2769
Japan	11646	11247	10329	7725	9809	7105	9530	6391	10353	8004
Korea, Republic of	1679	2993	2772	2046	2026	1146	2373	1469	2746	2127
Malaysia	90	302	461	901	319	621	375	681	448	989
OCEANIA	**1071**	**1403**	**1958**	**1447**	**1755**	**1331**	**1751**	**1228**	**1780**	**1604**
Australia	763	1164	1596	1247	1493	1190	1461	1080	1450	1400
New Zealand	308	233	352	189	254	133	282	140	321	193
EUROPE	**31178**	**39221**	**41853**	**30775**	**34207**	**25291**	**36227**	**26615**	**40908**	**36386**
EU-25	25791	33932	35680	25444	29920	21694	31231	22238	34721	30783
Austria	1271	1675	1381	531	1012	442	1111	465	1274	660
Finland	4248	5678	6340	3018	4531	2696	5096	2825	5941	6875
France	3407	3125	3655	3017	3434	2712	3378	2661	3485	3190
Germany	4259	5212	5224	3714	4610	3501	4695	3286	5225	4226
Italy	2465	3507	3454	2695	3279	2460	3217	2291	3434	2786
Russian Federation	4025	3404	3880	3095	2571	1982	3014	2371	3897	3217
Spain	1321	1798	2118	1764	2030	1636	1968	1531	2079	1860
Sweden	4595	6018	3813	1220	3087	787	3369	877	3677	1227
United Kingdom	1856	1184	2477	2782	2316	2583	2229	2374	2441	2940
DEVELOPED, ALL	**99761**	**102564**	**101005**	**70025**	**89303**	**60583**	**91793**	**59663**	**104131**	**82323**
DEVELOPING, ALL	**12892**	**26622**	**37853**	**41393**	**28583**	**27681**	**31614**	**31926**	**37824**	**38442**
WORLD	**112653**	**129185**	**138858**	**111418**	**117886**	**88264**	**123407**	**91588**	**141955**	**120765**

[1]Observations derived from FAO (2009), projections obtained with the Global Forest Products Model.

Table 33—Observed and projected mechanical pulp net trade (thousand mt) for world regions and selected countries in the Global Forest Products Model[1]

	Observed		Scenario A1B		Scenario A2		Scenario B2		Scenario A1B-Low Fuelwood	
	1992	2006	2030	2060	2030	2060	2030	2060	2030	2060
AFRICA	**-17**	**-19**	**-55**	**-133**	**-45**	**-84**	**-50**	**-138**	**-55**	**-170**
Egypt	0	-1	0	-1	0	0	0	0	0	0
Nigeria	0	-16	-48	-113	-40	-73	-43	-120	-48	-150
South Africa	3	0	0	0	0	0	0	0	0	0
NORTH/CENTRAL AMERICA	**189**	**10**	**-59**	**-484**	**-48**	**-183**	**-36**	**-359**	**-41**	**174**
Canada	244	101	25	7	35	62	27	89	25	45
Mexico	-17	-10	-74	-463	-74	-201	-74	-439	-74	-40
United States of America	-37	-81	-6	-21	-6	-44	13	-8	10	170
SOUTH AMERICA	**3**	**-5**	**0**	**0**	**0**	**0**	**0**	**0**	**0**	**0**
Argentina	-6	0	0	0	0	0	0	0	0	0
Brazil	9	-3	1	0	1	0	1	0	1	0
Chile	2	-2	0	0	0	0	0	0	0	0
ASIA	**-571**	**-556**	**-1079**	**-3271**	**-862**	**-1389**	**-996**	**-2787**	**-1096**	**-1909**
China	-77	-84	-370	-1088	-370	-155	-370	-1172	-370	-180
India	-22	-4	-278	-1304	-195	-661	-210	-884	-279	-1123
Indonesia	-42	-153	-165	-39	-32	-7	-147	-38	-177	-63
Japan	-374	-256	-62	-9	-91	-13	-79	-11	-64	-9
Korea, Republic of	-4	-1	-1	0	-1	0	-1	0	-1	0
Malaysia	0	-4	-8	-1	-5	-1	-6	-1	-7	-1
OCEANIA	**318**	**217**	**1314**	**5024**	**1122**	**1479**	**1188**	**3288**	**1311**	**1707**
Australia	0	-6	-21	-37	-6	-3	-3	0	-6	-1
New Zealand	318	223	1335	5062	1128	1482	1191	3288	1317	1707
EUROPE	**-27**	**58**	**-242**	**-1258**	**-288**	**57**	**-228**	**-125**	**-240**	**76**
EU-25	-195	-176	-396	-1285	-396	-434	-383	-976	-394	-694
Austria	-7	-5	-10	-34	-7	-2	-4	-2	-10	-2
Finland	30	25	5	2	5	37	5	37	5	5
France	-35	-33	-16	-51	-9	-1	-10	-1	-14	-2
Germany	-93	-78	-10	-8	-10	-4	-10	-1	-10	5
Italy	-109	-110	-36	-5	-55	-8	-45	-7	-37	-5
Russian Federation	1	0	0	0	0	0	0	0	0	0
Spain	6	-12	-71	-471	-71	-133	-71	-442	-71	-471
Sweden	176	103	25	8	25	4	26	34	25	17
United Kingdom	-130	-61	-239	-583	-239	-311	-239	-495	-239	-226
DEVELOPED, ALL	**101**	**23**	**969**	**3577**	**729**	**1450**	**877**	**3126**	**986**	**1838**
DEVELOPING, ALL	**-206**	**-318**	**-1090**	**-3698**	**-850**	**-1571**	**-998**	**-3247**	**-1107**	**-1959**
WORLD	**-105**	**-295**	**-121**	**-121**	**-121**	**-121**	**-121**	**-121**	**-121**	**-121**

[1]Observations derived from FAO (2009), projections obtained with the Global Forest Products Model.

Table 34—Observed and projected chemical pulp net trade (thousand mt) for world regions and selected countries in the Global Forest Products Model[1]

	Observed		Scenario A1B		Scenario A2		Scenario B2		Scenario A1B-Low Fuelwood	
	1992	2006	2030	2060	2030	2060	2030	2060	2030	2060
AFRICA	**222**	**303**	**1**	**-619**	**45**	**-246**	**51**	**-463**	**-4**	**-479**
Egypt	-53	-59	-103	-273	-157	-241	-103	-270	-109	-216
Nigeria	-2	-1	-3	-11	-3	-7	-3	-7	-3	-7
South Africa	165	173	120	-175	148	-73	120	-175	120	-175
NORTH/CENTRAL AMERICA	**9309**	**6843**	**13232**	**15181**	**13381**	**12015**	**14361**	**11665**	**13841**	**19268**
Canada	8205	8495	14112	17180	14112	19590	14112	18334	14112	12677
Mexico	-369	-1066	-601	-1241	-467	-563	-476	-965	-539	-377
United States of America	1487	-539	-194	-662	-194	-6942	802	-5619	354	7049
SOUTH AMERICA	**2503**	**8253**	**6204**	**3043**	**6494**	**3652**	**6191**	**3392**	**7279**	**3929**
Argentina	37	131	174	104	281	163	241	141	239	140
Brazil	1612	5841	4771	2635	4944	2836	4726	2610	5807	3200
Chile	1318	2638	1786	975	1643	898	1661	907	1795	980
ASIA	**-6042**	**-10706**	**-19008**	**-20592**	**-18641**	**-16893**	**-19678**	**-19418**	**-21062**	**-22199**
China	-963	-7045	-13182	-16542	-10639	-12226	-11916	-13459	-13537	-14092
India	-119	-366	-816	-984	-747	-873	-831	-1266	-834	-1543
Indonesia	-310	2253	1187	384	1319	708	1218	421	1298	688
Japan	-2479	-1675	-1124	-249	-3718	-949	-2820	-952	-2397	-1110
Korea, Republic of	-1516	-2216	-2126	-693	-1870	-839	-2182	-1150	-2334	-2052
Malaysia	-49	-243	-223	-138	-117	-28	-172	-62	-172	-45
OCEANIA	**89**	**155**	**165**	**230**	**166**	**123**	**166**	**123**	**165**	**123**
Australia	-203	-316	-104	-40	-104	-25	-104	-25	-104	-23
New Zealand	292	474	274	273	274	150	274	150	274	150
EUROPE	**-4904**	**-4332**	**-1658**	**1694**	**-2509**	**285**	**-2153**	**3637**	**-1282**	**-1706**
EU-25	-5655	-5727	-2723	712	-3407	-611	-3025	2788	-2302	-2538
Austria	-268	-385	-46	52	-46	74	-46	52	-46	33
Finland	1123	2268	3510	6373	3362	6050	3510	6136	3510	2730
France	-1605	-1571	-582	-674	-625	-105	-580	-65	-581	-65
Germany	-3468	-3741	-2362	-3714	-2744	-2808	-2727	-842	-2297	-469
Italy	-2380	-3461	-3402	-2468	-3265	-2453	-3201	-2283	-3399	-2778
Russian Federation	801	1734	1078	591	1078	602	1078	591	1078	591
Spain	88	124	479	341	327	345	458	371	414	305
Sweden	2470	2448	3190	5324	2866	1593	2697	2536	3579	1982
United Kingdom	-1730	-1184	-2477	-2782	-2316	-2583	-2229	-2374	-2441	-2940
DEVELOPED, ALL	**2476**	**2154**	**11157**	**17693**	**7801**	**11827**	**10015**	**15114**	**10820**	**16522**
DEVELOPING, ALL	**-1299**	**-1638**	**-12220**	**-18756**	**-8864**	**-12891**	**-11078**	**-16178**	**-11883**	**-17586**
WORLD	**1177**	**516**	**-1063**	**-1063**	**-1063**	**-1064**	**-1063**	**-1064**	**-1063**	**-1063**

[1]Observations derived from FAO (2009), projections obtained with the Global Forest Products Model.

Table 35—Observed and projected other fiber pulp consumption (thousand mt) for world regions and selected countries in the Global Forest Products Model[1]

	Observed		Scenario A1B		Scenario A2		Scenario B2		Scenario A1B-Low Fuelwood	
	1992	2006	2030	2060	2030	2060	2030	2060	2030	2060
AFRICA	**253**	**282**	**424**	**888**	**492**	**679**	**443**	**828**	**421**	**789**
Egypt	120	159	231	627	347	514	268	584	227	526
Nigeria	0	0	0	0	0	0	0	0	0	0
South Africa	87	94	138	123	100	76	127	125	139	128
NORTH/CENTRAL AMERICA	**426**	**356**	**352**	**308**	**369**	**300**	**358**	**265**	**350**	**250**
Canada	46	51	54	37	39	21	45	28	54	47
Mexico	238	133	131	173	170	191	150	151	127	99
United States of America	82	154	139	56	135	55	136	50	142	63
SOUTH AMERICA	**553**	**400**	**529**	**582**	**390**	**409**	**414**	**470**	**531**	**603**
Argentina	112	132	253	276	181	186	193	218	255	291
Brazil	127	73	111	122	81	81	86	96	112	131
Chile	0	0	0	0	0	0	0	0	0	0
ASIA	**15367**	**16836**	**25267**	**30113**	**18184**	**19186**	**20965**	**22317**	**25243**	**24831**
China	13395	13368	18645	21035	13573	14327	15419	15616	18676	16138
India	1109	2009	3879	4877	2593	2525	3163	3490	3881	4614
Indonesia	115	104	62	48	49	28	52	33	62	51
Japan	33	95	102	79	98	75	95	67	103	86
Korea, Republic of	4	10	8	10	6	6	7	7	8	10
Malaysia	1	4	6	28	6	24	6	25	6	36
OCEANIA	**11**	**3**	**14**	**137**	**14**	**59**	**13**	**130**	**11**	**8**
Australia	9	1	5	7	4	7	4	6	5	8
New Zealand	0	0	0	0	0	0	0	0	0	0
EUROPE	**388**	**341**	**446**	**479**	**409**	**419**	**406**	**410**	**446**	**506**
EU-25	347	331	420	433	388	383	383	374	420	465
Austria	1	9	10	5	7	4	8	4	9	7
Finland	1	0	1	1	1	1	1	1	1	2
France	32	0	0	0	0	0	0	0	0	0
Germany	37	24	29	34	26	32	26	30	30	37
Italy	100	190	198	161	189	148	184	138	199	170
Russian Federation	0	3	4	6	2	4	3	5	4	7
Spain	93	0	1	2	1	2	1	2	1	2
Sweden	0	7	4	2	3	1	3	1	5	2
United Kingdom	27	43	103	126	95	119	92	110	102	136
DEVELOPED, ALL	**647**	**738**	**884**	**782**	**784**	**653**	**814**	**685**	**888**	**837**
DEVELOPING, ALL	**16352**	**17480**	**26148**	**31726**	**19074**	**20399**	**21784**	**23735**	**26114**	**26149**
WORLD	**16999**	**18218**	**27032**	**32507**	**19858**	**21052**	**22598**	**24420**	**27002**	**26987**

[1]Observations derived from FAO (2009), projections obtained with the Global Forest Products Model.

Table 36—Observed and projected waste paper consumption (thousand mt) for world regions and selected countries in the Global Forest Products Model[1]

	Observed		Scenario A1B		Scenario A2		Scenario B2		Scenario A1B-Low Fuelwood	
	1992	2006	2030	2060	2030	2060	2030	2060	2030	2060
AFRICA	986	1776	4804	12401	3624	7907	4273	11529	4780	12615
Egypt	63	235	620	2307	639	1758	600	2032	585	2079
Nigeria	11	1	56	822	53	512	56	851	57	964
South Africa	455	1130	2563	4355	1827	2637	2346	4401	2579	4520
NORTH/CENTRAL AMERICA	21603	39083	68995	108090	62077	95223	63313	92220	74666	136999
Canada	1942	3678	13203	23261	10569	18685	11571	22001	12299	40124
Mexico	1863	3969	7035	11012	5262	7637	5526	8617	6989	10462
United States of America	17681	31132	47458	70704	45249	66664	45142	58870	54118	83295
SOUTH AMERICA	2168	2372	9187	18357	6871	12800	7293	15014	9153	19181
Argentina	269	736	1810	3339	1269	2205	1357	2587	1816	3456
Brazil	1173	329	4357	9596	3234	6511	3442	7608	4377	10224
Chile	71	264	842	1362	727	1078	731	1274	792	1367
ASIA	24580	78380	132740	241301	98876	160383	110546	177659	132047	210493
China	3393	45107	74323	136204	52521	91120	60507	99629	74346	106178
India	408	1723	5748	15733	3923	8060	4545	10945	5752	14142
Indonesia	867	3722	6885	11703	4668	6569	5518	7849	6898	12037
Japan	14027	14163	19230	25139	18255	23001	17742	20712	19267	25806
Korea, Republic of	3624	6089	9414	11833	7000	6917	8110	8493	9196	11905
Malaysia	481	753	1916	3759	1283	2284	1525	2624	1805	3777
OCEANIA	834	1562	4023	5438	3600	4891	3576	4590	3542	6052
Australia	756	1473	3363	4426	3123	4173	3047	3835	2938	5008
New Zealand	77	84	645	974	467	691	517	726	589	1007
EUROPE	25522	46319	79892	114254	67725	95484	70973	99284	77038	132152
EU-25	24054	41964	70504	95499	60959	82573	63173	83609	67645	111770
Austria	1144	2336	2734	2380	2140	1969	2314	2067	2488	2690
Finland	870	853	5989	8113	4347	7156	4896	7677	5504	18061
France	3168	5470	8379	11401	7729	9760	7745	10075	7618	11576
Germany	6738	12608	18231	20018	15544	19121	16566	18307	17580	24418
Italy	2907	5155	7269	9690	6890	8779	6771	8185	7202	9864
Russian Federation	360	2396	4802	9934	3247	6342	3774	7560	4820	10155
Spain	1893	4865	5734	7253	5524	6651	5346	6230	5573	7507
Sweden	1233	1934	3844	3537	3213	2547	3460	2772	3675	3540
United Kingdom	2592	3455	7495	11951	7100	10785	6800	9921	7378	12276
DEVELOPED, ALL	60559	98156	166902	244467	147641	212202	151803	210897	169334	293263
DEVELOPING, ALL	15134	71336	132739	255373	95131	164486	108171	189399	131891	224229
WORLD	75693	169491	299640	499840	242772	376688	259974	400296	301225	517491

[1]Observations derived from FAO (2009), projections obtained with the Global Forest Products Model.

Table 37—Observed and projected other fiber pulp net trade (thousand mt) for world regions and selected countries in the Global Forest Products Model[1]

	Observed		Scenario A1B		Scenario A2		Scenario B2		Scenario A1B-Low Fuelwood	
	1992	2006	2030	2060	2030	2060	2030	2060	2030	2060
AFRICA	**-58**	**-24**	**86**	**-47**	**-39**	**22**	**32**	**-79**	**85**	**-15**
Egypt	-73	-39	0	-218	-138	-160	-50	-219	0	-151
Nigeria	0	0	0	0	0	0	0	0	0	0
South Africa	12	9	69	164	83	169	65	129	69	132
NORTH/CENTRAL AMERICA	**99**	**63**	**223**	**423**	**134**	**321**	**172**	**380**	**225**	**414**
Canada	-6	-11	-3	20	3	27	0	22	-4	5
Mexico	2	-17	61	94	0	36	28	85	65	143
United States of America	105	91	166	318	134	263	146	281	164	275
SOUTH AMERICA	**-1**	**-4**	**172**	**398**	**211**	**379**	**221**	**372**	**169**	**309**
Argentina	0	-1	-30	0	0	0	0	0	-31	-18
Brazil	0	-3	16	54	31	68	31	59	16	29
Chile	0	0	0	0	0	0	0	0	0	0
ASIA	**-114**	**-77**	**-464**	**-726**	**-289**	**-691**	**-424**	**-648**	**-463**	**-623**
China	-26	-22	-411	-822	-295	-767	-376	-729	-416	-305
India	-10	-13	0	0	0	0	0	0	0	0
Indonesia	1	1	128	233	84	152	101	167	128	164
Japan	-29	-35	-29	-5	-45	-24	-35	-12	-30	-27
Korea, Republic of	-4	-10	-8	-10	-6	-6	-7	-7	-8	-10
Malaysia	0	-3	-4	-26	-4	-22	-4	-23	-4	-34
OCEANIA	**0**	**-1**	**-5**	**-7**	**-4**	**-7**	**-4**	**-6**	**-5**	**-8**
Australia	0	-1	-5	-7	-4	-7	-4	-6	-5	-8
New Zealand	0	0	0	0	0	0	0	0	0	0
EUROPE	**-45**	**-59**	**-98**	**-128**	**-101**	**-109**	**-83**	**-105**	**-98**	**-164**
EU-25	-35	-53	-90	-109	-95	-96	-77	-92	-90	-147
Austria	0	-9	-9	-3	-6	-3	-6	-3	-8	-5
Finland	-1	0	-1	-1	-1	-1	-1	-1	-1	-2
France	-9	56	70	81	62	69	65	71	70	73
Germany	-5	-24	-29	-34	-26	-32	-26	-30	-30	-37
Italy	-14	-9	0	0	-12	0	0	0	0	0
Russian Federation	2	-3	-4	-6	-2	-4	-3	-5	-4	-7
Spain	6	14	13	14	11	12	12	13	13	12
Sweden	0	-7	-4	-2	-3	-1	-3	-1	-5	-2
United Kingdom	-27	-43	-102	-124	-94	-118	-91	-108	-101	-135
DEVELOPED, ALL	**37**	**14**	**130**	**400**	**93**	**344**	**115**	**337**	**127**	**244**
DEVELOPING, ALL	**-156**	**-116**	**-217**	**-486**	**-180**	**-431**	**-202**	**-424**	**-214**	**-331**
WORLD	**-119**	**-102**	**-87**	**-87**	**-87**	**-87**	**-87**	**-87**	**-87**	**-87**

[1]Observations derived from FAO (2009), projections obtained with the Global Forest Products Model.

Table 38—Observed and projected waste paper net trade (thousand mt) for world regions and selected countries in the Global Forest Products Model[1]

	Observed		Scenario A1B		Scenario A2		Scenario B2		Scenario A1B-Low Fuelwood	
	1992	2006	2030	2060	2030	2060	2030	2060	2030	2060
AFRICA	**-56**	**-41**	**-55**	**-1674**	**112**	**-1204**	**84**	**-1901**	**-53**	**-1632**
Egypt	-3	-8	0	-174	0	-368	-1	-396	0	0
Nigeria	-1	-1	0	-442	0	-263	0	-556	0	-571
South Africa	-13	18	246	476	315	374	312	444	246	485
NORTH/CENTRAL AMERICA	**4210**	**12746**	**13533**	**-1266**	**5497**	**1753**	**7907**	**-2291**	**8550**	**-26683**
Canada	-464	-1028	-9438	-15600	-7398	-13697	-8256	-16127	-8505	-32189
Mexico	-1001	-1703	-2461	0	-1409	-298	-1498	0	-2380	188
United States of America	5724	15470	25658	15109	14465	16402	17832	14652	19641	6043
SOUTH AMERICA	**-320**	**-270**	**-1628**	**-1679**	**-1072**	**-1892**	**-1055**	**-2139**	**-1551**	**-1936**
Argentina	-33	-37	-349	0	-38	0	-68	0	-345	0
Brazil	-18	-11	-578	-1672	-515	-1352	-437	-1533	-578	-2018
Chile	-3	-46	-291	-55	-262	-226	-245	-272	-237	-14
ASIA	**-4985**	**-23351**	**-16508**	**-1836**	**-7237**	**-3543**	**-10257**	**2697**	**-15215**	**37645**
China	-1591	-20511	-10417	20013	-2802	5136	-5348	16483	-9958	56159
India	-252	-1722	-5748	-15733	-3923	-8060	-4545	-10945	-5752	-14142
Indonesia	-866	-2067	-2644	0	-1095	454	-1783	540	-2625	0
Japan	-405	3815	7394	6378	3488	6196	5188	5915	7590	6820
Korea, Republic of	-1503	-1086	-126	0	-116	-337	-122	0	-126	261
Malaysia	49	-189	-505	-504	-97	-164	-282	-129	-376	-406
OCEANIA	**77**	**1146**	**618**	**738**	**179**	**925**	**396**	**815**	**1085**	**381**
Australia	33	906	580	722	136	803	348	616	1039	365
New Zealand	44	242	33	0	37	112	42	187	41	0
EUROPE	**-1373**	**7578**	**3215**	**4893**	**1697**	**3135**	**2100**	**1995**	**6360**	**-8600**
EU-25	-1537	7148	3104	6752	644	4856	1527	4422	6184	-5672
Austria	-510	-901	-855	-260	-557	-9	-659	-154	-594	-497
Finland	-91	163	-4617	-6436	-2989	-5569	-3562	-6117	-4122	-16323
France	-409	952	1274	1438	154	2365	569	1031	2119	1813
Germany	1179	225	71	1151	55	606	137	0	494	-2471
Italy	-720	423	758	2424	25	875	142	2199	895	2655
Russian Federation	31	189	830	461	1352	142	1076	296	862	555
Spain	-492	-732	-553	1504	-1159	-74	-783	595	-353	1562
Sweden	-333	-599	-1999	-1669	-1659	-823	-1835	-986	-1827	-1617
United Kingdom	171	3856	4102	3078	2371	3338	3188	3123	4321	3332
DEVELOPED, ALL	**3508**	**26868**	**27273**	**10921**	**12408**	**12653**	**17216**	**6850**	**26039**	**-28123**
DEVELOPING, ALL	**-5955**	**-29060**	**-28099**	**-11746**	**-13233**	**-13478**	**-18041**	**-7675**	**-26864**	**27298**
WORLD	**-2447**	**-2192**	**-825**	**-825**	**-825**	**-825**	**-825**	**-825**	**-825**	**-825**

[1]Observations derived from FAO (2009), projections obtained with the Global Forest Products Model.

Table 39—Observed and projected newsprint prices (1997$/mt) for selected countries in the Global Forest Products Model[1]

	Observed		Scenario A1B		Scenario A2		Scenario B2		Scenario A1B- Low Fuelwood	
	1992	2006	2030	2060	2030	2060	2030	2060	2030	2060
AFRICA										
Egypt	602	660	551	612	504	458	515	486	532	503
Nigeria	613	686	545	625	514	467	525	499	534	515
South Africa	546	606	516	581	469	424	496	455	495	468
NORTH/CENTRAL AMERICA										
Canada	546	606	480	556	451	408	456	435	466	452
Mexico	573	636	511	573	479	427	484	455	504	454
United States of America	573	636	508	602	479	436	484	463	493	467
SOUTH AMERICA										
Argentina	659	731	564	582	517	432	527	459	553	484
Brazil	573	636	523	584	475	441	484	467	503	486
Chile	546	606	482	570	451	418	456	446	469	466
ASIA										
China	573	636	488	465	444	352	460	382	487	438
India	630	700	587	595	522	454	545	494	584	540
Indonesia	541	606	507	562	472	412	481	438	500	458
Japan	573	636	510	567	480	424	485	450	504	470
Korea, Republic of	573	606	473	556	449	406	450	435	465	440
Malaysia	573	636	523	579	483	436	493	463	516	480
OCEANIA										
Australia	573	636	502	550	466	411	470	431	488	449
New Zealand	546	606	488	556	454	408	462	435	471	459
EUROPE										
EU-25										
Austria	546	606	490	585	461	428	466	455	483	468
Finland	546	606	486	568	456	425	462	451	477	468
France	573	606	495	563	463	419	469	440	486	459
Germany	573	636	503	559	465	407	472	431	483	457
Italy	573	636	508	568	479	423	484	449	494	472
Russian Federation	546	606	488	548	454	405	461	432	478	449
Spain	573	636	507	556	476	424	481	434	494	459
Sweden	546	606	505	582	472	442	478	465	494	482
United Kingdom	568	644	492	536	461	397	466	424	487	448
DEVELOPED, ALL										
DEVELOPING, ALL										
WORLD	659	535	480	556	451	408	456	435	466	452

[1]Observations derived from FAO (2009), projections obtained with the Global Forest Products Model.

Table 40—Observed and projected printing and writing paper prices (1997$/mt) for selected countries in the Global Forest Products Model[1]

	Observed		Scenario A1B		Scenario A2		Scenario B2		Scenario A1B-Low Fuelwood	
	1992	2006	2030	2060	2030	2060	2030	2060	2030	2060
AFRICA										
Egypt	1194	1102	964	949	913	783	935	816	952	846
Nigeria	1194	1099	964	898	926	707	935	743	952	714
South Africa	995	863	780	836	731	652	758	682	758	662
NORTH/CENTRAL AMERICA										
Canada	939	863	750	804	716	642	724	663	738	653
Mexico	995	915	805	855	767	691	775	714	793	704
United States of America	995	915	784	875	757	711	758	722	751	659
SOUTH AMERICA										
Argentina	1164	1071	924	872	839	693	858	726	906	754
Brazil	939	863	784	833	732	674	743	697	766	686
Chile	995	915	801	855	767	693	775	714	789	704
ASIA										
China	995	863	822	838	761	684	779	708	813	708
India	939	1096	952	860	863	702	899	745	946	782
Indonesia	937	863	787	830	744	666	756	689	772	682
Japan	939	915	776	806	748	643	753	665	769	653
Korea, Republic of	935	859	761	827	728	661	732	692	746	669
Malaysia	995	915	801	855	767	679	775	708	789	701
OCEANIA										
Australia	995	913	780	802	740	646	743	659	757	645
New Zealand	995	915	801	855	767	693	775	714	789	704
EUROPE										
EU-25										
Austria	939	859	750	835	716	652	724	675	738	653
Finland	939	863	750	804	716	642	724	663	738	653
France	995	915	777	808	746	643	750	658	763	645
Germany	995	860	759	821	724	651	730	671	739	656
Italy	995	915	785	813	755	653	758	673	775	663
Russian Federation	1144	1046	807	784	771	625	778	647	790	634
Spain	995	915	785	842	755	668	758	679	775	660
Sweden	939	861	750	804	716	647	724	663	738	653
United Kingdom	979	912	800	817	767	655	771	677	789	664
DEVELOPED, ALL										
DEVELOPING, ALL										
WORLD	1133	857	750	804	716	642	724	663	738	653

[1]Observations derived from FAO (2009), projections obtained with the Global Forest Products Model.

Table 41—Observed and projected other paper and paperboard prices (1997$/mt) for selected countries in the Global Forest Products Model[1]

	Observed		Scenario A1B		Scenario A2		Scenario B2		Scenario A1B-Low Fuelwood	
	1992	2006	2030	2060	2030	2060	2030	2060	2030	2060
AFRICA										
Egypt	971	1032	866	792	826	671	837	705	849	751
Nigeria	928	982	828	765	788	629	800	661	811	695
South Africa	796	846	725	713	677	585	705	616	708	650
NORTH/CENTRAL AMERICA										
Canada	796	846	694	693	666	569	671	595	684	637
Mexico	844	897	725	680	692	571	699	600	722	625
United States of America	796	846	707	730	678	608	681	629	687	640
SOUTH AMERICA										
Argentina	971	1032	797	728	758	602	766	628	788	661
Brazil	796	846	731	721	679	600	690	627	717	660
Chile	844	846	724	739	689	612	696	641	713	678
ASIA										
China	844	897	774	724	714	609	735	638	773	685
India	1013	1073	875	736	788	617	825	662	876	739
Indonesia	790	846	724	707	689	578	697	605	718	641
Japan	796	897	722	700	694	578	699	604	718	639
Korea, Republic of	796	846	696	709	666	585	671	614	687	632
Malaysia	844	897	732	678	695	567	705	595	733	644
OCEANIA										
Australia	796	846	704	694	666	576	672	598	687	635
New Zealand	844	846	704	692	666	570	677	595	687	637
EUROPE										
EU-25										
Austria	796	846	701	715	668	584	677	611	690	640
Finland	796	846	701	709	666	588	677	614	687	646
France	844	846	700	692	666	569	676	590	690	627
Germany	844	846	704	693	666	563	677	590	687	637
Italy	844	897	728	702	701	581	702	607	722	642
Russian Federation	796	846	710	706	674	584	682	611	698	644
Spain	844	897	730	706	701	595	705	603	726	636
Sweden	796	846	704	717	672	599	677	623	690	656
United Kingdom	844	910	715	685	686	563	691	590	711	626
DEVELOPED, ALL										
DEVELOPING, ALL										
WORLD	971	788	704	692	666	561	677	590	687	637

[1]Observations derived from FAO (2009), projections obtained with the Global Forest Products Model.

Table 42—Observed and projected newsprint consumption (thousand mt) for world regions and selected countries in the Global Forest Products Model[1]

	Observed		Scenario A1B		Scenario A2		Scenario B2		Scenario A1B-Low Fuelwood	
	1992	2006	2030	2060	2030	2060	2030	2060	2030	2060
AFRICA	518	869	1773	3416	1157	1891	1428	3051	1787	3575
Egypt	117	127	332	616	216	371	239	464	335	648
Nigeria	18	37	107	231	66	119	85	222	108	242
South Africa	214	302	425	562	270	293	377	572	429	594
NORTH/CENTRAL AMERICA	12970	10322	10353	8800	9543	7888	9217	7084	10425	9353
Canada	267	469	589	623	557	573	549	507	593	656
Mexico	422	485	760	1012	487	575	537	741	763	1073
United States of America	12156	9077	8472	6353	8131	6209	7714	5132	8535	6774
SOUTH AMERICA	1013	1203	1988	2680	1314	1642	1441	2057	2002	2809
Argentina	302	253	402	513	263	302	284	371	404	537
Brazil	297	544	845	1122	547	644	595	799	853	1174
Chile	58	74	138	174	96	120	108	160	139	183
ASIA	7708	13702	27279	41079	18193	23271	21917	28526	27336	42391
China	1050	4204	9508	14589	6074	8808	7539	10167	9512	14808
India	566	1590	4036	7582	2284	3233	3190	5140	4041	7771
Indonesia	112	296	819	1355	474	635	605	806	821	1426
Japan	3707	3889	4079	3887	3834	3471	3693	3034	4089	4076
Korea, Republic of	813	1029	1859	1902	1081	867	1442	1217	1868	2020
Malaysia	223	337	800	990	492	514	622	649	803	1037
OCEANIA	672	848	1090	1185	1035	1116	1029	963	1097	1246
Australia	569	685	918	995	879	944	865	801	924	1046
New Zealand	101	152	139	151	136	151	139	136	141	159
EUROPE	9183	12394	14832	16063	12764	12926	13072	13251	14916	16870
EU-25	7712	10769	12335	12860	11215	11026	11144	10663	12406	13504
Austria	354	267	273	256	258	229	258	222	274	271
Finland	113	154	193	178	185	164	184	160	194	186
France	742	905	990	996	942	911	899	809	995	1049
Germany	2058	2613	2750	2674	2610	2412	2551	2184	2777	2813
Italy	578	832	824	786	776	696	752	631	830	823
Russian Federation	854	698	1263	1693	693	930	881	1191	1269	1780
Spain	454	486	656	669	624	602	606	553	660	702
Sweden	519	783	768	711	731	642	759	670	772	746
United Kingdom	1877	2451	2801	2928	2656	2674	2552	2406	2808	3062
DEVELOPED, ALL	26306	27211	29875	29220	26829	24890	26715	23879	30049	30788
DEVELOPING, ALL	5758	12127	27440	44002	17178	23843	21389	31052	27514	45455
WORLD	32064	39338	57315	73222	44007	48733	48104	54931	57563	76243

[1]Observations derived from FAO (2009), projections obtained with the Global Forest Products Model.

Table 43—Observed and projected printing and writing paper consumption (thousand mt) for world regions and selected countries in the Global Forest Products Model[1]

	Observed		Scenario A1B		Scenario A2		Scenario B2		Scenario A1B-Low Fuelwood	
	1992	2006	2030	2060	2030	2060	2030	2060	2030	2060
AFRICA	958	1709	3648	7665	2569	4892	3032	6999	3671	8191
Egypt	228	325	785	1726	563	1180	607	1398	789	1801
Nigeria	65	139	385	974	265	599	323	967	386	1055
South Africa	417	714	1034	1699	730	1056	946	1771	1045	1852
NORTH/CENTRAL AMERICA	25438	32859	37371	39957	35223	37451	34296	34340	37867	43954
Canada	2133	2482	4151	5765	3993	5523	3943	5026	4173	6224
Mexico	698	2289	3162	5234	2250	3448	2421	4197	3179	5622
United States of America	22168	27708	29281	27485	28406	27407	27301	23780	29736	30529
SOUTH AMERICA	1821	3751	6723	11227	4897	7760	5243	9229	6773	12011
Argentina	293	547	1339	2203	979	1499	1037	1747	1349	2321
Brazil	952	2049	3584	5917	2572	3938	2743	4645	3614	6352
Chile	72	184	298	476	225	363	247	455	299	512
ASIA	20533	36547	73450	127878	55218	89262	62590	99622	73744	136152
China	6387	17067	38623	70246	27557	48516	32529	54385	38781	74700
India	1056	1649	4580	10305	2982	5432	3841	7744	4589	10661
Indonesia	578	0	1225	2402	807	1363	972	1638	1233	2582
Japan	9440	10158	13808	17743	13184	16696	12803	15028	13853	19174
Korea, Republic of	988	1316	2119	2861	1400	1588	1747	2060	2134	3096
Malaysia	324	1588	2835	4414	1945	2737	2335	3268	2849	4748
OCEANIA	799	1722	2533	3600	2452	3528	2438	3149	2558	3891
Australia	681	1482	2138	3039	2077	2987	2052	2634	2161	3288
New Zealand	112	227	347	490	341	497	346	460	348	526
EUROPE	21865	32509	46252	64522	41817	56796	42295	57000	46541	69808
EU-25	20200	29793	41548	57126	38387	51525	38350	50535	41803	61829
Austria	168	439	539	676	519	640	517	624	542	740
Finland	684	236	599	747	581	720	578	707	602	807
France	3345	4414	6277	8452	6050	8089	5833	7390	6317	9175
Germany	5594	6980	9159	11782	8814	11139	8660	10317	9247	12800
Italy	2787	3700	4913	6331	4704	5899	4592	5471	4937	6823
Russian Federation	862	754	1456	2505	916	1611	1104	1952	1467	2705
Spain	1460	2560	3062	4088	2953	3894	2887	3642	3076	4471
Sweden	442	139	101	126	97	119	100	124	101	136
United Kingdom	3263	4912	6987	9673	6725	9225	6521	8505	7021	10436
DEVELOPED, ALL	56953	75652	97748	121999	91048	111767	90249	106709	98599	132751
DEVELOPING, ALL	14461	33445	72230	132851	51127	87923	59645	103629	72555	141256
WORLD	71414	109097	169978	254850	142175	199689	149894	210338	171154	274006

[1]Observations derived from FAO (2009), projections obtained with the Global Forest Products Model.

Table 44—Observed and projected other paper and paperboard consumption (thousand mt) for world regions and selected countries in the Global Forest Products Model[1]

	Observed		Scenario A1B		Scenario A2		Scenario B2		Scenario A1B-Low Fuelwood	
	1992	2006	2030	2060	2030	2060	2030	2060	2030	2060
AFRICA	2488	3900	7627	12224	5431	7676	6457	10990	7659	12455
Egypt	340	705	1390	2426	1005	1637	1083	1931	1396	2455
Nigeria	30	151	348	682	243	412	294	656	350	697
South Africa	1095	1633	3075	4116	2190	2503	2814	4119	3091	4204
NORTH/CENTRAL AMERICA	50491	65107	79347	94474	74185	86497	72438	78973	79768	97085
Canada	2952	3933	5024	5709	4810	5297	4761	4845	5040	5819
Mexico	2136	5475	8283	11257	5949	7288	6386	8800	8290	11474
United States of America	44723	54411	63619	73866	61619	71298	59313	62113	64011	76110
SOUTH AMERICA	5516	6408	12749	17343	9359	11866	10000	13999	12793	17683
Argentina	737	1264	1950	2540	1415	1697	1502	1975	1955	2595
Brazil	2799	2351	6453	8643	4668	5672	4970	6652	6482	8817
Chile	326	749	1189	1535	905	1150	992	1425	1193	1566
ASIA	41748	92295	152650	217208	112763	146636	129286	164532	152779	220332
China	15554	50578	90033	131913	64675	89769	75894	100275	90050	133594
India	1168	2065	4611	8133	3030	4279	3873	6033	4610	8126
Indonesia	1255	3777	7971	12586	5311	7095	6359	8471	7986	12868
Japan	15157	15917	17410	18295	16596	16647	16147	15086	17430	18677
Korea, Republic of	3610	5994	9173	10155	6141	5587	7593	7197	9199	10425
Malaysia	932	1370	2232	2874	1551	1747	1848	2077	2231	2907
OCEANIA	1658	2271	2843	3280	2737	3107	2730	2800	2858	3345
Australia	1269	1797	2237	2567	2164	2443	2139	2164	2249	2619
New Zealand	385	439	526	608	517	600	524	557	529	620
EUROPE	38327	57409	66523	77121	58208	63652	60047	66088	66721	78754
EU-25	32746	49474	54793	61501	50366	53459	50592	53073	54953	62806
Austria	880	1685	1672	1739	1606	1583	1602	1548	1678	1784
Finland	642	1304	1165	1191	1126	1108	1121	1091	1170	1217
France	4946	5639	6371	6967	6134	6453	5917	5913	6390	7124
Germany	8245	11797	11658	12392	11201	11353	11003	10547	11720	12632
Italy	4406	7162	7861	8280	7506	7479	7340	6967	7876	8449
Russian Federation	3831	4504	6930	9343	4433	5914	5301	7120	6955	9539
Spain	2965	5945	5803	6402	5582	5854	5462	5504	5811	6555
Sweden	1147	1303	1462	1496	1407	1373	1448	1418	1468	1527
United Kingdom	4675	4825	5910	6645	5670	6146	5507	5692	5917	6780
DEVELOPED, ALL	104239	136131	159341	183559	146737	163244	146465	156001	160001	188106
DEVELOPING, ALL	35988	91260	162398	238092	115947	156189	134492	181380	162576	241548
WORLD	140226	227391	321739	421650	262683	319433	280957	337381	322577	429654

[1]Observations derived from FAO (2009), projections obtained with the Global Forest Products Model.

Table 45—Observed and projected newsprint net trade (thousand mt) for world regions and selected countries in the Global Forest Products Model[1]

	Observed		Scenario A1B		Scenario A2		Scenario B2		Scenario A1B-Low Fuelwood	
	1992	2006	2030	2060	2030	2060	2030	2060	2030	2060
AFRICA	-36	-351	-692	-1436	-562	-953	-608	-1236	-694	-1476
Egypt	-73	-127	-257	-612	-216	-371	-232	-464	-257	-622
Nigeria	-5	-24	-48	-117	-39	-86	-50	-121	-49	-116
South Africa	116	41	26	10	26	10	26	10	26	10
NORTH/CENTRAL AMERICA	2691	1890	6936	6722	3531	3278	5728	6493	8069	13231
Canada	8664	6653	13305	11268	9861	9852	11379	12179	10896	15053
Mexico	-133	-214	-385	-183	-238	-128	-344	-237	-385	-487
United States of America	-5732	-4337	-5653	-3961	-5872	-6209	-5053	-5132	-2104	-903
SOUTH AMERICA	-341	-544	-723	-1687	-119	-687	-299	-1032	-867	-1430
Argentina	-96	-70	-32	-13	-32	-13	-32	-13	-32	-13
Brazil	-71	-409	-468	-999	-168	-335	-198	-484	-486	-651
Chile	103	260	351	141	473	201	366	147	230	92
ASIA	-2290	-2012	-4499	-2937	-2540	-1375	-4076	-3302	-4790	-8000
China	-460	-375	-382	-1	-311	81	-354	10	-442	-107
India	-246	-968	-1593	-1165	-431	-173	-1593	-1489	-1593	-3872
Indonesia	57	261	114	46	114	46	114	46	106	20
Japan	-452	-118	-612	-245	-657	-351	-613	-320	-612	-914
Korea, Republic of	-200	583	542	1309	820	1583	594	1155	345	874
Malaysia	-223	-87	-329	-319	-329	-424	-329	-489	-329	-691
OCEANIA	111	-55	104	188	-6	12	-1	26	45	27
Australia	-165	-270	-149	-60	-153	-61	-157	-63	-153	-61
New Zealand	278	215	259	239	146	59	159	77	204	82
EUROPE	162	950	-1070	-794	-247	-219	-688	-892	-1706	-2297
EU-25	-643	-622	-1607	-1154	-1074	-706	-1329	-1047	-2202	-2293
Austria	41	157	75	23	75	30	75	30	75	30
Finland	1144	431	217	87	215	86	216	87	217	87
France	-72	205	101	41	101	41	101	41	101	41
Germany	-836	-248	-99	34	-99	132	-99	86	-99	-40
Italy	-477	-613	-559	-224	-587	-270	-506	-203	-697	-544
Russian Federation	89	1295	633	626	694	541	686	502	633	343
Spain	-334	-106	-224	-8	-146	-59	-208	-54	-460	-262
Sweden	1605	1758	877	352	877	301	877	318	877	278
United Kingdom	-1177	-1359	-736	-201	-681	-210	-748	-237	-880	-343
DEVELOPED, ALL	2763	2900	5717	5945	2866	2805	4765	5467	6158	10413
DEVELOPING, ALL	-2466	-3022	-5661	-5889	-2809	-2749	-4709	-5410	-6101	-10357
WORLD	297	-122	56	56	56	56	57	57	57	56

[1]Observations derived from FAO (2009), projections obtained with the Global Forest Products Model.

Table 46—Observed and projected printing and writing paper net trade (thousand mt) for world regions and selected countries in the Global Forest Products Model[1]

	Observed		Scenario A1B		Scenario A2		Scenario B2		Scenario A1B-Low Fuelwood	
	1992	2006	2030	2060	2030	2060	2030	2060	2030	2060
AFRICA	**-435**	**-691**	**-1974**	**-2349**	**-928**	**-1033**	**-1397**	**-1693**	**-1941**	**-2828**
Egypt	-170	-225	-696	-552	-95	-20	-391	-126	-662	-1012
Nigeria	-65	-138	-383	-383	-264	-196	-322	-330	-384	-257
South Africa	-82	99	28	6	28	6	29	6	28	6
NORTH/CENTRAL AMERICA	**-977**	**-4199**	**1402**	**5747**	**328**	**1242**	**2512**	**4367**	**1398**	**8500**
Canada	1434	3632	5834	9713	3287	3519	4504	6892	5889	13519
Mexico	-153	-864	-1921	-2623	-639	-565	-996	-1920	-1975	-4129
United States of America	-1887	-6620	-1895	-735	-1895	-1277	-515	-55	-1895	-237
SOUTH AMERICA	**125**	**-292**	**-976**	**-1810**	**-676**	**-1237**	**-736**	**-1567**	**-965**	**-2001**
Argentina	-96	-155	-39	-8	-39	-8	-39	-8	-39	-8
Brazil	442	503	172	36	172	36	179	37	172	36
Chile	-72	-184	-298	-476	-225	-363	-247	-455	-299	-512
ASIA	**-1554**	**478**	**-9634**	**-10281**	**-3700**	**-5118**	**-6753**	**-7053**	**-9598**	**-27328**
China	-856	470	-3731	-2868	-56	-12	-2042	-1184	-3731	-18683
India	4	-118	-69	-14	-34	-7	-46	-10	-75	-16
Indonesia	157	2724	788	164	813	169	740	154	797	166
Japan	170	-239	-110	4	-110	-23	-110	-23	-110	4
Korea, Republic of	53	1442	453	94	445	92	418	87	451	94
Malaysia	-123	-1452	-2573	-2441	-1674	-1082	-2068	-1529	-2579	-2261
OCEANIA	**-478**	**-1059**	**-664**	**-611**	**-669**	**-602**	**-681**	**-570**	**-666**	**-597**
Australia	-377	-819	-269	-50	-294	-61	-295	-55	-269	6
New Zealand	-95	-227	-347	-490	-341	-497	-346	-460	-348	-526
EUROPE	**2819**	**7746**	**13994**	**11452**	**7794**	**8897**	**9205**	**8666**	**13921**	**26402**
EU-25	2872	8080	14604	10776	8062	7931	9682	8186	14530	25810
Austria	1378	2181	2308	673	1413	485	1649	572	2108	1170
Finland	4295	8922	12547	10181	8494	9210	9571	9364	12327	24872
France	-397	-1223	-333	-69	-340	-71	-336	20	-333	171
Germany	-421	1371	1071	223	394	82	457	95	1224	272
Italy	-390	-537	-164	-34	-171	-36	-166	-35	-164	-34
Russian Federation	-17	-151	-21	37	-21	37	-21	37	-21	80
Spain	-610	-967	-270	-56	-310	-64	-313	-65	-272	-57
Sweden	1363	3274	3513	1868	2336	486	2793	723	3815	1925
United Kingdom	-1672	-3655	-2446	-509	-2531	-526	-2459	-511	-2534	-527
DEVELOPED, ALL	**1914**	**3322**	**16985**	**19579**	**8302**	**10353**	**12274**	**14664**	**16969**	**38833**
DEVELOPING, ALL	**-2414**	**-1339**	**-14837**	**-17431**	**-6154**	**-8204**	**-10125**	**-12515**	**-14820**	**-36684**
WORLD	**-500**	**1983**	**2148**	**2149**	**2148**	**2149**	**2149**	**2149**	**2148**	**2149**

[1]Observations derived from FAO (2009), projections obtained with the Global Forest Products Model.

Table 47—Observed and projected other paper and paperboard net trade (thousand mt) for world regions and selected countries in the Global Forest Products Model[1]

	Observed		Scenario A1B		Scenario A2		Scenario B2		Scenario A1B-Low Fuelwood	
	1992	2006	2030	2060	2030	2060	2030	2060	2030	2060
AFRICA	**-524**	**-1114**	**-1705**	**-1178**	**-964**	**-643**	**-1133**	**-931**	**-1808**	**-1268**
Egypt	-197	-345	-564	-142	-274	-69	-296	-74	-643	-238
Nigeria	-22	-133	-245	-89	-122	-31	-171	-43	-246	-65
South Africa	40	126	99	25	99	25	99	25	99	25
NORTH/CENTRAL AMERICA	**4183**	**2536**	**5413**	**3308**	**4502**	**3369**	**6057**	**4410**	**12225**	**28188**
Canada	1135	1020	5134	3941	4621	3904	4651	4755	4931	19952
Mexico	-145	-1605	-602	-141	-498	-125	-479	-120	-651	-137
United States of America	3732	4077	1989	427	1185	255	2783	640	9102	9373
SOUTH AMERICA	**-51**	**-47**	**-91**	**-83**	**-9**	**-48**	**3**	**-55**	**-122**	**-83**
Argentina	-163	-294	-101	-25	-101	-25	-101	-25	-101	-25
Brazil	494	796	276	69	287	72	307	77	276	69
Chile	-61	19	1	-11	1	-11	1	-11	1	0
ASIA	**-2816**	**-6287**	**-22495**	**-13955**	**-16197**	**-12056**	**-20917**	**-16047**	**-23564**	**-48796**
China	-1626	-2418	-18293	-12780	-14646	-11309	-18293	-15148	-18293	-47041
India	-20	-33	-16	-4	-17	-4	-14	-3	-16	-4
Indonesia	105	192	55	14	55	14	55	14	55	14
Japan	302	-148	-40	-10	-40	-10	-40	-10	-40	-10
Korea, Republic of	241	341	366	646	885	223	678	476	199	613
Malaysia	-497	-687	-448	-99	-277	-70	-389	-98	-587	-148
OCEANIA	**-34**	**447**	**1723**	**683**	**1226**	**399**	**1258**	**667**	**954**	**1325**
Australia	13	346	1143	455	936	333	878	529	463	927
New Zealand	-43	135	656	328	343	127	445	213	568	499
EUROPE	**419**	**3515**	**15881**	**9951**	**10167**	**7702**	**13458**	**10683**	**11040**	**19360**
EU-25	4	3178	14827	9305	9103	7088	12414	10017	10025	17023
Austria	431	484	479	280	210	56	340	181	210	254
Finland	2274	3093	5515	2105	3989	1591	4757	2210	4231	5519
France	-873	67	1193	1702	693	347	1080	1809	94	1087
Germany	-1426	148	5837	3748	3232	4265	4953	4780	4714	8593
Italy	-864	-533	-248	-62	-248	-62	-248	-62	-248	-62
Russian Federation	146	336	125	31	249	63	173	44	125	150
Spain	-487	-1020	-303	-76	-316	-79	-310	-78	-303	73
Sweden	3302	4809	3609	907	2962	745	3178	799	2897	873
United Kingdom	-1806	-1724	-510	333	-518	-130	-511	-59	-510	146
DEVELOPED, ALL	**5413**	**8765**	**24526**	**14953**	**17154**	**12246**	**22087**	**16715**	**25753**	**49901**
DEVELOPING, ALL	**-4236**	**-9716**	**-25801**	**-16227**	**-18429**	**-13521**	**-23362**	**-17990**	**-27029**	**-51175**
WORLD	**1177**	**-951**	**-1275**	**-1275**	**-1275**	**-1275**	**-1275**	**-1274**	**-1275**	**-1274**

[1]Observations derived from FAO (2009), projections obtained with the Global Forest Products Model.

Table 48—Observed and projected value added to wood and fiber input in forest industries (million 1997$) for world regions and selected countries in the Global Forest Products Model[1]

	Observed		Scenario A1B		Scenario A2		Scenario B2		Scenario A1B-Low Fuelwood	
	1992	2006	2030	2060	2030	2060	2030	2060	2030	2060
AFRICA	2190	3354	5426	9510	4269	7292	4889	9298	5450	10370
Egypt	85	216	503	1581	557	1235	500	1422	487	1479
Nigeria	165	18	95	862	89	587	96	898	97	1004
South Africa	891	1694	2308	2667	1651	1749	2114	2836	2326	2946
NORTH/CENTRAL AMERICA	75808	99318	108239	102096	97172	75687	101048	81589	114539	127746
Canada	9782	19232	25313	26068	21234	26472	22180	26777	23472	33070
Mexico	1754	3878	5080	5646	4322	4953	4233	4510	5112	6064
United States of America	63849	75433	76573	68497	70601	42829	73554	48601	84701	86664
SOUTH AMERICA	6070	15085	18998	20995	16185	20310	16621	21046	19742	24968
Argentina	759	1552	2395	2628	1864	1854	1923	2135	2462	2847
Brazil	3482	8803	11613	12610	10090	13305	10330	13151	12325	16002
Chile	664	2505	2262	2155	2095	2074	2097	2218	2243	2304
ASIA	46381	116149	145313	180137	109543	126402	120737	138433	143098	169561
China	3870	54491	74152	99035	53715	69835	60454	76063	73979	87886
India	4925	5118	8526	12539	6012	7086	7238	9453	8553	12466
Indonesia	4169	6715	7406	8153	5416	4925	6132	5679	7463	8619
Japan	23665	24747	23614	20947	21038	19012	20776	17250	22595	20797
Korea, Republic of	3750	7999	9008	8456	6409	4824	7402	5977	8555	8116
Malaysia	1714	3808	3054	3723	2389	2624	2659	2877	3019	3968
OCEANIA	2376	4561	5752	5746	5196	4881	5244	4815	5409	5893
Australia	1590	2597	3831	3818	3595	3698	3550	3403	3561	4487
New Zealand	733	1938	1879	1865	1569	1131	1660	1356	1810	1340
EUROPE	63837	106127	112359	112033	95352	107124	99211	105603	109398	125951
EU-25	49535	90043	95107	93073	82224	91554	84717	88693	92190	105161
Austria	3086	5152	4114	2707	3291	2850	3486	2509	3755	3175
Finland	5933	11101	12829	9606	9788	10072	10671	9482	11856	16352
France	6527	9230	10425	9547	9763	8821	9681	8791	9860	10361
Germany	12711	21915	21089	15896	18375	15195	19115	15055	20719	19664
Italy	4394	7545	7584	7257	6993	6572	6726	5893	7353	7138
Russian Federation	10010	8653	9038	9583	6698	7478	7352	7693	9101	10364
Spain	2647	6502	6498	6195	6022	5851	5892	5477	6288	6635
Sweden	4951	9427	7378	7402	6852	12172	7210	9189	7771	6650
United Kingdom	3578	4703	7207	8462	6613	7793	6428	7245	6910	8548
DEVELOPED, ALL	164502	232137	246698	237173	215639	202955	223719	206969	248655	276713
DEVELOPING, ALL	32160	112455	149389	193344	112078	138743	124031	153816	148981	187777
WORLD	196662	344593	396087	430517	327717	341697	347750	360784	397637	464490

[1]Observations derived from FAO (2009), projections obtained with the Global Forest Products Model.

APPENDIX A

Global Forest Products Model formulation

The Global Forest Products Model (GFPM) has a static phase that computes the spatial economic equilibrium among the forest sectors of countries in a given year, and a dynamic phase that describes the changes in the conditions of this equilibrium over time.

Spatial global equilibrium

For each projected year, the GFPM computes a spatial equilibrium by maximizing the consumers and producers surplus:

$$\max Z = \sum_i \sum_k \int_0^{D_{ik}} P_{ik}(D_{ik})\, dD_{ik} - \sum_i \sum_k \int_0^{S_{ik}} P_{ik}(S_{ik})\, dS_{ik}$$
$$- \sum_i \sum_k \int_0^{Y_{ik}} m_{ik}(Y_{ik})\, dY_{ik} - \sum_i \sum_j \sum_k c_{ijk} T_{ijk} \qquad [1]$$

where: i,j = country, k = product, P = price in U.S. dollars of constant value, D = final product demand, S = raw material supply, Y = quantity manufactured, m = manufacturing cost, T = quantity transported, and c = cost of transportation, including tariff. All variables refer to a specific year.

End-product demand

$$D_{ik} = D_{ik}^* \left(\frac{P_{ik}}{P_{ik\text{-}1}} \right)^{\delta_{ik}} \qquad [2]$$

where: D^* = current demand at last year's price, P_{-1} = last year's price, and δ = price elasticity of demand. As shown in the section on market dynamics, below, D^* depends on last year's demand, and the growth of GDP in the country. In the base year, D^* is equal to the observed base-year consumption, and P_{-1} is equal to the observed base-year price.

Primary product supply

$$S_{ik} = S_{ik} \left(\frac{P_{ik}}{P_{ik\text{-}1}} \right)^{\lambda_{ik}} \qquad [3]$$

where: S^* = current supply at last year's price, and λ = price elasticity of supply. As shown in the section on market dynamics, below, S^* depend on last year's supply, and on exogenous or endogenous supply shifters. In the base year, S^* is equal to the base-year supply, and P_{-1} is equal to the observed base year price.

Total forest drain

$$S_i = (S_{ir} + S_{in} - \Theta_i S_{if})\, \mu_I \qquad [4]$$

r = industrial roundwood,
n = other industrial roundwood,
f = fuelwood,

$0 \leq \Theta \leq 1$ = fraction of fuelwood that comes from the forest,
$\mu \geq 1$ = ratio of drain to harvest.
$S_i \leq I_i$
I_i = forest stock.

Material balance

For each product and country, demand equals supply.

$$\sum T_{jik} + S_{ik} + Y_{ik} - D_{ik} - \sum a_{ikn} Y_{in} - \sum T_{ijk} Y_{in} = 0 \quad \forall i, k \qquad [5]$$

where: a_{ikn} = input of product k per unit of product n.

Trade Inertia constraints are used to dampen the annual changes in trade:

$$T^L_{ijk} \leq T_{jik} \leq T^U_{ijk} \qquad [6]$$

where the superscripts L and U refer to a lower bound, and upper bound, respectively.

Prices

The shadow prices of the material balance constraints [5] give the market-clearing prices for each commodity and country.

Manufacturing cost

Manufacturing is represented by activity analysis, with input-output coefficients and a manufacturing cost. The manufacturing cost is the marginal cost of the inputs not recognized explicitly by the model (labor, energy, capital, etc.);

$$m = m_{ik}^* \left(\frac{Y_{ik}}{Y_{ik\text{-}1}} \right)^{S_{ik}} \qquad [7]$$

where: m^* = current manufacturing cost, at last year's output, and s = elasticity of manufacturing cost with respect to output. As shown in the next section, m^* depend on last year's manufacturing cost, and on the exogenous rate of change of manufacturing cost. In the base year, m^* is equal to the observed base-year manufacturing cost and $Y_{ik,-1}$ is equal to the observed base-year quantity manufactured.

Transport cost

The transport cost per unit of volume for commodity k from country i to country j in any given year is given by:

$$C_{ijk} = f_{ijk} + t^I_{jk} (f_{ijk} + P_{ijk}) \qquad [8]$$

where: c = transport cost, per unit of volume, f = freight cost, per unit of volume, t^I = import ad-valorem tariff, and P_{-1} is equal to the previous year world export price.

Market dynamics

Unless otherwise indicated, the following variables refer to one country, one commodity, and one year.

Demand shifts

$$D^* = D_{-1} (1 + a_y g_y + a_0)$$ [9]

g_y = GDP annual growth rate, a_y = elasticity with respect to GDP, a_0 = annual trend.

Supply shifts

The supply of fuelwood and industrial roundwood shifts over time with the changes in growing stock:

$$S^* = S_{-1} (1 + \beta_l g_l) \text{ for } k = r, n, f$$ [10]

where: g_l = annual rate of change of forest stock (endogenous, see below), and β = elasticity.

The supply of waste paper and other fiber pulp shifts with GDP growth:

$$S^* = S_{-1} (1 + \beta_y g_y)$$ [11]

Changes in forest area and forest stock

$$A = (1 + g_a) A_{-1}$$ [12]

where: A = forest area, and g_a = annual rate of forest area change equation [9] and the annual rate of forest area change, g_a defined by:

$$g_a = a_0 + a_1 y' + a_2 y'^2 \text{ for } y' <= y'^*, \text{ else } g_a = 0$$ [13]

Where, for each country, α_0 is calibrated so that in the base year the observed g_a is equal to the g_a, predicted by [15] given the income per capita y'.

y' = income per capita, predicted from:

$$y' = (1 + g_y) y'_{-1}$$ [14]

$$y'^* \text{ is defined by } g_a = a_0 + a_1 y'^* =+ a_2 y'^{*2} = 0$$ [15]

$$\text{and } y'^* > -a_1/2a_2$$

Forest stock evolves over time according to a growth-drain equation:

$$I = I_{-1} + G_{-1} - S_{-1}$$ [16]

where $G = (g_a + g_u) I$ is the periodic change of forest stock without harvest, g_u = periodic rate of forest growth on a given area, without harvest[1].

The annual rate of forest growth, g_u, is defined by:

$$g_u = \gamma_0 \left(\frac{I}{A}\right)^\sigma$$ [17]

where σ is negative, so that g_u decreases with stock per unit area. For each country, γ_0 is calibrated so that in the base year the observed g_u is equal to the g_u predicted by [17] given the stock per unit area, I/A.

---

[1] The forest stock, I, is: $I_t = U_t A_t$ where A_t is the area and U_t is the stock per unit area (stock density). Without harvest, the stock annual growth rate is $dI /I = dU / U + dA /$ or $g_l = g_u + g_a$. Thus, the level of stock, without harvest, changes according to $I_t = I_{t-1} (1 + g_l) = I_{t-1} (1 + g_u + g_a)$. With a harvest S_{t-1} from t-1 to t this becomes $I_t = I_{t-1} (1 + g_u + g_a) - S_{t-1}$. With the above notations, $I_{t-1} (1 + g_u + g_a) = G_{t-1}$ the change in forest stock without harvest, which leads to equation [18].

The annual rate of change of forest stock net of harvest, used in equation [10] is then:

$$g_l = \frac{I - I_{-1}}{I_{-1}}$$ [18]

Changes in manufacturing coefficients and costs

The input-output coefficients a in equation [5], may change exogenously over time, for example to reflect increasing use of recycled paper in paper manufacturing:

$$a = a_{-1} + \Delta a$$ [19]

where Δa = annual change in input-output coefficient.

The manufacturing cost function shifts exogenously over time:

$$m^* = m_{-1} (1 + g_m)$$ [20]

where g_m = the exogenous rate of annual change in manufacturing cost.

Changes in transport cost

The transport cost function [8] shifts exogenously over time according to the recursion:

$$c^* = c_{-1} + \Delta f + t^l (f + P_{-1}) - t^l_{-1} (f_{-1} + P_{-2})$$

with:

$$f = f_{-1} + \Delta f, \ t = t_{-1} + \Delta t$$ [21]

where Δf and Δt are periodic changes in freight cost and taxes, respectively.

Changes in trade inertia bounds

$$T^L = T_{-1} (1 - \varepsilon)^p$$ [22]
$$T^U = T_{-1} (1 + \varepsilon)^p$$

ε = absolute value of maximum annual relative change in trade flow (exogenous).

Linear approximation of demand, supply, and manufacturing cost

For example, consider a demand equation such as [2]. Omitting the subscripts for region and product, the inverse demand equation in any given year is:

$$P = P_{-1} \left(\frac{D}{D^*}\right)^{1/\sigma}$$

The linear approximation is:

$$P = a + bD \text{ with } a = P_{-1} - bD^* \text{ and } b = \frac{P_{-1}}{\sigma D^*} \text{ for D}^* \geq 1, \text{ else}$$

$$b = \frac{P_{-1}}{\sigma} \text{ for D}^* \geq 1, \text{ and } a = P_{-1}$$ [23]

$b = 0$ if $\sigma = 0$. The same method is used for the supply, and the manufacturing cost equations.

APPENDIX B

Gross Domestic Product growth assumptions

The national population projections were taken directly from the Intergovernmental Panel on Climate Change (IPCC) scenarios. National Gross Domestic Product (GDP) projections were obtained by first predicting national GDP per capita and then multiplying by national population, except for the United States for which future GDP growth rates were established separately (USDA Forest Service, 2012). Wanted was GDP per capita from 2006 to 2060 for each of the other 179 countries used in the GFPM. Given were the GDP per capita of each country in 2006, and the GDP per capita projections of the IPCC for each scenario A1B, A2 and B2.

The main assumption was that the GDP per capita of the different countries would converge during the period 2006 to 2060 (Sala-i-Martin 2006). Specifically by the year 2100, that is 40 years after the time horizon of the study, the GDP per capita of all the countries within a region would be the same, and equal to the average regional GDP per capita predicted by each IPCC scenario.

A secondary assumption was that the ratio of the GDP per capita of a particular country to the GDP per capita of its region would evolve from its observed value in 2060 to the assumed value of 1.0 in 2100 according to a logarithmic difference equation described below.

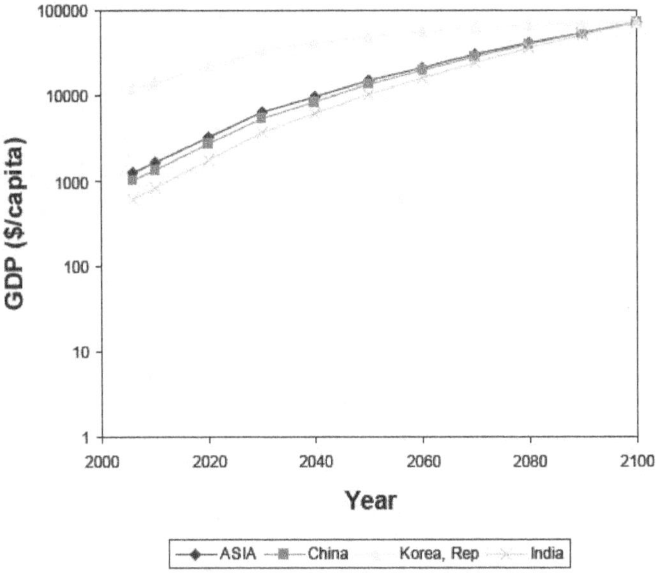

Figure B1 shows the projections from 2006 to 2100 for selected countries of Asia, for scenario A1B. Only the years 2006 to 2060 were used in this study.

Algebraically, let y_{it} be GDP per capita in country i and year t, y_{Rt} the GDP per capita in region R in year t, ε, t=0 the base year, 2006, T=2100-2006 the number of years from the base to the horizon.

The initial ratio of country to region GDP per capita was:

$$r_{i0} = \frac{y_{i0}}{y^{R0}}$$

Logarithmic convergence of this ratio was obtained by:

$$r_{i0} = r_{i,t-1} \left(\frac{r_{iT}}{r_{i0}}\right)^{1/T} \text{ for } t = 1 \text{ to } T,$$

where r_{iT} was the target ratio at the horizon, r_{iT} was equal to 1 in this application.
Then:
$y_{it} = r_{it} y_{Rt}$ for $t = 1$ to T.

Figure B1 —Projection of GDP per capita in China, the Republic of Korea, and India, given the IPCC projection of GDP per capita for Asia.

APPENDIX C

Fuelwood demand assumptions

For fuelwood demand the objective was to match the fuelwood consumption from 2006 to 2060 projected with the Global Forest Products Model (GPFM) for each of the 180 countries, and the Intergovernmental Panel on Climate Change (IPCC) assumptions regarding the future world demand for biofuels. Given were the fuelwood consumption of each country in 2006, the assumptions on GDP growth by country (see Appendix B), and the IPCC projections of biofuel consumption in scenarios A1B, A2 and B2.

It was assumed that from 2006 to 2060 the world fuelwood consumption would grow by the same factor as the world biofuel demand predicted by the IPCC, i.e., approximately 5.5 times for scenario A1B, 2.7 times for scenario A2 and 2.9 times for scenario B2. Another assumption was that the international fuelwood consumption would converge in the sense that by 2060 the ratio of national to world fuelwood consumption was equal to the ratio of national GDP to world GDP.

These assumptions gave the national fuelwood consumptions in 2060 and the annual growth rates of demand needed from 2006 to 2060 at constant price to achieve this 2060 consumption.

This demand growth rate applied to the GFPM led to a world consumption that differed from the IPCC level due to the endogenous change in prices. This gap was decreased by adjusting the national demand growth rates and running the GFPM again. This was repeated until the IPCC level of global consumption was nearly achieved.

The algebraic procedure can be summarized as follows. The goal was fuelwood consumption growing to the same fraction of each country's GDP in 2060.

$$\frac{c_{i,60}}{y_{i,60}} = \frac{\sum_j c_{j,60}}{\sum_j y_{j,60}}, \forall i$$

Where $c_{i,60}$ was fuelwood consumption in country i in 2060, and $y_{i,60}$ is the gross domestic computed above. The world fuelwood consumption in 2060 was:

$$\sum_j c_{j,60} = g \sum_j c_{j,60}$$

Where g was the growth of biofuel consumption from 2006 to 2060 predicted by the IPCC. Thus, the fuelwood consumption in 2060 for each country was:

$$c_{i,60} = \frac{y_{j,60}}{\sum_j y_{j,60}} g \sum c_{j,60}$$

An initial estimate of the exogenous annual growth rate of fuelwood demand, r_1^0, to cause a country to reach $c_{i,60}$ was:

$$r_1^0 = \left(\frac{c_{i,60}}{c_{i,60}}\right)^{\frac{i}{54}} - 1$$

Due to the price change, this growth rate led to a consumption level in 2060, $c_{i,60}^0$, generally different from $c_{i,60}$. Then, the rate of shift of demand was revised to r_i^1, to achieve the target, $c_{i,60}$:

$$r_i^1 = \left(\frac{c_{i,60}}{c_{i,60}}\right)^{\frac{i}{54}} (1 + r_1^0) - 1$$

A new GFPM projection was then computed with the demand rate of shift r_i^1. Repeating this gave GFPM projections that converged to the target fuelwood consumption levels $c_{i,60}$.

APPENDIX D
Technical change assumptions

For wood products other than paper and paperboard, manufacture is represented in the Global Forest Products Model with an input of industrial roundwood and all other inputs are covered by the manufacturing cost.

To minimize the effects of statistical errors, the best current technology was deducted from the data of the major producing countries only, those that produced more than 5 percent of the global output in 2006.

Among these countries, the country with the best manufacturing technology, Bk, was the country with the least total unit cost of production:

$$p_w a_{Bk,k} + m_{Bk,k} = \min_{\forall i} (p_w a_{ik} + m_{i,k})$$

Where:
p_w world price of industrial roundwood in 2006
$a_{i,k}$ m^3 of industrial roundwood per m^3 of product k for country i,
$m_{i,k}$ manufacturing cost excluding wood input per m^3 of product k.
$a_{Bk,k}$ best current technology input-output coefficient for product k,
$m_{Bk,k}$ best current technology manufacturing cost for product k.

This best technology was assumed to improve further by 2060, to the levels $a_{60,k}$ and $m_{60,k}$. Then, the input-output coefficient and manufacturing cost of each country converged from their value in 2006 to these best 2060 values at a constant annual rate.

For paper and paperboard the same procedure was applied, with the assumption that the least expensive input, waste paper, increased 2006 to 2060 and the most expensive inputs, chemical pulp and other fiber pulp decreased from by the same proportion, while mechanical pulp compensated to change the total fiber input to a common total.